New Perspectives on

Japanese Language Learning,

Linguistics, and Culture

NFLRC Monographs is a refereed series sponsored by the National Foreign Language Resource Center at the University of Hawai'i under the supervision of the series editor, J. D. Brown. NFLRC Monographs present the findings of recent work in applied linguistics that is of relevance to language teaching and learning, with a focus on the less commonly-taught languages of Asia and the Pacific.

Developing, using, and analyzing rubrics in language assessment with case studies in Asian and Pacific languages
   James Dean Brown (Editor), 2012
   ISBN 978–0–9835816–1–1

Toward useful program evaluation in college foreign language education
   John M. Norris, John McE. Davis, Castle Sinicrope, Yukiko Watanabe (Editors), 2009
   ISBN 978–0–9800459–3–2

Second language teaching and learning in the Net Generation
   Raquel Oxford & Jeffrey Oxford (Editors), 2009
   ISBN 978–0–9800459–2–5

Case studies in foreign language placement: Practices and possibilities
   Thom Hudson & Martyn Clark (Editors), 2008
   ISBN 978–0–9800459–0–1

Chinese as a heritage language: Fostering rooted world citizenry
   Agnes Weiyun He & Yun Xiao (Editors), 2008
   ISBN 978–0–8248328–6–5

Perspectives on teaching connected speech to second language speakers
   James Dean Brown & Kimi Kondo-Brown (Editors), 2006
   ISBN 978–0–8248313–6–3

ordering information at nflrc.hawaii.edu

New Perspectives on Japanese Language Learning, Linguistics, and Culture

edited by
KIMI KONDO-BROWN
YOSHIKO SAITO-ABBOTT
SHINGO SATSUTANI
MICHIO TSUTSUI &
ANN WEHMEYER

NATIONAL FOREIGN LANGUAGE RESOURCE CENTER
University of Hawai'i at Mānoa

(cc) 2013 Kimi Kondo-Brown, Yoshiko Saito-Abbott, Shingo Satsutani, Michio Tsutsui, Ann Wehmeyer

This work is licensed under the Creative Commons Attribution-NonCommercial-ShareAlike 3.0 Unported License. To view a copy of this license, visit http://creativecommons.org/licenses/by-nc-sa/3.0/

Manufactured in the United States of America.

The contents of this publication were developed in part under a grant from the U.S. Department of Education (CFDA 84.229, P229A100001). However, the contents do not necessarily represent the policy of the Department of Education, and one should not assume endorsement by the Federal Government.

ISBN: 978–0–9835816–3–5

Library of Congress Control Number: 2012952500

cover photo ©2005 Ann Wehmeyer
　　　　　　　taken at *Kumano Nachi Shrine, Wakayama Prefecture* 熊野那智大社，和歌山県

book design by Deborah Masterson

distributed by
National Foreign Language Resource Center
University of Hawai'i
1859 East-West Road #106
Honolulu HI 96822–2322
nflrc.hawaii.edu

About the
National Foreign Language Resource Center

THE NATIONAL FOREIGN LANGUAGE RESOURCE CENTER, located in the College of Languages, Linguistics, & Literature at the University of Hawai'i at Mānoa, has conducted research, developed materials, and trained language professionals since 1990 under a series of grants from the U.S. Department of Education (Language Resource Centers Program). A national advisory board sets the general direction of the resource center. With the goal of improving foreign language instruction in the United States, the center publishes research reports and teaching materials that focus primarily on the languages of Asia and the Pacific. The center also sponsors summer intensive teacher training institutes and other professional development opportunities. For additional information about center programs, contact us.

James Dean Brown, Director
National Foreign Language Resource Center
University of Hawai'i at Mānoa
1859 East-West Road #106
Honolulu, HI 96822–2322

email: nflrc@hawaii.edu
website: nflrc.hawaii.edu

NFLRC Advisory Board 2010–2014

Robert Blake
University of California, Davis

Mary Hammond
East-West Center

Madeline Spring
Arizona State University

Carol Chapelle
Iowa State University

Contents

Preface ix

1 日本語イマージョンプログラムに在籍するJHL児童の物語産出力と言語力の発達について [Development of Narrative Writing Ability and Language Proficiency in Young JHL Learners in a Japanese Immersion Program]
    Masako O. Douglas, Kiyomi Chinen, & Hiroko C. Kataoka 1

2 Using N Desu in Small Talk: JFL Learners' Pragmatic Development [スモールトークにおける「んです」の使用：海外日本語学習者の語用論的能力の発達]
    Tomoko Iwai 27

3 Effects of Dynamic Written Corrective Feedback on JFL Students' Homework [JFL学習者の宿題へのDynamic Written Corrective Feedbackの効果]
    Yuka Akiyama & Mayumi Fleshler 49

4 内容重視の言語教育の理論と実践：「批判的」日本語教育に向けて [Theories and Practices of Content-Based Language Instruction: Toward "Critical" Japanese Language Education]
    Shinji Sato, Atsushi Hasegawa, Yuri Kumagai, & Uichi Kamiyoshi . 69

5 Social Network Development during Study Abroad in Japan [日本での留学期間中の社会的ネットワーク形成]
    Spencer A. Ring, Daniel Gardner, & Dan P. Dewey 95

6 Grammar and Interactional Discourse: Marking Non-topical Subject in Japanese Conversation [インターアクションと文法：日本語の会話における「が」の非トピック明示機能]
    Michiko Kaneyasu 123

7 「の」名詞化構文についての一考察:主要部内在型関係節とその周辺
   [A Study of the *No*-Clause Construction in Japanese: Internally Headed Relative Clauses and Beyond]
   Xiaoman Miao 145

8 **Transmissive Feminism: The Evolutive Mind as Displayed in the Overseas Letters of Yamada Kakichi to Yamada Waka** [伝達されるフェミニズム:山田嘉吉から山田わかへ, 二人の往復書簡が明かす女性思想の新たなかたち]
   Rika Saito 163

About the Contributors 183

Preface

This volume contains eight papers, all of which were presented at the Association of Teachers of Japanese (ATJ) Annual Spring Conference held at the University of Hawai'i at Mānoa in March, 2011. In January 2012, the ATJ became the American Association of Teachers of Japanese (AATJ) after consolidating with its sister organization the National Council of Japanese Language Teachers. This consolidation was intended to create better collaboration across various levels of instruction and also to provide stronger advocacy. This publication project came about partly to celebrate this major transition.

The ATJ/AATJ annual spring conferences are refereed conferences with more than 200 participants and usually feature more than 100 presentations on various aspects of Japanese language acquisition and pedagogy, linguistics, and literature. For this volume, we initially received over 40 manuscripts, which were peer-reviewed by professionals in the field. The eight articles selected for this volume are all original studies, appearing in print for the first time, and have been recommended for publication by the anonymous external reviewers. All of the chapters went through revisions based on the external reviews.

The present collection deals with several important topics in the fields of Japanese language learning, linguistics, and culture. Chapters 1 through 3 are empirical classroom research papers that examine issues that may be of interest to Japanese language professionals in the field—the development of narrative writing of young learners in a two-way Japanese immersion program (Chapter 1–Douglas, Chinen, & Kataoka), the effect of instruction on pragmatics including the use of *n desu* among beginning-level Japanese as a Foreign Language (JFL) university students (Chapter 2–Iwai), and the effect of "dynamic written corrective feedback" on beginning-level JFL university students (Chapter 3–Akiyama & Fleshler). Chapter 4 (Sato, Hasegawa, Kumagai, & Kamiyashi) discusses theoretical issues and practical examples concerning content-based instruction, with an emphasis on its connection to the community and the development of critical thinking. In Chapter 5 (Ring, Gardner, & Dewey), based on their questionnaire data on social networks collected from students studying abroad, the authors argue that study abroad program interventions and locations can play a large role in facilitating the students' interactions with Japanese-speaking individuals in Japan. Chapters 6 and 7 are linguistics papers that shed new light on the functions of specific linguistic items. Chapter 6 (Kaneyasu) examines data obtained from face-to-face and telephone conversations and analyzes the role of the case marker *ga* in sustaining the participants' orientation to a common topic. In Chapter 7, Miao argues that the "internally headed relative clause" be regarded as a *no*-clause construction rather than a relative clause and claims that this construction shares features with other complex sentences including relative clauses, adverbials clauses, complements, and coordination. Chapter 8 (Saito) examines handwritten letters exchanged between a distinguished female social activist in Japanese history, Yamada Waka (1879–1957) and her husband, Yamada Kakichi, in 1922, which reveal new information about her advancement as a feminist thinker and the role of English in their respective communications.

We would very much like to thank the anonymous reviewers for their thoughtful and valuable feedback. We would also like to give special thanks to Ms. Susan Schmidt, who has provided generous and impeccable assistance during the review process.

We hope that this volume will prove useful to professionals and students in the field.

Mahalo,
Volume editors
August, 2012

日本語イマージョンプログラムに在籍するJHL児童の物語産出力と言語力の発達について

Development of Narrative Writing Ability and Language Proficiency in Young JHL Learners in a Japanese Immersion Program

NFLRC monographs

ダグラス昌子 (Masako O. Douglas)
知念聖美 (Kiyomi Chinen)
片岡裕子 (Hiroko C. Kataoka)

カリフォルニア州立大学ロングビーチ校
(California State University, Long Beach)

要旨

米国西海岸都市部の小学校の双方向日本語イマージョンプログラムに在籍する幼稚園から5年生231人を対象に、継承日本語(JHL)の子どもたちの物語産出力と言語力の発達を外国語(JFL) の子どもたちと比較研究した結果を報告する。連続する4つの絵について書いた話をデータとして収集し、物語産出力は評定尺度表で、そして言語力は、流暢さ、複雑さ、正確さの領域で測り、比較分析を行った。その結果次のことが分かった。1) 物語産出力と言語力は、JHLもJFLも特に低学年で上昇がみられたが、正確さは、両グループともに伸びが少なかった。2) JHLはJFLに比べ、量的、質的にも常にJFLを上回り、5年生ではトピックが明確で、詳細な情報がある物語が書けるようになるが、JFLの物語産出力は、物語とみなせるレベルには達していなかった。本研究の知見は、研究が希

Douglas, M.O., Chinen, K, & Kataoka, H. (2013). 日本語イマージョンプログラムに在籍するJHL児童の物語産出力と言語力の発達について [Development of narrative writing ability and language proficiency in young JHL learners in a Japanese immersion program]. In K. Kondo-Brown, Y. Saito-Abbott, S. Satsutani, M. Tsutsui, & A. Wehmeyer (Eds.), *New perspectives on Japanese language learning, linguistics, and culture* (pp. 1–25). Honolulu: University of Hawai'i, National Foreign Language Resource Center.

少である異族言語のイマージョンプログラムにおける継承語の発達を理解する一助となると考える。

Abstract

This chapter presents the results of a study of development of narrative writing ability and language proficiency in young learners of Japanese as a heritage language (JHL) as compared with learners of Japanese as a foreign language (JFL) in a two-way Japanese immersion program. Students attended a suburban elementary school on the West Coast of the U.S., and 231 students from grades K–5 participated in the study. Using a rubric, we measured students' narrative writing ability language proficiency by fluency, complexity, and accuracy of language use in the stories that students had written about a series of four drawings. The results indicated that: 1) narrative writing ability and Japanese proficiency developed with grade level in both JHL and JFL groups, especially at lower grade levels. However, linguistic accuracy development was very slow. 2) JHL students consistently exceeded JFL students in terms of quantity and quality of their writing samples and language proficiency development. The narratives written by JHL 5th graders produced a clear topic and detailed information. In contrast, JFL children's narrative ability stayed at the pre-narrative level. The findings from this study further our understanding of heritage language development in immersion programs of non-cognate languages, a topic deserving further research.

はじめに

米国では,英語以外の言語を母語とする児童の英語力の発達と,英語を母語とする児童の外国語の力,および学力の向上と文化の理解を同時にバランスよく促進させることを目標に,小学校教育に双方向イマージョンプログラムが1963年に初めて導入され,1980年代後半には多くの双方向イマージョンが設立された(Christian, Howard, & Loeb, 2000)。米国における双方向イマージョンに共通する基本理念は,ある外国語を母語とする児童と,英語を母語とする児童がほぼ半分の割合で在籍し,低学年では学習言語には外国語を主体として使用し,学年が上がるにつれ徐々に英語での学習時間を増やしていき,最終的には50パーセントずつになるというものである。しかし,初期の学科学習に使われる2言語の割合は,プログラムにより異なる。米国における双方向イマージョンは英語とスペイン語のものが殆どで,実際に教室で使用される言語の割合はプログラムによって異なる(Christian, 2008)。

アメリカにおける日本語イマージョンプログラムは1988年にオレゴン州で始まった。翌年には3校が加わり,2000年には全米で12の小学校が日本語イマージョンプログラムを実施していた[1]。2011年現在,CAL (Center for Applied Linguistics)によると,日本語イマージョンプログラムは31校あり,それは全米におけるイマージョンプログラムの5.3パーセントを占める。31校の内訳は,保育園・幼稚園2校,小学校19校,中学校6校,高等学校4校となっている。しかし,その中には日本語での授業時間が50パーセントに満たないプログラムや,既に廃止されているプログラム,日本語学校に英語話者の子どもたちが加わっているプログラムなども含まれており,厳密にイマージョンと呼べるプログラムは,CALのリストにはまだ含まれていない1校を加えて,小学校16校におけるプログラムだけではないかと思われる[2]。このうち,4校が双方向イマージョンのカリキュラムを取り入れている。

---

[1] 本研究チームの1人が2001年に国際交流基金及びAAS-NEACに提出したプロポーザルに提示されたイマージョンプログラムのリストによる。

[2] CALのリストに含まれているほとんどの中学,高校の日本語コースはイマージョンプログラム卒

英語と日本語を扱う双方向イマージョンには，日本語を継承学習言語として学習する児童が多く在籍するプログラムも存在する。双方向イマージョンの基本理念は英語を母語とする児童と目標言語(マイノリティー言語を以下目標言語と呼ぶ)を母語とする児童が同一のクラスに在籍するというものであるが，日本語のイマージョンの場合，目標言語のグループは，入学時に目標言語を母語とする児童(例．母国から米国に来て間もない児童)と，英語のほうが目標言語より強い児童などから構成されていて，日本語の母語話者のみとは言えない。本研究は，米国の日本語双方向イマージョンプログラムに通う，日本語を継承語として学習する子どもたちに焦点をあてて調査を行ったものである。

先行研究

米国における双方向イマージョン教育

イマージョン教育をとりいれるプログラム数の増加とともに，その教育効果を検証する研究が行われてきたが，イマージョンアプローチは，学科の内容学習と言語の習得の両方に効果があるという肯定的な結果が報告されている (Collier & Thomas, 2004; Cummins, 1998; Snow, 1986; Thomas & Collier, 2002)。例えば，Thomas & Collier (2002) は，米国の5つの学校区のイマージョンプログラムを調査し，これらのプログラムに在籍する児童は，学校の環境や社会・文化的背景は異なるものの，1つの言語で学習をする児童と比べ，全教科の成績がよいという共通点があることを指摘している。

また双方向イマージョンプログラム導入の際，常に懸念される目標言語と主流言語(社会で使用されている言語を以下主流言語と呼ぶ)両言語グループの児童の英語力の発達についても，イマージョンプログラムの児童は英語だけのプログラムや英語での学習への移行を最終目的とする移行型バイリンガルプログラムの児童と比べ，英語の標準到達度試験で同等かそれ以上の成績を修めていることが報告されている(Bae, 2001, 2007; Cazabon, Nicoladis, & Lambert, 1998; Cummins, 1998; Howard, Christian, & Genesee, 2004; Lindholm-Leary, 2001)。Bae (2001, 2007)は，韓国語・英語のイマージョンの研究で，イマージョンプログラムに在籍して3年目(小学校2年生)の児童が物語を英語で書く力を測定した結果，イマージョンの児童が物語を書く平均的な力(以後物語産出力)は，英語のみのプログラムに在籍する児童のうちで標準テストで上位にいる児童の物語産出力と同等であったことを報告している。

一方，目標言語の伸びについては，Howard et al. (2004)がスペイン語・英語イマージョンプログラムの研究で，小学校5年生の終わりには両言語グループの児童がスペイン語にも顕著な伸びが見られたことを報告している。Sugarman & Howard (2001)の書く力の研究でも，スペイン語の文法，作文，綴りや句読点などの言語面において，3年間に5段階の評定尺度表 (rubric)でスペイン語グループは平均が 2.5 から 3.8 へ，英語グループは 2.2 から 3.7 へと伸びが見られたことが報告されている。しかし，この結果とは対照的に，カナダのフランス語・英語のイマージョンプログラムの研究では，イマージョンプログラムの最終学年である小学校6年生のフランス語の聞く・読む力は，同年齢のフランス語母語話者の学習者との差がほとんどなくなるまでに飛躍的に伸びたものの，話す・書く力では母語話者の言語力とかなりの差があると報告されている (Harley, Allen, Cummins, & Swain, 1991)。

業生を対象としており，CALのデータではpartial immersion(部分イマージョン)として扱われている。しかし，これらの学校は実際には1日1, 2時間の日本語の授業をもうけているだけであり，イマージョンの定義からは外れる。このようなプログラムはimmersion continuation program(イマージョン継続プログラム)と呼ばれるべきであろう。

また,目標言語が母語である子どもの話し言葉と読み書きの力の強化が,第2言語である英語の読み書きの力と学習言語力の習得に欠かせないという結果が報告されている(Edelsky, 1982; Carson, Carrell, Silberstein, Kroll, & Kuehn, 1990; Lanauze & Snow, 1989)。別の研究では,イマージョンは異文化理解の向上にも貢献しているという結果が報告されている(Cazabon, Lambert, & Hall 1993; Freeman, 1998)。

イマージョン教育の効果に関する研究結果は,上記のように肯定的なものがある反面,いくつかの問題点も指摘されている。Bae (2001, 2007)は,米国におけるイマージョン教育の児童の英語力の発達の研究では,スペイン語と英語のプログラムの研究の量に比べ,それ以外の目標言語でかつ異族言語のイマージョン教育における英語力の発達の研究が限られていることを指摘している。

上記の Bae の研究も含め現在までのところ,英語力の発達に焦点を当てた研究が主流で,目標言語である継承語の保持発達に焦点をあてた研究は充分なされていない。Kondo-Brown (2010)は,イマージョンプログラムが継承語保持発達に効果があるという研究結果を幾つか挙げているが(Montrul & Potowski, 2007; Sohn & Merrill, 2008),総じて,イマージョン教育における表記法が異なる言語の継承語学習者の研究は非常に少なく,Christian (2008)は,そのような言語のイマージョンプログラムが継承語発達に有効であるかどうかを研究する必要があると述べている。

さらにイマージョンプログラムでの継承語の保持発達研究で,その継承語が英語と同属か異族かが,保持発達にどのように影響するのかという研究も数が限られている。継承日本語(JHL: Japanese as a Heritage Language)に関しては,小学校のイマージョンプログラムを卒業した11・12年生の日本語会話能力調査の結果が報告されているが(Chinen, Douglas, & Kataoka, 2009),その報告の中で日本語イマージョンの卒業生たちの日本語力は,スペイン語やフランス語のイマージョンの各言語の到達レベルと比較してかなり低いことが指摘されている。また,言語力の発達の測定対象については,話し言葉の発達の研究が主流であり,書く力を検証した研究が限られているという指摘がある(Bae 2001, 2007; Howard et al., 2004)。さらに,イマージョンプログラムにおける継承語の発達を評価する測定ツールの研究の必要性も指摘されている(Kondo-Brown, 2010)。

継承日本語教育

米国で継承語および継承語教育の研究の必要性が指摘された時期に(Kondo-Brown 2003; Peyton, Ranard, & McGinnis, 2001; University of California Los Angeles, 2001),継承日本語教育の分野でも,カリキュラムと教材開発,教師研修,言語力の発達,アイデンティティ,学習動機など多岐の分野にわたる研究の必要性が指摘された(井川 2003; 片岡・古山・越山 2001; Sasaki, 2001)。以来,継承日本語学習者の大学生を対象として,プレースメントテストの結果と言語背景との関係の研究(Kondo-Brown, 2004),日本語を外国語として学習する学生との日本語力の違いの研究(Kanno, Hasegawa, Ikeda, Ito, & Long, 2008; Kondo-Brown, 2005),漢字力分析(ダグラス 2010)など言語面に焦点をあてた研究や,学習者のアイデンティティに焦点を当てた研究(Kondo-Brown, 2000),継承日本語教育に関する研究(Douglas, 2002, 2003, 2007; Kondo-Brown, 2005),および先行研究のまとめと JHLも含めた継承語教育のこれからの実践と研究への提言(Kondo-Brown, 2003, 2010)などへと研究の広がりを見せている。

また大学生以外に,JHLの児童・生徒を対象として,アイデンティティ形成に果たす日本語補習授業校の役割の研究(Chinen & Tucker, 2005),学習動機 の研究(Nunn, 2009),

JHL カリキュラムデザインのための理論的枠組みの研究(Douglas, 2005, 2008), JHL 児童の家庭の言語背景と言語力に関する保護者の期待度の研究(ダグラス・片岡・岸本 2003)など多岐の分野にわたる研究が行われてきた。JHL 児童の言語力の測定では, 米国西海岸の都市部にある日本語補習授業校の児童・生徒(小学校から中学校まで)を対象にした Kataoka, Koshiyama, & Shibata (2008)の研究がある。Kataoka et al. (2008)は, 日本語の語彙, 文型, 助詞と英語の語彙の測定では, 日本語が母語である子どもたちと比べると年齢が上がるにつれ日本語力の差は大きくなるものの, JHLの子どもたちの日本語力は, 年齢とともにのびているという結果を報告している。米国では, 義務教育の年齢の JHL の子どもたちの JHL 教育の主流を担うのが, 補習授業校や継承日本語学校など公共教育以外の教育機関であるため, 既存の JHL 研究も, 週1回土曜日だけの日本語補習授業校や継承日本語学校という環境での研究が中心となっている。

物語文

Minami (2002)は, 物語文の定義には研究者間に一致したものがないことを指摘し, 自身の研究では, Hicks (1994)の定義をもとに, 物語文とは, 「時間的, テーマ的に関係した出来事に言及したもの」であるとしている(Minami, 2002, p. 217)。本研究も, この定義をもとにしている。

物語文の先行研究では物語産出のタスク(課題)の種類に多様性が見られる。口頭で産出された物語のデータとしては, 自身に起こった出来事のモノローグ(Minami, 1996, 2002), 絵本の絵をもとに話を語ったもの(内田 1996, 2003; Kajiwara & Minami, 2008; Minami, 2008), 聞いた話の続きを語ったもの(内田 1996, 2003)などがある。また書き言葉では, 自身の個人的体験を書いたもの (Howard et al., 2004), 絵本の絵をもとに話を書いたもの(Bae 2001, 2007; 内田 1996, 2003), 聞いた話の続きを書いたもの(内田 1996, 2003)などがある。本研究ではこれらのタスクのうちで, 絵をもとに物語を書くというのを選んだが, その理由を以下に記す。

「語る」という活動は年齢を問わず子どもに共通の経験であり(Bae, 2001), 物語ることは社会でも学校でも重要視されるスキルなので, 読み書きを発達させるために, 子どもに, 家や学校で物語を語らせるという活動がよく見られる(Peterson & Dodsworth, 1991)。また, 比較的早期に子どもが体験する活動であることから, 小学校の低学年でも馴染みのある活動である。Minami (2002)は4歳児ですでに物語ることの基盤ができていると報告している。与えられた絵について物語を書くというタスクを採用したのは, 絵が書かれる内容について書き手と読み手に共通のスキーマを与えるため, 物語の分析にあたり, 書かれた内容の理解が困難であるという事態が回避されるからである(Bae, 2007)。また, 自身の経験を自発的に語るというタイプの物語の場合は, 産出される内容が子どもによって異なるが, 絵という外的手がかりを使った場合は, 同じコンテクストでの比較が可能になる(Berman & Slobin, 1994)。さらに内容に関連のある一連の絵をもとに産出された物語では, 単文のレベルをこえた談話レベルでの言語力を調査することができる(Ripich & Griffith, 1990)という理由もある。

先行研究で物語産出力の発達を測定するために用いられた項目については, 年齢と学年, 言語力, 物語産出力と関係する言語力, 物語る技法の4項目が共通して使用されている(モノリンガル対象の研究: 内田 1996, 2003; Minami, 1996, 2002; バイリンガル対象の研究: Bae, 2001, 2007; Howard et al., 2004; Kajiwara & Minami, 2008)。以下, それぞれについて簡単に説明する。

1. 年齢と学年：先行研究では，年齢と学年はともに物語産出力の発達と相関する項目であることが実証されている(Bae, 2007; Minami, 2008)。つまり，物語産出力の発達には，モノリンガルでもバイリンガルでも，認知力の発達(年齢が関与)と，学校教育でのリテラシーの教育年数(学年)という2つの要因が関与していることがわかっている。

2. 言語力の発達の測定：言語力の発達を測定する項目としては，産出されたテキストの長さ(総語数の測定)，語彙の豊かさ(異なる語の数が総語数に占める割合)，文法の正確度がある。

3. 物語産出力の発達に関係する言語力の測定：物語産出力に関係する言語力の発達を測る手段として，結束性(cohesion)の測定がされている(Bae, 2001, 2007)。日本語の研究では，結束性を表現する言語形式である以下の項目が分析対象となっている：主語を表す助詞の「が」と談話レベルでトピックを表す「は」の的確な使い分け，同一のトピックで話が続いていることを示す談話ストラテジーとして使われるトピックの省略，出来事の時間の流れを表したり，原因と結果を表す接続表現(例．接続語：そして・それで，けれども・しかし；接続助詞：〜から・〜ので，〜けれども・〜が；動詞の接続形式：〜て形)(Kajiwara & Minami, 2008; Minami 1996, 2002, 2008; 内田 1996, 2003)。

4. 物語技法：物語技法とは，物語の筋の展開のために使う方略である(内田 2003)。物語技法の評価には，プロット(中心となる出来事やアクションと状況描写)，話の完結度，トピックの展開といった基準が使われている。日本語の物語産出力の先行研究では，物語技法について，大人と子どもに共通性が発見されている。内田(2003)は，金魚が金魚鉢から出て冒険を始めるところまで話を読み聞かせ，その続きを口頭で作るというタスクを使ったモノリンガル児童対象の研究で，5歳児が使う話の筋の展開構造方略が大人のそれと共通するという結果を述べている[3]。Minami (2008)は，少年と犬が逃げ出した蛙を探す旅に出るという内容の絵を見せて，口頭で話を作るというタスクを使い，日本語・英語のバイルンガルの幼児と児童(4歳から12歳)の研究をした。その中で，大人の日本語母語話者が高く評価した子どもの物語は，出来事やアクションが生起する順に並べられた構造の頻度が高いものであるという結果をもとに，日本語の物語は，出来事やアクションを時間の流れにそって描写するという構成方略をとるという結論に達している。一方英語の物語では，出来事やアクションの流れの描写とともに，語り手が登場人物や場所についてどう思っているかという情意表現が高く評価されると述べている。このようにプロットの構成に関しては，Minami (2008)は，社会的・文化的な違いが物語産出に影響するという結果を述べている。

本研究は，イマージョン教育の研究においてまだ研究が充分とはいえない異族言語のイマージョンにおける目標言語(継承語)の書く力と言語力の発達に焦点をあてた研究として，米国の日本語イマージョンプログラムに在籍するJHLの子どもの物語産出力と日本語力の発達を幼稚園から最終学年(5年生)までの全学年を対象に調査したものである。異族言語を対象としたイマージョンの先行研究では，研究対象が小学校1年生と

---

[3] 内田(2002)は，大人も子どもも話の筋が「出発-障害-到着-交遊-事件」か「出発-障害-到着-交遊-(変身)-友達になる」という筋をたどるものが多いという結果を報告している。しかし，子どもと大人が作った物語はむろん全く同じというわけではなく，子どもが作った物語には語彙の豊かさ，細かな主人公の状況説明，主人公の心理状態の描写，話の筋の構成の複雑さが欠けているとしている。

2年生で物語産出力を測ったもの(Bae, 2001, 2007)に限られており, 全学年を対象に書く力の発達を調査した研究は, 筆者らの知る限りではまだ無い。

調査方法

研究課題

研究課題は次の2項目からなる。

1. JHLの子どもの物語産出力と言語力は, 学年が上がるにつれどのように変化するのか。
2. JHLの子どもの物語産出力と言語力は, 同プログラムに在籍する外国語としての日本語(JFL)を学ぶ子どものそれと比べて違いがあるのか。あるとすればどのような違いがあるのか。この研究課題は次の理由により選んだ。程度の差はあれ, 英語と日本語のバイリンガルであるJHLの子どもにとって日本語は母語でもなく外国語でもない。このJHLの子どもの日本語を書く力の特徴は, 日本語が外国語である児童のそれとを比較することで把握することが可能となる。

調査対象

調査サイト

本研究が行われた西海岸の都市は, 日系コミュニティーの活力も強く, 戦前からの一世や二世の日系人, 戦後移民してきた新一世の日系人, また仕事の関係などで渡米してきた短期滞在者などが共存する。2010年の米国国勢調査(California Department of Finance, 2010)によると, およそ10万人の日系人や日本人がこの地域に在住している。日本語教育を行う機関も数多く存在し, 補習授業校, 継承日本語学校, 塾, イマージョンプログラムなどがある。日系のマスメディア, 日系の食料品店, 日本食レストラン, また日本語で対応可能な病院やカウンセリング, 弁護士, 社会福祉のサービスなどもあり, 日本語でコミュニケーションが図れる社会的領域が全米の中でも非常に広い。

調査対象プログラム

本研究は, 米国西海岸都市部にある公立小学校の日本語イマージョンプログラムを対象とした。このプログラムにはデータ収集時には13名の教師がおり, 幼稚園から小学5年生251人が在籍していた。1年生の算数や理科の教科では90パーセントが日本語で授業が行われているが, 学年が上がるにつれ日本語の割合が減少し, 5年になると50パーセントになる。当プログラムの教師によると, 主流言語グループの子どもたちは授業外は常に英語を使い, またJHLの子どもたちは, 主流言語グループの子ども達に話しかけるときは英語を使うとのことである。

調査対象児童

調査対象児童は, 上記のプログラムに在籍する幼稚園児から小学5年生の231名で, 子どもの数は, 最多の学年は幼稚園と小学校1年生と4年生で41名, 最少は小学3年生で35名であった。このうちJHLの子どもは108人, JFLは123人であった。JHLとJFLのグループ分けは保護者が学校に提出した家庭言語環境調査表と教師からの情報によって行った。学年別内訳は表1の通りである。

表1　調査対象児童の学年別内訳

	JHL		JFL		合計	
	人	%	人	%	人	%
幼稚園	21	19.4	20	16.3	41	17.7
1年生	23	21.3	18	14.6	41	17.7
2年生	18	16.7	19	15.4	37	16.0
3年生	12	11.1	23	18.7	35	15.2
4年生	20	18.5	21	17.1	41	17.8
5年生	14	13.0	22	17.9	36	15.6
合計	108	100	123	100	231	100

次に，この調査に参加した子どもたちの英語力について，2年生以上を対象に実施された英語標準テストの結果を，各学年，JHL/JFL別に図1に示す。標準テストは，得点によってFar Below Basic, Below Basic, Basic, Proficient, Advanced の5つのレベルに分けられている。図1は，それぞれのレベルにいる子どもの割合をパーセントで出したものである。図1が示すように，JHLとJFLともに Far Below Basic のレベルにいる子どもの比率はゼロであった。JHLとJFLの英語力の差は2年生と3年生では，統計的に有意差（t 検定の結果[4]）をもって，JFLの得点の平均値がJHLを上回っているが，4年生，5年生では，両者の平均値に有意差がみられず，高学年で JHL の子どもたちの英語力が伸びていることがわかる。特に図1の5年生の英語力のレベルの分布をみると，JHLとJFLがよく似たパターンになっていることからもわかる。

データ収集法

本研究のデータは，一連の4つの絵で表された話に基づいて児童が書いた物語を使用した。この物語作成は，児童の日本語力評価の一部として学校が実施したもので，本研究チームは評価に関連するデータ収集方法のデザインと集めたデータの分析を一任された。なお，研究結果の発表については当小学校より許可を得ている。

---

[4]

JHLとJFLの英語標準テストの各学年の平均値の比較

	JHL			JFL			t 検定		
学年	n	平均値	標準偏差値	n	平均値	標準偏差値	t	df	有意差検定結果
2	13	379.46	50.14	16	423.50	41.44	−2.59	27	.015
3	10	353.20	38.92	23	395.78	47.83	−2.48	31	.019
4	12	359.50	56.90	16	390.37	50.71	−1.51	26	.142
5	8	416.75	44.99	22	431.27	43.33	−.80	28	.428

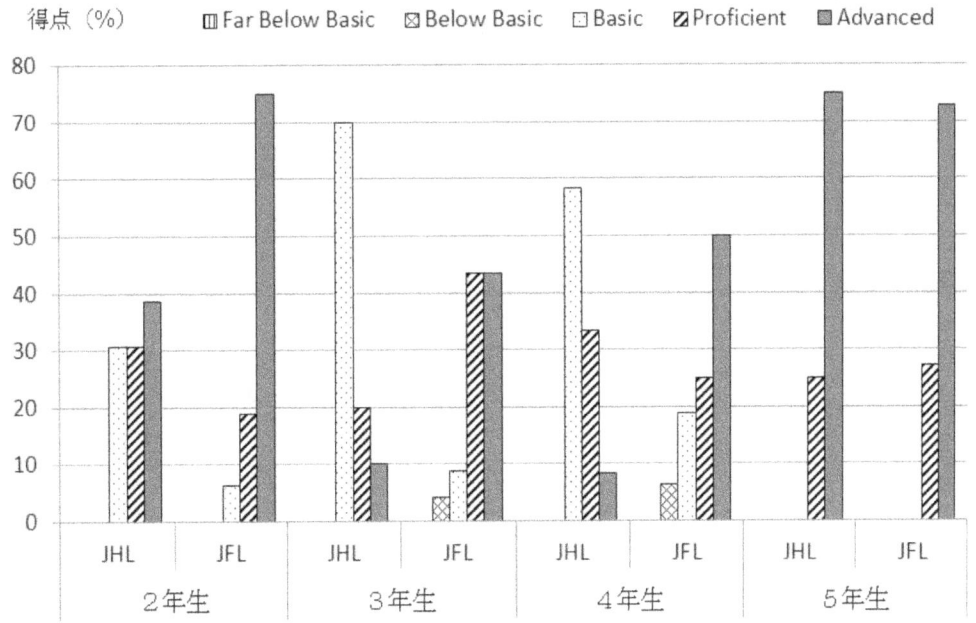

| 図1 | 英語標準テストのレベル別人数の割合 |

プロンプト(物語産出のための題材：4つの絵からなる物語)

先行研究で述べたように，「語る」という活動は年齢を問わず子どもに共通する経験で(Bae, 2001)，小学生の低学年でも馴染みのある活動である。また絵を物語作成のプロンプトとすることにより書き手と読み手で同じスキーマを作ることができ，それによって書かれた内容を読み手が理解しやすくなる(Bae, 2007)。さらに全員が同じ絵をもとに物語を書くと，物語産出力と言語力を同じコンテクストで比較することが可能になる(Berman & Slobin, 1994)。

4つの絵からなる話の内容は，無人島にいるおなかがすいた犬が，海に浮いている卵をみつけて食べようとしたら，中からワニが出てきたので，逃げるために木に登り，結局卵が食べられなかったというものである[5]。カラープリントされた絵の横には書き込みができる余白があり，子どもたちが一番慣れている様式を使用するために，その余白に升目をつけたり，線を引いたりするかどうかは担任の判断にまかせた。なお，使用した絵は，今回の物語産出力と言語力を測定するために用意したもので，教師も児童も今回初めて見たものである。

手順

2010年5月に幼稚園から5年生の各クラスで，担当教師が4つの絵のカラープリントを児童一人一人に与え，「おなかがすいた犬のお話です。お話を日本語で書いてください。」という指示を英語と日本語で与えた後に，子どもたちが物語を書いた。幼稚園児に関しては文を書くのがまだ困難なため，単語や絵でもいいという指示を出した。制限時間は学年により異なった。書かれた物語の評価はイマージョンプログラムの教師らと本研究

---

[5] 本研究で使用した4つの犬の絵は著者不明のため連絡が出来ず，掲載許可を求めることができなかったため，当論文には掲載をすることができなかった。

チームが全員で採点法の擦り合わせ調整をするために, 児童が書いたものを各学年から無作為に5つから6つ選び, あらかじめ作成した評定尺度表(rubric)を使い各自が評価をし, 評価にずれがある場合は話し合って基準を設定した。そして評価に統一性が確立されたことを確認した後, 別々に評価を実施した。教師らは, 担当する子ども以外の子どもの物語を名前を伏せて数人で読み, 協議の上で得点を決定した。また, 本研究チームの3人による評価も協議の上で決定した。教師らが決定した得点と本研究チームが決定した得点の評価を検証したところ, 評定者間信頼性は非常に高かった($r=.93, p<.001$)。そのため分析に際しては, 教師と研究チームの各得点の平均値を使用した。

データ分析方法

物語産出力の評価方法として評定尺度表(rubric)を用いるため, 本研究チームがNational Center for Research on Evaluation, Standards, and Student Testing (CRESST)のElementary Narrative Analytic Scaleを基に Advance Japanese (AP) Japanese Language and Culture Examination の Narrative Rubric を参考にして, 評価尺度表を構築した。Elementary Narrative Analytic Scale を基にした理由は, この評定尺度表の妥当性の検証がされているためである。Elementary Narrative Analytic Scale は, CRESST がカリフォルニアのシリコンバレーにある小学校の1年, 3年, 4年の3学年を対象に妥当性を検証したものである。結果は, 各学年の人数の差がありすぎることと, 1年と4年の児童数が極端に少ないことから妥当性についての最終的な結論は見送っているものの, 暫定的に, 1元配置分散分析(One-Way ANOVA)の結果から, 各学年間の物語産出力の差を測ることができるものであるとしている(Gearhart, Herman, Baker, & Whittaker, 1992)。

Elementary Narrative Analytic Scale は Focus/Organization, Development, Mechanics の3項目からなっているが, Mechanics の項目には誤用についての詳細な記述が無いため, 本研究で使用した評定尺度表では細かい基準を設け, 言語使用という項目とした。また, 言語の産出量を評価するため, テキストタイプという項目を追加した。従って, 本研究の評定尺度表は, 1)テキストタイプ, 2)テキスト構成, 3)話の精緻度と話の進展度, 4)言語使用(漢字も含む)の4項目からなる。テキストタイプというのは, 語, 単文, 複文のどのレベルで産出されたかを評価するものである。テキスト構成は, 物語のトピックの有無や維持力, 話の筋, 話としての体裁(始め・中・終わり)などを構成していく力を評価するものである。話の精緻度・話の進展度は, プロット, 話の設定, 主人公の描写, 詳細を描写する力を評価するものである。言語使用は, スタイルの維持, 使用されている文型の種類, 語彙, 漢字, 文法などの適切な使用を評価するものである。レベルは, 幼稚園から小学校5年生までの物語産出力を評価するため, ACTFL の K–12 Performance Guidelines(NoviceからPre-advanced)を参考に1(Novice-Low)から12(Advanced)のレベルを設けた。

以下に評価尺度表の各レベルの基準をまとめる。テキストタイプは, レベル1は単語が数個, 2はいろいろな単語および句があるもの, 3は単文が現れはじめているものとそれぞれに違いがあるが, テキスト構成や話の精緻度・話の進展度は1から3ではまだ見られない。4は単文がいくつか並んでいるが, ときとして単語レベルに落ち, トピックもはっきりせず, 物語との内容の関連がない。5は, 明確な接続詞はまだ使われていないものの, ようやく単文間に内容の関連が出始めるが, トピックは明確ではない。また話の精緻度・話の進展度は4, 5ともに最低限に限られている。6で物語としての体裁が整い始める。テキストタイプは6では, 複文の使用か接続詞の使用が見られ, 文どうしに内容的に関連が見られる。7は6に加えて接続詞や複文の使用が幾つか見られ, 8は接続詞や複文の使用が定着してみられるものとなっている。テキスト構成は, 6と7ではトピックが明白

ではあるが, 話の始め・中・終わりがはっきりしない。8になると, 話の進展がはっきりと書かれるようになる。話の精緻度・話の進展度では, 6と7は話の詳細が欠けているが, 8はいくつか詳細な情報が書かれていることが必要となる。9と10では, テキストタイプは段落となり, テキスト構成はトピックが明白で, 話に結束性を持たせるストラテジーが誤用の有無を問わず使われはじめる。話の筋がほぼ通っていて, 話の始め・中・終わりがはっきりしているものになる。このレベルでは, 話の精緻度・進展度では, 物語のプロットや主人公の描写, 話の設定ができて, 生き生きとした描写がところどころにあることが必要となる。9と10の違いは言語形式の項目で, 習った漢字が適切に使えるか (9), ほとんどの場合に適切に使われているか (10)にある。11と12は, テキストタイプに違いがあり, 11は複数の段落があり複文や接続詞の使用があるもの, 12は複数の段落に加え, 複文や接続詞が安定して使われていることが必要となる。話の構成や精緻度・進展度は, 11と12は共通しており, 明確なトピック, 話の筋が通っていること, 話の始め・中・終わりが明確であること, 結束性を出すストラテジーの継続した使用, 物語のプロットや主人公の描写, 話の設定が緻密で, 詳細な記述や生き生きとした描写が必要とされる。

言語力の測定ツールとしては, 書く力の中の流暢さ, 文法の複雑さ, 及び正確さ[6]の発達レベルを測る最も良い指標として Wolf-Quintero, Inagaki, & Kim (1998)が選んだ 測定方法を使用した。Wolf-Quintero et al. (1998)は, 第2言語の書く力の先行研究で使われている100以上の測定方法のメタアナリシスを行い, 書く力のプロフィシエンシーレベルに関して, 各測定方法の構成概念妥当性(construct validity)と並存的妥当性(concurrent validity)の検証をおこなった。その結果, 最も信頼できる方法として, 流暢さの測定には語数[7]を T-unit[8]数で割る方法, 複雑さの測定には節の数を T-unit 数で割る方法, 正確さの測定には誤りのない T-unit 数を T-unit 全体数で割る方法を薦めている。なお, 言語力の分析にあたり, T-unit 数, 誤りのない T-unit 数, 節数, 誤りのない節数, 語数, 誤りのない語数を本研究チームの1人が数え, 1ヶ月後に再度, データの25パーセントを Predictive Analytics Software (PASW) Version 18で無作為に抽出し, 同一の手順で数えた。評定者内信頼性(Intra-rater reliability)は, 誤りのない T-unit 数の2回の測定の信頼性が.97で, 他は.98から.99(いずれも $p<.001$)の高い信頼性が得られた。

分析結果

JHL/JFLの物語産出力と言語力の関係

本研究で測定した物語産出力と言語力の分析結果をここで述べる。表2は, JHLと JFL別の, 物語産出力の得点と書く力を構成する3項目の得点の平均値と標準偏差値を示している。JHL/JFLの各グループで, 物語産出力の得点と言語力の3項目間に有意な正の

---

[6] Wolf-Quintero, Inagaki & Kim (1998)は流暢さ, 文法の複雑さ, 及び正確さをそれぞれ, "rapid production of language," "use of varied and sophisticated structures and vocabulary," "error free production"と定義している。

[7] 語と語の間にスペースがある英語と比べ, 膠着言語である日本語は, 語と語の境界が明確ではなく, 何を語とするかには明確な定義がない。先行研究では名詞句(例.「本を」), 動詞句(例。「読んでみよう」)をそれぞれ一語と数える方法と, 形態素(例.「本」「を」)を1語と数える方法がある。Douglas (1992, 1994)は, クローズテストのデザインで形態素を語と数える方法が句を語と数える方法より, 他のテストと有意の相関があったと報告している。従って, 本研究では形態素で語を数えた。

[8] Wolf-Quintero et al. (1998)は, T-unit (terminable unit)を主文とそれに関係する従属文と定義している。

相関関係が見られた(JHLの物語産出力の得点と流暢さ: r=.38, p<.001; 物語産出力の得点と複雑さ: r=.36, p<.001; 物語産出力の得点と正確さ: r=.54, p<.001) (JFL 物語の産出力の得点と流暢さ: r=.63, p<.001; 物語産出力の得点と複雑さ: r=.67, p<.001; 物語産出力の得点と正確さ: r=.51, p<.001)。この結果より, 物語産出力と言語力は, 相互に関連しながら発達していくことがわかった。

表2　JHL/JFL物語産出力の得点と言語力の得点の平均値と標準偏差値

	JHL (n=97)		JFL (n=119)	
	平均値	標準偏差値	平均値	標準偏差値
物語産出力の得点	6.61	1.79	4.57	1.57
流暢さ	8.52	4.20	6.13	2.53
複雑さ	1.70	.82	1.16	.45
正確さ	.54	.29	.20	.23

JHL/JFLの物語産出力の学年別比較

ここでは, JHL/JFLの物語産出力の学年別の比較の結果を報告する。図2の JHL/JFLグループの各学年の平均値分布から, 各学年とも JHL の得点が JFL の得点を上回っていることがわかる。学校教育におけるリテラシー教育の初期である幼稚園から2年生までの JHL/JFL 各グループの物語産出力の得点の平均値(表3)をみると, JHL/JFLの幼稚園がそれぞれ 4.58, 2.45, 1年生が 5.86, 4.00, 2年生が 7.12, 5.41となっている。評定尺度表では, 書かれたものに物語としての体裁が出始めるのは, 得点が5のレベルとなる。このレベルに到達する時期をJHL/JFLで比べると, JHL は1年生, JFL は2年生となっていて, 1年の差がある。しかしその後の伸びを比べると, JHL は2年生以降物語産出力の得点が7以上となり, 5年生では8に近くなっていて, 物語産出力が急速に伸びていることがわかる。一方 JFL は, 2年生で5に達したものの, そのあと3年生から5年生まで5のまま, すなわち物語になりかけた状態で停滞していることがわかる。

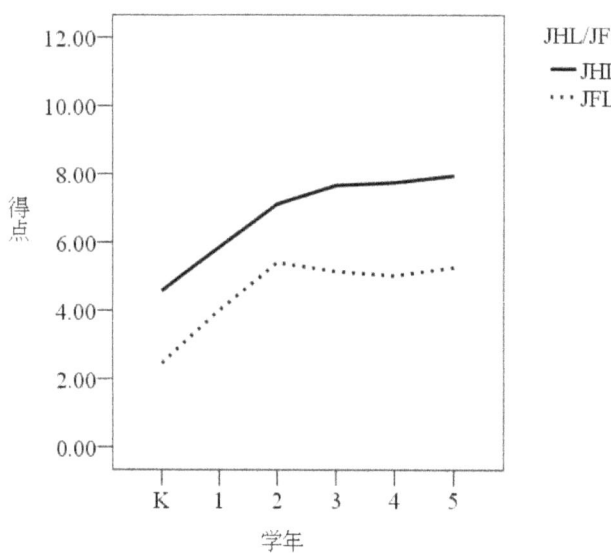

図2　JHL/JFL学年別物語産出力の得点の分布

このJHL/JFLの差の度合いをさらに調べるため, t 検定(t-test)による分析を行った。表3にその結果を示す。各学年ともJHLの物語産出力の得点の平均値は, JFLより有意差をもって高いことがわかる(2年生はp<.01, 2年生以外の学年 p<.001)。

次に, JHL/JFL別に各学年の平均値の比較を1元配置分散分析(one-way ANOVA)を用いて行った結果, JHL/JFLとも物語産出力の得点には学年間に有意差があることがわかった(JHL: $F[5, 91]=19.16, p<.001$; JFL: $F[5, 113]=18.35, p<.001$)。

表3　各学年のJHL/JFL別物語産出力の得点の平均値の比較

学年	JHL			JFL			JHL/JFL
	n (97)	平均値	標準偏差値	n (119)	平均値	標準偏差値	平均値差
幼稚園	20	4.58	1.50	20	2.45	1.29	2.13**
1年生	21	5.86	.65	17	4.00	1.25	1.86**
2年生	13	7.12	1.89	17	5.41	1.21	1.70*
3年生	12	7.67	1.19	23	5.15	1.12	2.51**
4年生	20	7.75	.91	20	5.02	1.16	2.73**
5年生	11	7.95	1.54	22	5.27	1.13	2.68**

* p<.01; ** p<.001

注)　物語産出力の評価点がついていない欠測値があったため, 表3のJHL/JFLそれぞれの数値は調査対象者より少なくなっている.

さらにこの有意差がどの学年間にあるのかを検証するため事後検定(post hoc test)を実施した。独立サンプルの検定の等分散性(equality of variances)を調べるLevene検定をPASW Version 18 を使って行った結果, 等分散性が仮定されなかったため, Tamhaneを用いて多重比較分析を行った。その結果, 表4が示すように, JHLでは幼稚園と1年生, 2年生, 3年生, 4年生, 5年生, 及び1年生と3年生, 4年生, 5年生との間に有意差がみられた($p<.05$)。JFLでは, 幼稚園と1年生, 2年生, 3年生, 4年生, 5年生との間, 及び1年生と2年生, 5年生との間に有意差がみられた($p<.05$)。

物語産出力は, 高学年の学年間には有意差が見られなかったが, 低学年では, 学年が上がるにつれ得点も上がっていた。この結果から, 特に低学年の物語産出力は, 学年(つまり学校教育におけるリテラシー教育の年数)とそれに伴う年齢(認知力の発達)に関係することがわかる。

表4　JHL/JFLの学年別物語産出力の得点比較(Tamhane)

物語文の得点	(I)学年	(J)学年	平均値の差(I-J)	有意差検定結果
JHL	幼稚園	1	−1.28	.024
		2	−2.54	.008
		3	−3.09	.000
		4	−3.18	.000
		5	−3.38	.000
	1年生	3	−1.81	.003
		4	−1.89	.000
		5	−2.10	.015
JFL	幼稚園	1	−1.55	.011
		2	−2.96	.000
		3	−2.70	.000
		4	−2.58	.000
		5	−2.82	.000
	1年生	2	−1.41	.032
		5	−1.27	.036

注）　表中では, (I)から(J)を引いたために, 平均値の差はマイナスで表示されているが, 実際は学年が上になるほど得点は高くなっている.

JHL/JFL間の言語力比較

　図3, 4, 5はそれぞれ流暢さ, 複雑さ, 正確さの項目を学年ごとにJHL/JFL間で比べたものである。これらの図から, 流暢さと複雑さの2項目は, JHLとJFL間で1年生の平均値が比較的近いがその他の学年では差が大きくなっていることがわかる。正確さは, 幼稚園からすでにJHLとJFL間で正確さを表す数値(誤りを含まないT-unitの数がT-unit全体数に占める割合)に約30パーセントの差があり, 3年生と4年生では, さらにその差が大きくなっている。

　今回の調査では, JHLは5年生の正確さが4年生を下回る結果となったが, 担任によると, クラスで観察した限りにおいて5年生は4年生に比べ, 日本語力全体が弱いグループであったということである。また, JFLの3年と4年は正確さの得点が他の学年に比べ低くなっているが, その原因は今回のデータ分析からは解明できなかった。

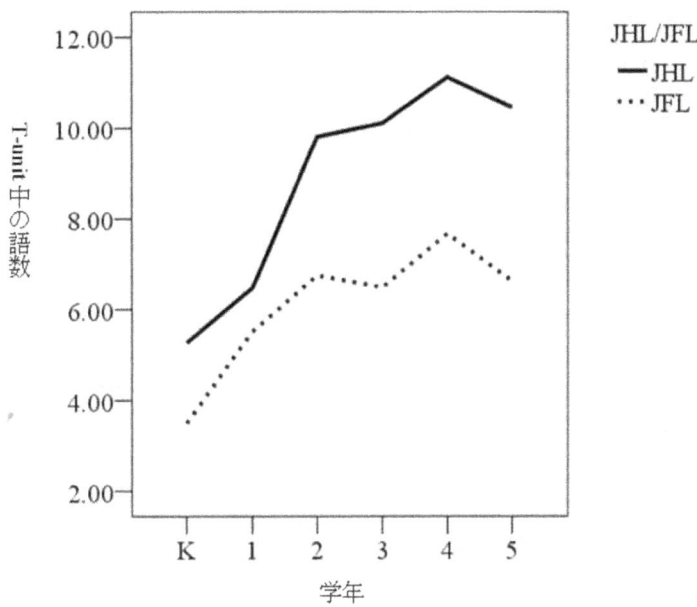

図3　流暢さのJHL/JFL間学年別比較

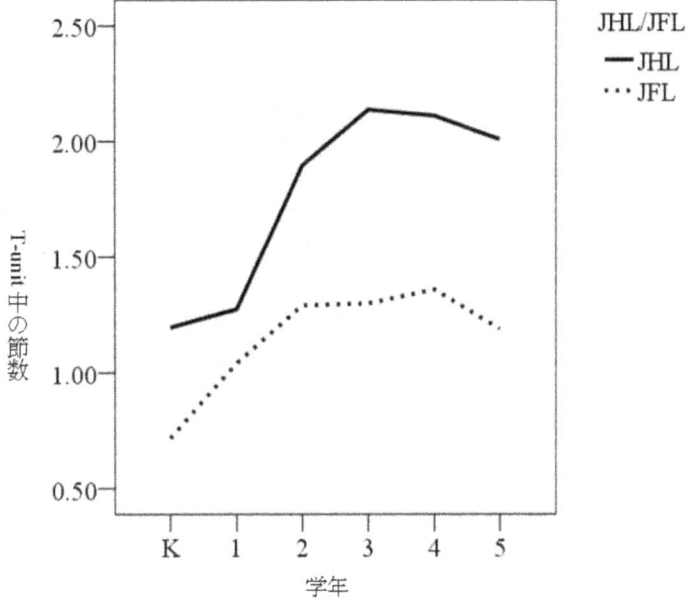

図4　複雑さのJHL/JFL間学年別比較

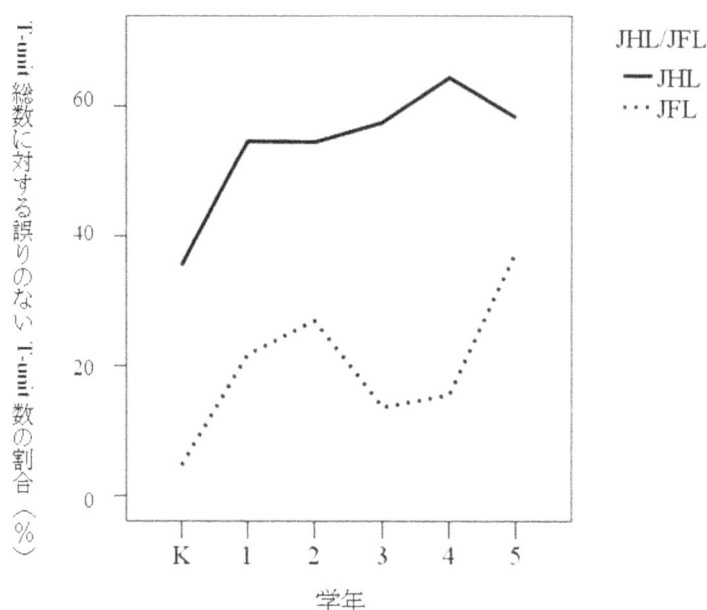

図5　正確さのJHL/JFL間学年別比較

　JHL と JFL 間の差の大きさを調べるため, 3項目について学年別に t 検定分析を行った。表5にその結果を示す。流暢さは, 幼稚園と1年生と3年生では JHL/JFL 間に有意差はなく, 2年生と4年生, 5年生で有意差が出ている。この結果から, JHL は高学年になると, 誤りのある語も含めて使える語彙が顕著に増えていることがわかる。一方, JHL と JFL 間で有意差のある学年の数が多いのは複雑さと正確さの項目である。JHLと JFL 間の違いは幼稚園からすでに有意な差となって現れており, 特に正確さにおける差が際立っている。JHL の複雑さの伸びを学年で比較すると, T-unit 中の節の数が幼稚園の1.20から最大で3年生の 2.14に増加し, 1つの節が文を構成するレベルから, 2並列文, または従属節と主節の構造の文のレベルへの伸びが見られる。一方 JFL は T-unit 中の節の割合の平均が最大でも1.36 (4年生)で 2つの節には達していない。また正確さでは, JHL は誤りのない T-unit の T-unit 全体に対する割合が, 幼稚園の35パーセントから最大で4年生の64パーセントへと伸びている。一方, JFL は幼稚園の5%が5年生では38パーセントとなってはいるが正確さはかなり低い。

表5　JHLとJFL間の言語力の学年別比較

	学年	JHL (n=108)			JFL (n=123)			t 検定		
		n	平均値	標準偏差値	n	平均値	標準偏差値	t	df	有意差検定結果
流暢さ	幼稚園	21	5.27	2.43	20	3.50	3.96	1.71	31.23	.097
	1	23	6.47	1.24	18	5.51	1.81	2.01	39	.051
	2	18	9.81	4.21	19	6.75	1.49	2.98	35	.005
	3	12	10.11	6.37	23	6.49	1.60	1.94	11.73	.077
	4	20	11.12	2.78	21	7.67	1.57	4.91	39	.000
	5	14	10.45	3.47	22	6.63	1.56	3.88	16.42	.001
複雑さ	幼稚園	21	1.20	.60	20	.72	.72	2.31	37.11	.026
	1	23	1.28	.24	18	1.04	.30	2.74	39	.009
	2	18	1.90	.61	19	1.29	.24	4.00	35	.000
	3	12	2.14	1.37	23	1.30	.29	2.01	11.51	.059
	4	20	2.11	.67	21	1.36	.30	4.60	25.82	.000
	5	14	2.01	.68	22	1.19	.30	4.25	16.25	.001
正確さ	幼稚園	21	.35	.30	20	.05	.14	4.23	29.00	.000
	1	23	.55	.29	18	.22	.31	3.48	39	.001
	2	18	.54	.27	19	.27	.21	3.48	35	.001
	3	12	.58	.23	23	.14	.17	6.52	33	.000
	4	20	.64	.20	21	.16	.16	8.54	39	.000
	5	14	.58	.35	22	.38	.22	1.99	19.9	.061

以上, JHL と JFL 間比較では, 文の質的な差や, 正確さの量的な差が見られたが, これらの差がどの程度であるのかを検証するために, JHL/JFL 別に1元配置分散分析(one-way ANOVA)を実施した。分析の結果, JHL/JFLともに言語力の3項目は, 学年間で有意差があることがわかった(JHL: 流暢さ $F[5, 102]=9.60, p<.001$, 複雑さ $F[5, 102]=6.98, p<.001$, 正確さ $F[5, 102]=2.58, p<.005$; JFL: 流暢さ $F[5, 117]=8.97, p<.001$, 複雑さ $F[5, 117]=7.62, p<.001$, 正確さ $F[5, 117]=6.37, p<.001$)。さらに, どの学年に有意差があるかを調べるため, 事後検定(Tamhane)を行った。表6にその結果を示す。

表6　言語力の学年間の差の分析(Tamhane)

	(I)学年	(J)学年	平均値の差(I–J)	有意差検定結果
JHL				
流暢さ(words/T-units)	幼稚園	2	−4.54	.006
		4	−5.85	.000
		5	−5.18	.001
	1年生	4	−4.65	.000
		5	−3.98	.013
複雑さ(clauses/T-units)	幼稚園	2	−.70	.015
		4	−.91	.001
		5	−.81	.019
	1年生	2	−.62	.008
		4	−.84	.000
		5	−.73	.022
正確さ(error free T-units/T-units)	幼稚園	4	−.29	.013
JFL				
流暢さ(words/T-units)	幼稚園	2	−3.26	.032
		4	−4.17	.003
		5	−3.13	.043
	1年生	4	2.16	.006
複雑さ(clauses/T-units)	幼稚園	2	−.57	.037
		3	−.58	.035
		4	−.64	.015
	1年生	4	−.31	.032
正確さ(error free T-units/T-units)	幼稚園	2	−.22	.010
		5	−.33	.000

　この結果から，JHL/JFLとも低学年(幼稚園, 1年生)と高学年(4年生, 5年生)間に有意差があるが，2年生から5年生の間には有意差が無いことがわかった。つまり，言語力の伸びは低学年で顕著であり，前述の物語産出力と同様に言語力も低学年で学年(学校教育におけるリテラシー教育の年数)とそれに伴う年齢(認知力の発達)に関係があることを示している。

考察

JHL/JFLの物語産出力と言語力の関係

　JHL/JFLの各グループで，物語の産出力の得点と言語力の3項目(流暢さ, 複雑さ, 正確さ)間の関係を調べた結果，それぞれに有意な正の関係があることがわかった。つまり，物語を産出する力と言語力は，相互に関連しながら発達していくということである。物

語を書くという作業には構成を考えたり、話の筋が通るようにするなど、考える力が必要になる。

考える力と言語力の関係は、Takano & Noda (1995)が"foreign language effect"として説明している。Takano & Noda (1995)の研究は実験手法を用いて、考える力を必要とする課題(算数の足し算)をしながら、母語または外国語で質問を聞いて答えるという課題を与え、言語の難しさ(母語対外国語)が考える課題の達成にどのぐらい影響するかを調べたものである。この実験結果では、外国語での課題をこなす時の方が足し算の結果が悪くなり、Takano & Noda は、両課題を同時に行うと言語が難しいときはそちらに負荷がかかるため、考える方に充分な力が使えなくなるためだと説明している。Takano & Nodaの研究は外国語の処理についてであるが、JHLの物語を書くという課題にも同等のことが言えるのではないだろうか。言語処理が難しいときは考えること、つまり物語る力が低下すると考えられる。特に物語を書くという作業は、文字の存在の認識にはじまり、音と字をつなぐ作業など、初期リテラシー獲得のための新しい経験をする時に言語面の処理の負荷が増大すると考えられる。この関係は以下の各セクションで、物語産出力と言語力の伸びの考察の中で論じる。

JHL/JFLの物語産出力の学年別比較

JHLの物語産出力を学年別で分析した結果、1年生で物語らしきものが書けるようになり、2年生になると不完全ながらトピックが明白な物語としての体裁を持つものが書け、5年生では話の始め・中・終わりがはっきりして、いくつか詳細な情報が入った物語に近づいていくという顕著な伸びが見られた。一方 JFL は、JHL に1年遅れて物語らしきものが書けるようになるが、その後は5年生までこのレベルが続き、顕著な伸びが見られなかった。

日本語を家庭言語として育った JHL の児童は、学習者間の言語力の差という継承語話者共通の特徴があるにしても(Kondo-Brown, 2005)、話す力については、入学後に日本語を学習し始める JFL の子どもと比べ差があることは予想され、このことが入学以後のリテラシー教育に影響を与えている可能性がある。Lü & Koda (2011)は、英語と継承中国語のバイリンガル児童の家庭での中国語の発達の度合いが、入学時の初期リテラシーの発達、とくに音を聞いて認識できる語彙の習得に影響するという結果を報告している。イマージョンの JHL の子どもたちも、Lü & Koda (2011)の研究の中の継承中国語の子ども達のように、すでに家庭で発達した話す日本語力をばねに初期リテラシーを発達させ、以後、物語産出力の学年差の顕著な伸びに見られるように、継続してリテラシーを発達させていく。これが学校教育で初めて日本語に接する JFL の子どもたちの日本語の物語産出力に大きく差をつける要因であろう。

また、学年差の分析において、JHL/JFLとも幼稚園及び1年生の物語産出力の得点と、他の学年の得点との間に顕著な差がみられたということから、学校教育での初期リテラシーの獲得が特に幼稚園では負荷が大きいことがうかがえる。JHL の子どもたちは幼稚園から1年生にかけて初期リテラシーを獲得し、書くという作業がコントロールできるようになると、すでに習得している話し言葉にある語彙力を使って物語を書き始めるのであろう。この初期リテラシー獲得期の物語を書く力の低迷は、日本語を母語とする子どもたちにも幼稚園から小学校1年にかけて見られるという結果が報告されており(内田 1990, 2003)、JHL の子どもたちと共通するものがある。

JHL/JFL間の言語力比較

JHL/JFL別に見ると, 各グループは学年が上がるにつれ言語力も上昇していくという結果が出たが, 言語力と相関関係がある物語産出力にも同じ結果が見られた。言語力と物語産出力の発達には, 学年(リテラシー教育の期間)と年齢(認知力)という2つの要因が関係しているという先行研究と一致する結果となった(Bae, 2007; Minami, 2008)。一方, JHL/JFL間の言語力の発達を比較分析した結果, 流暢さ, 複雑さ, 正確さの3項目で, どの学年でもJHLはJFLより言語力が高く, 学年が上がってもその差が狭まらず, 流暢さと複雑においては逆に差が広がることがわかった。JHLの幼稚園から高学年までの言語力の発達には著しいものがあり, 単文から始まり, 高学年では節数が増え, 並列文や従属節を持つ主節の使用へと発達している。しかしながら正確さをみると, 最高でも64パーセントにしか達せず, 高学年になっても正確さが充分に発達していないことがわかる。JFLの場合は高学年になっても平均節数が2つ以上になることはなく, 単文のレベルにとどまっている。小学校6年間という時間を考えた場合, これでいいのだろうかという疑問と, 異族言語のイマージョンではこれ以上を期待することはできないのかという疑問が同時に湧いてくる。以上の結果については, 次のセクションの教育への示唆のところでさらに論じる。

まとめと今後の課題

ここでは, 本研究のまとめと, 本研究の結果をもとにした教育への示唆, 及び今後の課題を述べる。

まとめ

本研究の課題は, 次の2つであった：1) JHLの子どもの物語産出力と言語力は, 学年が上がるにつれどのように変化するのか。2) JHLの子どもの物語産出力と言語力は, 同プログラムに在籍するJFLの子どものそれと比べて違いがあるのか。あるとすればどのような違いがあるのか。

まず研究課題1については, JHLの子どもの物語産出力と言語力は相関しながら, 学年の上昇とともに上がっていくことがわかった。低学年での初期リテラシーの獲得後は, 物語産出力, 言語力ともに顕著な伸びがみられた。5年生になるとトピックが明確で, 詳細な情報が盛り込まれた物語が書けるようになる。しかしながら言語力の中の正確さは, 高学年に至っても最大で4年生の64パーセントにまでしか達していないことがわかった。ただし, 複雑な文を書く事により, 間違いが増え, 正確さが下がるという可能性も考えられる。

次に研究課題2については, 各学年で, JHLの子どもの物語産出力と言語力は, JFLのそれを顕著に上回り, その差は狭まることはない。しかし, 両グループともそれなりに学年が上がると物語産出力と言語力の上昇がみられ, これは先行研究の結果と一致する。一方, JFLの物語産出力は物語になる手前のレベルにとどまり, また言語力も単文のレベルに終始していることがわかった。

教育への示唆

以上の結果を教育への示唆という観点から検討したい。本研究はJHLに焦点をあてたものであるが, 今回比較分析のためにデータ分析を行ったJFLについても同じイマージョンクラスの学習者ということで, 両グループにとっての教育支援ということから, JFLを含めた考察を行う。まず, 同じクラスに物語産出力, 言語力が大きく異なるJHLとJFLの子どもがいて, その差は学年があがっても狭まることはないことから, 物語を書く指導

に関しては区別化(differentiation)が必要となる。本研究で使った単純なプロットから,より複雑で高度な物語(すなわち,単に話しの順を追うだけではなく,主人公の心理や物語中の問題解決のための計画とその結果などがあるもの)を書くプロットまでレベル別のものを揃え,JFLとJHLのそれぞれの子どもの物語を書く力にあったものを適宜与え,指導する必要があると思われる。またJFLは,初期リテラシーの獲得後も物語産出力が物語になる前でとどまっているため,口頭で物語を充分聞かせたり,物語に必要な要素(話の始め・中・終わり,トピックの維持)の指導を定期的に行う必要があると思われる。

次に,JHL,JFLともに正確さの発達が充分でないことと,JFLのグループの言語力の発達が単文レベルに終始していることから,言語力の指導(会話,書きの両方の指導)を強化する必要がある。言語形式に焦点をあてた学習活動で,文法の正確さを習得させることや,単文を複文へとつなぐいろいろなタイプの練習(例えば,関係節やモダリティーの使用)などをいれた学習活動を行う必要があると思われる。

今後の課題

本研究の結果から,JHLとJFLの物語産出力と言語力の違いが明らかになったが,JHLの特性をさらに知る上で,日本語を母語とする子どもたちの物語産出力と言語力との比較も必要だと思われる。これを今後の研究課題としたい。また本研究は,幼稚園から5年生までの横断研究だったが,現在もイマージョンプログラムに在籍する子どもたちを引き続き研究し,同じ子どもが学年が上がるにつれ物語産出力や言語力にどのような変化が見られるかを調べる縦断研究を行う予定である。

本研究では,物語産出力に関して低学年で著しく伸びるが,3年生以上になると学年間には大差が見られないという結果が出た。Donovan (2001)の英語を母語とする幼稚園から5年生までの児童の物語産出力,話の精緻度・話の進展度の発達研究でも,低学年から高学年への伸びはあるものの,顕著な伸びは低学年でみられることが報告されている。Donovanはこの結果について,高学年での顕著な伸びがみられないことの原因は,学校教育の中でより複雑でいろいろな種類の物語を書く機会が限られていることではないかと推測している。本研究で使った4つの絵の物語もプロットが単純であるため,複数の段落を書く力は測れず,とくにJHL高学年では産出力の測定が頭打ちになった可能性がある。もしそうであるなら,この種の物語は低学年での物語産出力を測定するのには適しているが,高学年用にはより複雑なプロットを与える必要があり,今後の研究の課題としたい。

本研究では一連の4つの絵についての話を書くという方法で物語産出力を検証したが,物語には他にも種類があり,個人の体験についての物語か絵についての物語かなど,語る内容の違いで,産出された物語の質が違うことが先行研究で指摘されている(Minami, 2008)。また,内田(2003)は,経験や出来事について物語ることはすでにある知識を再生的に利用できるが,絵という補助手段を使わずに物語る場合は想像力が必要なファンタジーの世界の語りとなり,幼児にとっては難しく,認知力の発達が関係すると指摘している。また,とくに言語力の発達過程にいる子どもの場合,物語の産出手段が話し言葉によるのか書き言葉によるのかによって差が出る。さらにバイリンガル環境で育つ子ども達は,2言語の言語差,およびMinami (2002, 2008)の研究で指摘されているように,文化の違いが物語産出力の発達に与えていることを考慮する必要がある。これらの先行研究の知見は,研究結果の一般化は慎重に行うことが必要であることを示している。

最後に，双方向イマージョンプログラムの効果に関して簡単に述べる。JHL の子どもたちは，高学年になると英語力が JFL とほぼ同等レベルまで伸び，また日本語力も大きく伸びていくという結果からみて，双方向イマージョンプログラムは JHL の子どもたちにとっては非常に効果のあるプログラムだといえよう。一方，JFL の子どもたちの日本語力は，小学校高学年になってもゆるやかな伸びにとどまっており，双方向イマージョンの効果はJHLほどには見られなかった。同族言語のイマージョンプログラムでは目標言語と主流言語がともに習得されることが実証されているが，本研究の結果をみると，異族言語の双方向イマージョンプログラムの場合，JFLの子どもにとっての効果はさらに検証する必要があると思われる。例えば，教師からの話しかけの質と量の研究や，先にも述べた区別化の効果の検証などを，今後の課題として記しておきたい。

引用文献

井川チャールズ (2003) 「南加日系社会における日本語教育の今日的課題」羅府新報(1月1日・4日・7日)

内田伸子 (1996) 『ことばと学び』金子書房

内田伸子 (2003) 『子どもの文章』東京大学出版会第3刷

片岡裕子・古山弘子・越山泰子 (2001) 「南カリフォルニア日本語学園教師アンケート結果分析報告<http://www.jflalc.org/teaching/jflc/fclty_rpt/jpz_kyoushi/heritage2.html> (2004年1月8日)

ダグラス昌子 (2010) 「継承日本語学習者の漢字力分析」JHL Journal, 3. <http://www.aatj.org/atj/SIG/heritage/ejournal/vol3.pdf> (2011年11月1日)

ダグラス昌子・片岡裕子・岸本俊子 (2003) 「継承語校と日本語補習校における学習者の言語背景調査」『国際評論』1, 1–13.

Bae, J. (2001). Cohesion and coherence in children's written English: Immersion and English-only classes. *Issues in Applied Linguistics, 12*(1), 51 88.

Bae, J. (2007). Development of English skills need not suffer as a result of immersion: Grades 1 and 2 writing assessment in a Korean/English two-way immersion program. *Language Learning, 57*(2), 299–332.

Berman, R. A., & Slobin, D. I. (1994). *Relating events in narrative: A cross-linguistic developmental study*. Hillsdale, NJ: Erlbaum.

California Department of Finance. (2010). 2010 *Census: Demographic profiles, table 3a— population by race, including detailed Asian race*. Retrieved from http://www.dof.ca.gov/research/demographic/state_census_data_center/census_2010/view.php#DP

Carson, J. E., Carrell, P. L., Silberstein, S., Kroll, B., & Kuehn, P. A. (1990). Reading writing relationships in first and second language. *TESOL Quarterly, 24*(2), 245–266.

Cazabon, M., Lambert, W. E., & Hall, G. (1993). *Two-way bilingual education: A progress report on the Amigos program* (Report No. 7). Washington, DC: National Center for Research on Cultural Diversity and Second Language Learning.

Cazabon, M. T., Nicoladis, E., & Lambert, W. E. (1998). *Becoming bilingual in the Amigos two-way immersion program* (Research Report 3). Santa Cruz, CA and Washington, DC: Center for Applied Linguistics.

Center for Applied Linguistics. (2011). *Directory of foreign language immersion programs in U.S. schools*. Retrieved from http://www.cal.org/resources/immersion

Chinen, K., Douglas, M. O., & Kataoka, H. C. (2009). *Ex-immersion students' Japanese proficiency: A report on four west coast high school Japanese programs*. A research paper submitted to Center for Applied Second Language Studies (CASLS), University of Oregon.

Chinen, K., & Tucker, G. R. (2005). Heritage language development: Understanding the roles of ethnic identity and Saturday school participation. *Heritage Language Journal*, *3*(1), 60–83. Retrieved from http://www.heritagelanguages.org/

Christian, D. (2008). School-based programs for heritage language learners: Two-way immersion. In D. Brinton, O. Kagan, & S. Baucks (Eds.), *Heritage language education: A new field emerging* (pp. 257–268). New York, NY: Routledge.

Christian, D., Howard, E. R., & Loeb, M. I. (2000). Bilingualism for all: Two-way immersion education in the United States. *Theory into Practice*, *39*(4), 258–266.

Collier, V. P., & Thomas, W. P. (2004). The astounding effectiveness of dual language education for all. *NABE Journal of Research and Practice*, *2*(1), 1–20.

Cummins, J. (1998). Immersion education for the millennium: What have we learned from 30 years of research on second language immersion? In M. R. Childs & R. M. Bostwick (Eds.), *Learning through two languages: Research and practice. Second Katoh Gakuen International symposium on immersion and bilingual education* (pp. 34–47). Numazu, Japan: Katoh Gakuen.

Donovan, C. (2001). Children's development and control of written story and informational genres: Insights from one elementary school. *Research in the Teaching of English*, *35*(3), 394–447.

Douglas, M. (1992). *Development of orthography-related reading/writing strategies by learners of Japanese as a foreign language* (Unpublished doctoral dissertation). University of Southern California, Los Angeles.

Douglas, M. (1994). Japanese cloze tests: Toward their construction. *Japanese-Language Education around the Globe*, *4*, 117–131.

Douglas, M. (2002). Teaching heritage language: Individualized learning. In K. Nakajima (Ed.), *Learning Japanese in the network* (pp. 149–173). Calgary, Canada: University of Calgary Press.

Douglas, M. (2003, April). *Assessing Japanese heritage language learners' needs from community service learning*. Paper presented at the meeting of the National Council of Less Commonly Taught Languages, University of California, Los Angeles.

Douglas, M. (2005). Pedagogical theories and approaches to teach young learners of Japanese as a heritage language. *Heritage Language Journal*, *3*(1), 60–83. Retrieved from http://www.heritagelanguages.org/

Douglas, M. (2007). A profile of Japanese heritage learners, individualized curriculum and its effectiveness. In D. M. Brinton, O. Kagan, & S. Bauckus (Eds.), *Heritage language acquisition: A new field emerging* (pp. 215–228). Mahwah, NJ: Erlbaum.

Douglas, M. (2008). Curriculum design for young learners of Japanese as a heritage language. In K. Kondo-Brown & J. D. Brown (Eds.), *Teaching Chinese, Japanese, and Korean heritage language students: Curriculum needs, materials, and assessment* (pp. 237–270). New York, NY: Routledge.

Edelsky, C. (1982). Writing in a bilingual program: The relation of L1 and L2 texts. *TESOL Quarterly*, *16*(2), 211–228.

Freeman, R. D. (1998). *Bilingual education and social change*. Philadelphia, PA: Multilingual Matters.

Gearhart, M., Herman, J. L., Baker, E. L., & Whittaker, A. K. (1992). *Writing portfolios at the elementary level: A study of methods for writing assessment.* (CSE Tech. Rep. No. 337). Los Angeles: University of California, Center for the Study of Evaluation.

Harley, B., Allen, P., Cummins, J., & Swain, M. (1991). *The development of second language proficiency.* Cambridge, United Kingdom: Cambridge University Press.

Hicks, D. (1994). Individual and social meanings. *Journal of Narrative and Life History, 4*(3), 215–240.

Howard, E. R., Christian, D., & Genesee, F. (2004). *The development of bilingualism and biliteracy from grade 3 to 5: A summary of findings from the CAL/CREDE study of two-way immersion education* (Report No. 13). Santa Cruz, CA and Washington, DC: Center for Research on Education, Diversity & Excellence.

Kajiwara, M., & Minami, M. (2008). Narrative construction by bilingual children: Referential topic management. *Studies in Language Science, 7,* 79–90.

Kanno, K., Hasegawa, T., Ikeda, K., Ito, Y., & Long, M. H. (2008). Prior language-learning experience and variation in the linguistic profiles of advanced English-speaking learners of Japanese. In D. M. Brinton, O. Kagan, & S. Bauckus (Eds.), *Heritage language education: A new field emerging* (pp. 165–180). New York, NY: Routledge.

Kataoka, H. C., Koshiyama, Y., & Shibata, S. (2008). Japanese and English language ability of students at supplementary Japanese schools in the United States. In K. Kondo-Brown & J. D. Brown (Eds.), *Teaching Chinese, Japanese, and Korean heritage language students* (pp. 47–76). New York, NY: Earlbaum.

Kondo-Brown, K. (2000). Acculturation and identity of bilingual heritage students of Japanese in Hawai'i. *Japan Journal of Multilingualism and Multiculturalism, 6,* 1–19.

Kondo-Brown, K. (2003). Heritage language instruction for post-secondary students from immigrant backgrounds. *Heritage Language Journal, 1*(1), 1–25. Retrieved from http://www.heritagelanguages.org/

Kondo-Brown, K. (2004). Do background variables predict students' scores on a proficiency test?: Implications for placing heritage language learners. *Journal of the National Council of Less Commonly Taught Languages, 1,* 1–19.

Kondo-Brown, K. (2005, May). *Recent work on teaching heritage students in East Asian languages: What have we accomplished so far and what should we do next?* Paper presented at the Heritage Language Instruction Symposium, Los Angeles, CA.

Kondo-Brown, K. (2010). Curriculum development for advancing heritage language competence: Recent research, current practice, and a future agenda. *Annual Review of Applied Linguistics, 30,* 24–41.

Lanauze, M., & Snow, C. (1989). The relation between first and second language writing skills: Evidence from Puerto Rican elementary school children in bilingual programs. *Theory into Practice, 31,* 132–141.

Lindholm-Leary, K. J. (2001). *Dual language education.* Buffalo, NY: Multilingual Matters.

Lü, C., & Koda, K. (2011). The impact of home language and literacy support on English Chinese biliteracy acquisition among Chinese heritage language learners. *Heritage Language Journal, 8*(2), 44–80. Retrieved from http://www.heritagelanguages.org/

Minami, M. (1996). Japanese preschool children's narrative development. *First Language, 16,* 339–363. Retrieved from http://fla.sagepub.com.mcc1.library.csulb.edu/content/16/48/339.refs.html

Minami, M. (2002). *Culture-specific language styles: The development of oral narrative and literacy child language and child development.* New York, NY: Multilingual Matters.

Minami, M. (2008). Telling good stories in different languages: Bilingual children's styles of story construction and their linguistic and educational implications. *Narrative Inquiry, 18*(1), 83–110.

Montrul, S., & Potowski, K. (2007). Command of gender agreement in school-age Spanish-English bilingual children. *International Journal of Bilingualism, 11,* 301–328.

Nunn, M. (2009). Socio-cultural differences in U.S., high school students' motivation to learn the Japanese Language. *JHL Journal, 3.* Retrieved from http://www.aatj.org/atj/SIG/heritage/ejournal/vol2.pdf

Peterson, C., & Dodsworth, P. (1991). A longitudinal analysis of young children's cohesion and noun specification in narratives. *Journal of Child Language, 18,* 397–415.

Peyton, J. K., Ranard, D. A., & McGinnis, S. (Eds.). (2001). *Heritage languages in America: Preserving a national resource.* McHenry: Center for Applied Linguistics and Delta Systems.

Ripich, D. N., & Griffith, P. L. (1990). Narrative abilities of children with learning disabilities and nondisabled children: Story structure, cohesion, and propositions. *Journal of Learning Disabilities, 21,* 165–173.

Sasaki, M. (2001, March). *Japanese as a heritage language (JHL) classes in Brazil and Hawai'i: Their differences and similarities.* Paper presented at the meeting of the Association of Teachers of Japanese, Chicago, IL.

Snow, M. A. (1986). *Innovative second language education: Bilingual immersion programs* (Education Report No 1). Retrieved from http://eric.ed.gov/PDFS/ED278258.pdf.

Sohn, S-O., & Merrill, C. (2008). The Korean-English dual language program in the Los Angeles unified school district. In D. M. Brinton, O. Kagan, & S. Bauckus (Eds.), *Heritage language education: A new field emerging* (pp. 269–288). New York, NY: Routledge.

Sugarman, J., & Howard, E. R. (2001). *Development and maintenance of two-way immersion programs: Advice from practitioners* (Practitioner Brief No. 2). Santa Cruz, CA and Washington, DC: Center for Research on Education, Diversity & Excellence website: http://www.cal.org/crede/pubs/PracBrief2.htm

Takano, Y., & Noda, A. (1995). Interlanguage dissimilarity enhances the decline of thinking ability during foreign language processing. *Language Learning, 45*(4), 657–681.

Thomas, W. P., & Collier, V. P. (2002). *A national study of school effectiveness for language minority students' long-term academic achievement.* CREDE/CAL. Retrieved from http://crede.berkeley.edu/research/crede/research/llaa/1.1_final.html

University of California Los Angeles. (2001). *Heritage language research priorities conference report.* Retrieved from http://www.cal.org/heritage

Wolf-Quintero, K., Inagaki, S., & Kim, H. (1998). *Second language development in writing: Measures of fluency, accuracy, and complexity.* Honolulu, HI: Second Language Teaching and Curriculum Center, University of Hawai'i.

Using N *Desu* in Small Talk: JFL Learners' Pragmatic Development

スモールトークにおける「んです」の使用：
海外日本語学習者の語用論的能力の発達

Tomoko Iwai
University of Hawai'i at Mānoa

Abstract

Despite widespread use in authentic discourse, the extended predicate n desu does not receive the coverage it deserves. Japanese language textbooks do not account for the important function of extending talk and creating a conversational tone. In this longitudinal study, n desu was taught in two second-semester university JFL classes, with an instructional approach that placed heavy emphasis on pragmatics. This pragmatics-focused instruction featured a) awareness raising, b) explicit instruction, c) communicative practice, and d) feedback sessions. Pre- and post-data were collected from conversations between the students and Japanese exchange students, and analyzed both quantitatively and qualitatively to examine 1) whether the pragmatics-focused instruction resulted in increased use of n desu by the students, 2) what effect the length of instruction had on the students' use of n desu, and 3) what effect the use of n desu had on the students' participation with regard to its contribution to small talk. The results are compared to those of another group of students who received grammar-focused instruction. The students in the pragmatics-focused group (PFG) increased the use of n desu in various turn types, while the students in the grammar-focused group produced no instances of n desu in either conversational session. Furthermore, in many cases PFG students' use of n desu contributed to the co-construction of involved small talk in a way that is more consistent with natural conversation.

要旨

自然会話では「んです」の使用が頻繁であるが、日本語の教科書では、人間関係を重視したスモールトークで、話題を展開し話を続けていくことにより相手への興味や話者の社交性を表すという「んです」の重要な機能がほとんど紹介されていない。本研究では、アメリカの大学の初級二学期目の学生に、一学期間語用論を中心とした教授法を用いて、相手とスモールトークを相互に構築することを目標に、「んです」及びスモールトークの中で同時に使われる主な語用論項目の使い方を教えた。教授に当たっては、意識化活動、語用論の明示的説明、会話練習、教師によるフィードバック等の手法を使った。本研究では、1) 語用論を重視した教授法により学生の「んです」の使用が増加するか、2) 習得期間の違いが学生の「んです」の使用にどのような効果を持つか、3)「んです」の使用が学生のスモールトークの構築にどのような影響を与えるか、の三点を縦断的に調査した。データは日本語の会話専門のコースの学生と日本人留学生との会話を学期の初めと終わりにビデオを採取し、文法中心クラスの学生のデータと比べた。分析の結果、語用論グループの多くが「んです」を使ったが、文法グループで使用した学生はいなかった。また、「んです」を使った学生の中の多くは、「んです」を使ってより自然な会話に近い相互参加型のスモールトークを構築することに成功した。

Introduction

The extended predicate *n desu* is essential in everyday conversation in Japanese, but its coverage in Japanese language textbooks does not reflect its widespread use in natural conversation. Well known and most commonly-used elementary Japanese textbooks tend to focus only on one or two functions of *n desu*, usually that of explanation and/or showing a speaker's assumptions. As a result, learners, especially those who do not have extensive exposure to authentic spoken Japanese, tend to use the distal *-masu* form of verbs as a default sentence ending for all purposes, which deviates from authentic use of the language by native speakers. In this study, *n desu* was taught along with other pragmatic resources as an indispensable resource for everyday conversation, in particular, small talk, using a pragmatics-focused instructional approach. The instruction focused on the common use of *n desu* which contributes to the creation of a conversational tone, and conveys various social meanings such as friendliness, interest, involvement, and an orientation to engage further in the ongoing talk. The learners' conversations with native speaker peers were videotaped for analysis before and after the instruction. Another set of conversational data was collected from learners in a second-semester class who received grammar-focused instruction for comparison.

Previous research

N *desu* in L1 literature

The extended predicate *n desu* has been an object of vigorous study in Japanese linguistics. It is a pragmatic resource that is widely used in Japanese spoken discourse and consists of the sentence-final particle *no* and the copula *desu*. The primary function of *n desu* has been described in past studies as showing that there is some information or evidence in the linguistic or extra linguistic context that forms the basis for the claim or proposition made in the utterance (Alfonso, 1980; Aoki, 1986; Kuno, 1973; Makino & Tsutsui, 1986). Thus the interpretation of the utterance marked with *n desu* depends on this extra information that is not in the utterance itself. The use of *n desu* in an utterance does not change the referential meaning of the utterance but it adds certain overtones to the statement such as explanation (Alfonso, 1980; Aoki, 1986; Kuno, 1973; Makino & Tsutsui, 1986), emphasis, and mild correction (Alfonso, 1980).

N *desu* in conversation

The above studies captured the fundamental function of *n desu* as indexing evidence/information outside of the utterance in which *n desu* is used. However, this explanation does not fully account for the use of *n desu* in small talk where there is no apparent evidence or information that *n desu* is referencing. In Japanese conversation, including narratives, *n desu* is used frequently to convey information that is not shared with the interlocutor. Makino & Tsutsui (1986) explain that if no information is shared by the interlocutors, the speaker is speaking emotively as if some information were shared with the hearer, with the effects of involving the hearer in his talk or to impose his idea upon the hearer. This function of *n desu* that shows involvement may be linked to the cohesive function of *n desu* used in place of the distal *masu* form observed in narrative studies (Clancy, 1982; Iwasaki, 1992). Iwasaki (1992) observes that over 90% of the all the finite clauses in the narrative data are produced with *n desu* (Iwasaki, 1992). While nearly 50% of the bare clause (-*masu* form) appears with no related clauses, only 1.8 % of *n desu* clauses occur with no related clauses in the spoken discourse data. This shows that *n desu* has a function of relating the clause in which it is used to another clause somewhere in the discourse.

Wang (2009) also observed this cohesive function of *n desu* in the spoken discourse data; 90% of the yes-no questions marked with *n desu* occur in the middle of the discourse while most of the *ka*-marked yes-no questions without *n desu* occur at a discourse boundary often to introduce a new topic. N *desu*-marked yes-no questions are rarely used to introduce a brand new topic but are mostly used to develop, deepen, or specify an ongoing topic or to shift to a subtopic. The transcript of the data shows that these yes-no questions are followed by answers and elaborations also marked by *n desu* contributing to the topic development.

Yoshimi (2001a) compares the utterances with and without *n desu* in small talk and offers an explanation on the difference: one of the functions of *n desu* in small talk is "to help the speaker maintain a conversational tone in his/her talk" and "too many missed uses of *n desu* result in speech that is 'dry', 'speechy', 'flat', and 'dull' or 'disinterested'" (Yoshimi, 2001a, p. 9). Yoshimi explains that, when used in a question, *n desu* indexes shared understanding of the context/situation, creating a sense of solidarity with the interlocutor and this leads to the conversational and friendly tone. When answering a question, the speaker uses *n desu* to retain the same conversational tone, to index the shared understanding about the topic at hand, and to indicate that they are engaging in a friendly chat. It is important to note that *n desu* does not always index friendliness in all contexts. Cook (1990) states that *n desu* indexes group authority for knowledge in social contexts such as parents socializing their children. However, *n desu* has the function of indexing engagement in extended discourse. This engagement is often friendly, especially when used with other co-occurring pragmatic resources that also index engagement and friendliness, such as listener responses and evaluative comments.

The following two dialogues illustrate the differences between the conversational exchanges with and without the use of *n desu*.

(1)
1 A: *Lee san, shuumatsu wa nani o shita <u>n desu</u> ka?*
        'What did you do this weekend, Lee?'
2 B: *Shuumatsu desu ka? Shuumatsu wa tomodachi to issho ni benkyoo shita <u>n desu</u>.*
3   'Weekend? I studied with my friends this weekend.'
        Getsuyoobi ni shiken ga atta kara.
        'There was an exam on Monday, so…'

4   A: *Hee, taihen deshita ne.*
         'Oh, that's too bad."
5   B: *Ee. Yamada san wa?*
         'Yeah, how about you?'
6   A: *Watashi wa tomodachi no uchi de paatii ga atta <u>n desu</u>.*
         'I had a party at my friend's house'
7   B: *Hee, ii naa. Tanoshikatta desu ka?*
         'Oh, how nice. Was it fun?'
8   A: *Un, sugoku tanoshikatta desu yo.*
         'Yeah, it was really fun.'

(2)
1   A: *Lee san, shuumatsu wa nani o shita <u>n desu</u> ka?*
         'What did you do this weekend, Lee?'
2   B: *Shuumatsu desu ka? Shuumatsu wa eiga o mimashita.*
         'This weekend? I saw a movie.'
3   A: *A soo desu ka. Nani o mita n desu ka?*
         'Oh, really. What did you see?'
4   B: *Rasuto samurai o mimashita.*
         'I saw Last Samurai.'
5   A: *Hee, omoshirokatta desu ka?*
         'Oh, was it good?'
6   B: *Hai sugoku yokatta desu.*
         'Yes, it was really good.'
7   A: *Hee watashi mo mitai naa.*
         'Oh I want to see it too.'

In dialogue (1), both A and B use *n desu*. This creates a tone in which both participants are engaged in a friendly chat, as opposed to simply eliciting information. The friendly tone is created through the use of *n desu* and other resources as well, such as listener responses, evaluative comments (line 4, 7), as well as follow ups that elaborate (line 3) and ask a further question (line 7). The use of *n desu* indexes the participants' orientation to one of a friendly chat and an orientation that keeps the conversation going. In dialogue (2), while A's turns are similar to dialogue (1) with *n desu* and other resources to show interest and engagement, B's turns end in the distal form –*mashita,* and sound more abrupt and a bit unfriendly. B's use of -*mashita* in line 4 sounds especially abrupt because its tone signals that she is finished with what she is saying. It does not have the same function as *n desu,* which shows an orientation to engage more in talk, especially when A is trying to develop the topic by asking a follow-up question (line 3). Thus, the use of *n desu* in line 4 would make B's participation more engaging and friendly since it is used in small talk.

Instruction of *n desu* in small talk

The use of *n desu* presents a challenge in a Japanese as a foreign language (JFL) classroom on two fronts. First, the English speaking JFL learners do not have the same pragmatic phenomenon in their native languages and they do not have extensive exposure to spoken Japanese which might clue them into this pragmatic phenomenon; and secondly, *n desu* seems to be a slippery and elusive pragmatic resource to many Japanese instructors because of its heavy dependence on contextual variables which makes its use seem inconsistent and puzzling at times.

Previous research on learner use of *n desu* indicates that *n desu* responds well to explicit pragmatics-focused instruction in the case of conversational narratives at a second- and third-year level (Iwai, 2000; Yoshimi, 2001b; Yoshimi & Iwai, 2001). Yet, in the case of small talk, the pilot study for this research did not support this. It indicated that *n desu* was resistant to instruction with only three of 13 students producing *n desu* in small talk after a semester of instruction (Iwai, 2005). However, the small number of the subjects in the pilot study put into question the reliability of this finding, and it was subsequently addressed in the present study.

Another factor that may have contributed to the low number of students who produced *n desu* in the pilot study was the length of instruction. Although everyone in this group received a semester of instruction during this study, two of them had received instruction on *n desu* in the previous semester using the same instructional approach. One of the two students produced *n desu* in both the beginning and the end of the semester while the other did not produce any. The issue of how much time it takes learners to start using pragmatic resources has been raised in previous studies. For example, Yoshimi (2001b) found that despite gains in the use of *n desu* to maintain the flow of a narrative, the students did not make use of variants of *n desu* to mark shifts in scene or perspective, or to build up the suspense or to highlight the point of the story. Yoshimi suggests that the question of time must also be considered in determining whether some aspect of pragmatics is more resistant to teaching (Yoshimi, 2001b:243). In a recent study, Ishida (2009) found that the students who received instruction on speech style in Japanese for two semesters outperformed those students who only received instruction for one semester. In Ishida's study, the students who received two semesters of instruction did better than those with one semester of instruction not only in their understanding of the forms for indexing different stances but also in the production of those forms (Ishida, 2009). These results suggest the importance of sustained instruction of pragmatics over time (Yoshimi, 2009) and the benefit of curriculum that implements long-term, sustained instruction of pragmatics.

Instructional approach

Previous studies on the effectiveness of the instruction of pragmatics showed promise in the case of explicit instruction, an instructional approach that featured awareness raising, metapragmatic explanation of the target pragmatic features, modeling, communicative practice and feedback (House, 1996; Iwai, 2000; Kasper & Rose, 2002; Rose & Kasper, 2001; Tateyama, 2001; Yoshimi, 2001b). Iwai (2005) used all of the above instructional components in a semester-long pilot study on the instruction of small talk as an activity in a beginning JFL class. This study sets itself apart from other studies in one important aspect; the instruction used pragmatics-focused instructional approach as a mainstay of instruction throughout the semester rather than treatments added on to an existing curriculum. The study found significant improvement in the students' ability to co-construct more involved small talk where students displayed their affective stances much more than before the instruction.

Research questions

This study examined the effectiveness of the pragmatics-focused instruction on the students' use of *n desu* in small talk. Based on the previous research, the study aims to answer the following research questions.

1. Did the pragmatics-focused instruction result in increased use of *n desu* by the students after the instruction?

2. What effect did the length of instruction have on the use of instructed pragmatic resources by the students?

3. What effect did the use of *n desu* have on the students' participation with regard to its contribution to small talk?

Methods

N desu was taught as one of the indispensable resources that are used to co-construct the activity of small talk in this study. The ability to co-construct an involved small talk was coined *conversational competence* and was operationalized for instruction by identifying eight pragmatic resources deemed essential through the analysis of naturally occurring conversations by native speakers, as well as previously-obtained conversational data between a native speaker and a JFL student. These pragmatic resources include *n desu*, listener responses, evaluative comments, repair, and four conversational moves that follow a question-and-answer sequence, namely: a follow-up question, an expansion that relates to the content in the preceding talk, a return question that asks the same or similar question to that asked by the interlocutor, and a question or statement that introduces a new topic. Of course, it must be recognized that the resources used in small talk generally go beyond this limited list of resources. For this study, conversational competence was conceived to be part of communicative competence (Hymes, 1972), a construct that covers small talk at the elementary level of JFL instruction. This study will mainly focus on the contribution to small talk of *n desu* and four conversational moves through quantitative and qualitative analysis of the students' conversational data.

Participants

There were 28 students in the pragmatics-focused-group (PFG) and 11 students in the grammar-focused-group (GFG). Both groups were enrolled in a second-semester Japanese course at an American university. Students in both groups were of college age except for three mature graduate students (late 20s and early 30s) in the PFG. Of the 28 students in the PFG, 14 had taken the first-semester PF class in the previous semester. The other fourteen came from the first- and second-semester GF classes or were placed in this course by a placement exam.

The instructor for the PFG was the author, a female native speaker with over 20 years of teaching experience in university and community settings in and outside the United States. The instructor for the GFG was a bilingual, male instructor with more than 20 years of experience at the same institution.

Data collection and analysis

Data consists of video-recorded conversations between students and native speakers from Japan who came as exchange students. Each student initially met a native speaker peer (one of three conversation partners, [CP1] for example) in a *conversation session* at the beginning of the semester (CS1), and another conversation partners [CP2] or [CP3]) at the end of the semester (CS2) in which they engaged in small talk for five minutes. Students met with a different native speaker each time to ensure the authenticity of the encounter. The videotaped conversations were transcribed for analysis. Quantitative analysis was conducted to examine whether *n desu* was used by each of the students in CS1 and CS2. Each instance of *n desu* produced by students was coded, counted, and classified as to the type of conversational moves in which *n desu* occurred. The instruction of conversational competence included such conversational moves as: a) follow-up questions, b) expansions (statements related to the self's or the interlocutor's utterance in the prior discourse), c) return questions (ones that repeat or partially modify the interlocutor's question), and d) new-topic-introducing turns (either questions or statements) as these turns contribute to the development of the topic and provide an environment for *n desu* to occur. *N desu* can occur in any of the above conversational moves, and together they contribute to creating a friendly and involved tone for small talk. These turns marked with *n desu* can occur after an initial question-and-answer sequence followed by an acknowledgment turn, and contribute to the development of the topic at hand. Thus, students who do not produce these turns have much less opportunities to use *n desu* compared to the students who do, leading to a less involved, passive participation in small talk.

Types of turns

The students' conversational data was analyzed quantitatively and qualitatively to examine how students used *n desu* in terms of its placement in different conversational moves, and the impact the use of *n desu* had on the overall quality of small talk.

The following are the examples of the conversational moves that were part of the instruction of conversational competence.

Follow-up questions

Follow-up questions relate to the ongoing topic by asking for more detailed information. The use of follow-up questions indicates interest in the interlocutor's answers and develops the topic further.

    1   S1:   *Yuki san Hawai wa doo desu ka?*
                    'How do you like Hawai'i, Yuki?'
    2   CP2: *n. suki desu.*
                    'Yes, I like it.'
    3   S1:   *a suki desu ka.*
                    'Oh you like it.'
    4   CP2: *hai.*
                    'Yes.'
    5   S1:   *e saafin (.)*
                    'Oh surfing (.)'
    6   CP2: *.hh mada shita koto ga nai n desu.*
                    '.hh I haven't tried that yet.'
    7   S1:   *a soodesu ka.* [*hee.*
                    'Oh okay. [I see.'
    8   CP2:   [*hai:.*
                    ['Yes.'
→   9   S1:   *doo-dooshite hawai suki na n dseu ka?*
                    'Why do you like Hawai'i?'
    10   CP2: ((laughs)) *samuku nai kara desu.*
                    'Because it's not cold.'
    11   S1:   ((laughs)) *a soodesu ka.*
                    'Oh I see.'

Expansion

An expansion turn is usually a statement that is related to the previous discourse. Participants can use this turn to explain or elaborate on his/her previous statement or offer his/her thoughts/experience regarding the interlocutor's utterance.

    91   CP2: *shumi wa nandesu ka?*
                    'What's your hobby?'
    92   S8:   *shumi wa:: supootsu ga suki desu.*
                    'My hobby is: I like sports.'

```
     93    CP2: donna supootsu ga su [ki desu ka?
                'What kind of sports [do you like?'
     94    S8:                       [basket boru: [uh: to: =
                                     ['basketball: [uh: and:' =
     95    CP2:                                    [n.
                                                   ['uh huh'
→    96    S8:  = football [to: volleyball. Uh: kinoo    [basket =
                = 'football [and: volleyball. Uh: yesterday [basket' =
     97    CP2:            [N.                           [n
                           ['uh huh                      uh huh'
→    98    S8:  = ball- UH basket ball ni-ni itta n desu.
                = 'all- I went to UH basketball.'
     99    CP2: ↑ aa soo desu ka. doodeshita ka?
                ↑ 'Ohh I see! How was it?'
    100    S8:  hai. Uh: uh °iidesu ne.
                'Yes. Uh: uh °good, aren't they.'
    101    CP2: ↑ nn.
                ↑ 'nn.'
```

Return question

A return question is used to ask the same question back to the interlocutor. It can be the same question verbatim or a reformulated question that has a similar referential content.

```
     32    CP2: hai. Nani o benkyoo shite iru n desu ka?
                'Yes. What are you studying?'
     33    S1:  eeto ne. eigo de: (.) second language acquisition desu kedo [:]
                'Um: in English: (.) it's called second language acquisition but'
     34    CP2: [Hai.
                'uh huh'
     35    S1:  nihongo de: aa: eigo kyooiku ka naa?
                'in Japanese aa: English education? I wonder'
     36    CP2: n. ((nodding)) ↑ soo desu kaa.
                'N. ((nodding)) I see.'
     37         (.5)
→    38    S1:  de nani o (.) benkyoo suru n desu ka?
                'So what (.) do you study?'
     39    CP2: koko de
                'here'
→    40    S1:  hai. Senkoo wa
                'Yes, your major is'
     41    CP2: women's stadiizu.
                'Women's studies'
     42    S1:  a women's studies desu kaa.
                'Oh women's studies. I see.'
     43    CP2: hai.
                'Yes.'
```

New-topic introduction

New topics were introduced from time to time in both questions and statements.

42	CP1:	*ima nannensei desu ka?*
		'What year are you?'
43	S21:	*ima: wa ninensei desu.*
		'Now: I'm a sophomore.'
44	CP1:	*nnnnn.*
		'nnnnn'
→ 45	S21:	*kongakki wa nani o toru n desu ka?*
		'What do you take this semester?'
46	CP1:	*kongakki- wa: bijinesu no jugyoo o futatsu to:*
		'This semester- I'm taking: two business courses:
47		*keizai no jugyoo hitotsu to eigono jugyoo o hitotsu totte imasu.*
		one economics class and one English class.'

Instruction of *n desu* in the pragmatics-focused group

The PFG received instruction in a course that focused on oral communication with a pragmatics-based curriculum. The instruction used in this study adopted the explicit instruction approach that many studies found to be beneficial for teaching pragmatics (House, 1996; Iwai, 2000; Kasper & Rose, 2002; Rose & Kasper, 2001, Tateyama, 2001; Yoshimi, 2001b).

The metapragmatic information about *n desu* was made salient to students mainly through explanation of its use in model dialogues. The students were required to read the usage notes that had extensive and in-depth explanations about *n desu* contained in the instructional materials. Then, the instructor involved the students in the analysis of the model dialogue that contained *n desu*. In this activity, a dialogue was analyzed into actions such as question, answer, acknowledgment, evaluative comment, follow-up question, etc. (Yoshimi, 2003) and the use of pragmatic resources was discussed with regard to the actions they help accomplish. The main functions of *n desu* were explained as a) creating a conversational tone, e.g., a friendly and interested tone in an action of a question, and b) the willing participation in the action of an answer or an elaboration.

Native speaker modeling
The instructor often initiated small talk with students at the beginning of class using *n desu*. This impromptu conversational exchange between the instructor and one of the students gave the other students opportunities to observe a native speaker model of small talk. The students were instructed to pay attention to the conversation and listen for the resources that were used by the instructor. The instructor asked the students what resources were used in the conversation and what they thought of the conversation in terms of its tone, such as friendliness and display of interest among other things. The model dialogues in the textbook with audio recordings between native speakers also functioned as models for the students (Appendix A).

Communicative practice after explicit instruction
The explicit instruction through usage notes and dialogue analysis was followed by a communicative practice session where students engaged in various small talk topics in pairs and with the instructor. During the communicative practice after instruction on *n desu* in small talk, students used activity sheets provided by the instructor that contained information regarding the goals of the interaction, the situation, and who they are talking to

(See Appendix B) in order to perform a task. The tasks involved engaging in mostly open-ended conversation about various topics along with various goals.

In addition to the communicative practice with activity sheets, there were also impromptu communicative practices two to three times a week where students were directed to have a chat with each other for three to five minutes at the beginning of class. The instructor asked students to talk about the past weekend's activities on Mondays, their plans for the coming weekend on Fridays, as well as plans for Thanksgiving and Christmas vacation. The practice of talking about weekends and holidays was frequent, and became routine (Coulmas, 1981) by the end of the semester.

Feedback

The communicative practice after the explicit instruction was always followed by opportunities to provide feedback. The feedback aimed to raise students' awareness by providing them with an opportunity to observe and evaluate other students' performances. After students had practiced working in pairs, the instructor either a) asked two students to chat with each other (usually a new pair who had not talked to each other during the practice) in front of the whole class, or b) called on a student and chatted with him or her. Then the instructor solicited feedback from other students. After discussion, students were provided feedback on what each did well, and ways each could improve. During feedback sessions, the instructor commented on students' use and non-use of the pragmatic resources appropriate for the talk, as well as the use of tone of voice and facial expression. Feedback after the routine impromptu small talk at the beginning of class was not as extensive as that held after the communicative practice. After the routine small talk, the instructor simply asked students if they used appropriate actions such as follow-up questions and listener responses, as well as appropriate resources for small talk, such as *n desu,* to remind them of the appropriate actions and resources for small talk.

Instruction of *n desu* in the grammar-focused group

The GFG received instruction in a four-skilled course that had a grammar-based curriculum that included some conversational practice. The instruction for this group consisted of demonstrations of grammatical structures, *kanji*, reading and writing centering on the grammatical structures presented in the lesson. Though the curriculum for this class did not contain a treatment of *n desu* in small talk, it did include *n desu* as a grammar structure having the function of explanatory ending in one of the chapters. The examples in this chapter are exchanges that start with a question, *doo shita n desu ka?* "What's the matter," where the answer is to be given with the *n desu* ending indicating that it is an explanation. For students who took a first-semester grammar-focused (GF) class, *n desu* was also covered in the last chapter, which focused on the use of the dictionary form of verbs. In this chapter, *n desu* was also presented as having an explanatory function. It was included in the Grammar Note of the chapter and used with the dictionary form of verbs introduced. It was also included in the Strategies section serving two functions: to introduce a main topic, and to ask for information about a word. In both courses, *n desu* is treated as a grammar point rather than a pragmatic resource, and its inclusion is largely limited to its explanatory function. Though *n desu* was used in the example sentences for introducing a main topic, the explanation was given on the unfinished sentence using the conjunction *kedo instead.* There was no mention of *n desu* in the explanation.

The instructor for the GFG regularly assigned reading on a grammar point along with structure drills and an exercise handout for oral practice before a class meeting. In class, the instructor answered students' questions about the grammatical point in question, and had the students work in pairs using the grammatical structure in a question-and-answer sequence as instructed in the handout. The instructor encouraged the students to expand and follow-up if the answer was interesting but this was not part of the required task. In addition to the grammar instruction and practice, the instructor also included conversational practice using a handout in mid-semester. The handout included such resources for small talk as acknowledgment and evaluative comments but *n desu* was not included as a resource for small talk.

Results and discussion

Use of *n desu* by students in PFG and GFG

In this study, there was a notable gain in the use of *n desu* among the students in the PFG after the semester of instruction. The following table shows the number of students who used *n desu* before and/or after the instruction as well as the number of tokens used (in the parentheses).

Table 1. Number of students who used *n desu* in CS1 and CS2 and total number of tokens used

	did not use CS1 or CS2	used CS2 only	used CS1 & CS2	used CS1 only
PFG (n=28)	7	12 (22)	8 (42)	1 (3)
GFG (n=11)	11	0	0	0

There was a sharp difference between the GFG and the PFG in the gains in the production of *n desu* in the conversation sessions. Of the 28 students who received instruction on *n desu* in the PFG, 20 students produced *n desu* in their conversation session with a native speaker at the end of the semester. Seven students did not use any instances of *n desu* either at the beginning or the end of the semester. Eight students used *n desu* in both conversation sessions. In comparison, the GFG did not produce any instances of *n desu* in conversation sessions at the beginning or at the end of the semester. As mentioned earlier, the GFG did receive instruction on *n desu* with an explanatory function in exchanges starting with *doo shita n desu ka?* 'What's the matter?' in one of the chapters. Those who took the first-semester GF class in the previous semester had been exposed to routine expressions such as *kono kanji nante yomu n desu ka* "how do you read this *kanji?*" introduced in the last chapter of the previous semester. Students also covered the use of *n desu* as a main topic introduction as in *keejiban ni kore ga hatte atta n desu kedo* 'this was posted on the notice board but…' in another chapter of the book. However, they did not receive instruction on the use of *n desu* to create a conversational tone that was taught in the experimental classes for this study. These results support the benefit of the pragmatics-focused (PF) instruction over the GF instruction in the use of *n desu*.

Effect of length in pragmatics-focused instruction

Analysis of the students' previous study background yielded an interesting insight into the time it takes to develop pragmatic competence. The students in the PFG can be categorized into two groups based on the length of PF instruction they received.

1. PF2SEM Group had two consecutive semesters of PF instruction
2. PF1SEM Group had one semester of PF instruction

Fourteen students had received pragmatics-focused instruction on *n desu* during the previous semester (PF2SEM). Students in this group received two semesters of PF instruction when the study concluded at semester's end. The remaining fourteen received instruction that did not focus on pragmatics (PF1SEM) prior to this study, so they had only one semester of PF instruction.

Table 4. Number of students who used *n desu* in CS1 and CS2 in PFG by length of PF instruction

	did not use CS1 or CS2	used CS2 only	used CS1 & CS2	used CS1 only
PFG (28)				
PF2SEM (14)	0	7	7	0
PF1SEM (14)	7	5 (1)*	1	1
total (28)	7	12	8	1

* incomplete *n desu*. Production of "n" only without "desu" included in 5.

The table above shows that the students who received two semester of PF instruction on the use of *n desu* all produced *n desu* at the end of the semester. Six out of fourteen produced *n desu* in both CS1 and CS2, meaning that they produced *n desu* after one semester of instruction. The other seven did not produce *n desu* after one semester of instruction but did so after two semesters of instruction. More students from this group produced *n desu* at the end of the semester when compared to the PF1SEM group. All seven students who did not produce *n desu* in either CS1 or CS2 are in the PF1SEM group. This suggests that one semester of PF instruction was insufficient for all students to learn to use *n desu*, while two semesters of instruction was sufficient. This is consistent with the findings in Ishida's (2009) study on speech styles in Japanese in which students who received instruction on speech styles the previous semester outperformed those who did not.

Patterns of use and involvement

This section discusses the learners' use of *n desu* in terms of its contribution to involved small talk and how its use co-occurs with other resources of small talk. Learners used *n desu* in a variety of turn types, e.g., question (new topic introduction), answer, follow-up question, expansion, statement (new topic introduction), listener response, and repair. These turn types were presented as an indispensable part of small talk for this study. Use of *n desu* creates a conversational tone signaling the speaker's willingness to engage and extend talk. This often results in extended talk through the speaker's involved participation using such turns that follow up on the previous turns, adds onto one's own answers, or introduces a new topic. These turns accomplish important actions of developing the topic at hand and displaying the speaker's affective stances (Ochs, 1993, 1996), and are indispensable in co-constructing friendly and comfortable small talk.

Table 5. Number of occurrences of *n desu* in various types of turns in CS1 and CS2

	CS1	CS2	total
new topic question	2	16	18
expansion	2	17	19
follow-up question	3	9	12
repair	0	1	1
answer	5	3	8

In both CS1 and CS2, the learners used *n desu* most in expansion turns when they elaborated on their own turn, or expanded on their interlocutor's turn (19 tokens). The learners also introduced a new topic either by asking a question or by making a statement (18 tokens). Follow-up questions were also produced with *n desu* frequently (12 tokens). *N desu* was also used to answer questions (8 tokens). This shows that expansion, new topic introduction, and follow-up question turns were major environments for using *n desu*. Qualitative analysis of the learners' conversations indicates that many had a relatively passive participation in CS1, where they answered questions and allowed the native speaker to take the role of an "interactional manager" (Kasper, 2004), that is, a native speaker that takes the role of facilitating the conversation by asking questions and introducing topics. Many learners had very few opportunities to use n desu because of their passive participation in CS 1. Thus, when they used more conversational moves and participated more actively in the conversation, they had more opportunities to use *n desu*. Only when learners became more active in topic introduction and used more conversational moves were they able to use *n desu*.

An obvious case for this is where learners did not use any of these turn types in CS1, but did so in CS2. In doing so, they also used *n desu*. For example, Student 25 did not use any instances of *n desu* in CS1; in CS2, he used *n desu* once each in a follow up question and an expansion. The use of those turn types increased from 0 to 2 for follow-up questions and 1 to 4 for expansions from CS1 to CS2. The following conversational excerpt between S25 and CP2 in CS1 shows that S25's participation is limited to answering questions. Throughout the conversation, S25 did not use any follow-up questions and only one expansion turn. In the excerpt below, S25 asks a return question in line 19 and a new topic question in line 23. He does not follow-up with a related question, using only a minimal expansion to add more information after *hai* "Yes" (line 31). There were very few opportunities for him to use *n desu* because he did not use follow-up questions and elaborations that could have presented opportunities for using *n desu*. His lack of follow-up on the interlocutors' turns as well as the lack of *n desu* makes this interaction an awkward and uninvolved one-sided exchange. His lack of follow-up after the listener response in line 25 abruptly cuts off the topic of CP2's hobby after she asks S25 what his hobby is.

Excerpt 1. S25 (PFG) and CP2 in CS1

   13   CP2: ((nodding)) *ima nannensei desu ka?*
            ((nodding)) 'what year are you?'
   14   S25: *sannensei desu.*
            'I'm a junior.'
   15   CP2: ((nodding)) *nnn. nani o senkoo shite imasu ka?*
            ((nodding)) 'Nnn. What are you majoring in?'
   16   S25: *bijinesu desu.*
            'In business.'
   17   CP2: ((smiling and nodding)) *omoshiroi desu ka?*
            ((smiling and nodding)) 'Is it interesting?'
   18   S25: *ee maa maa.*
            'Yeah so-so.'
   19   CP2: ((laughing)) *maa maa desu ka?*
            ((laughing)) 'so-so?'
→ 20   S25: ((smiling)) *ee.* ((hand extended)) *Ko-i-zumi san wa?*
            ((smiling)) 'yeah. ((hand extended)) How about you?'
   21   CP2: *eto hawai daigaku de women's studies o benkyoo shite imasu.*
            'Um I'm studying women's study at UH.'
   22   S25: *a soo desu ka.*
            Oh I see.
   23   CP2: *hai.*
            'Yes.'
→ 24   S25: *uh shumi wa nan desu ka?*
            'Uh what are your hobbies?'

	25	CP2: *eiga o miru no ga suki desu.*
		'I like watching movies.'
→	26	S25: *a soo desu ka.*
		'Oh okay.'
	27	CP2: *shumi wa nan desu ka?*
		'What are your hobbies?'
	28	S25: *eeto: weighto toraining to: kanuu-paddling?*
		'uhm: weight training and canoe paddling?'
	29	CP2: *kanuu paddling?*
		'Canoe paddling?'
	30	S25: *yeah. Hai.*
		'Yeah. Yes.'
	31	CP2: ((nodding/smiling)) *omoshiroi desu ka?*
		((nodding/smiling)) 'Is that fun?'
	32	S25: *hai.* ((nodding)) [*sugoku omoshiroi desu.*
		Yes. ((nodding)) ['it's really fun.'
	33	CP2: [*nn.* (.) *omoshiroi desu ka.*
		['nn. (.) it's fun, I see.'
	34	((nodding)) *nihon ni itta koto: ga arimasu ka?*
		((nodding)) 'Have you been to Japan?'
	35	S25 ((puzzled face))
	36	CP2: *nihon ni ikimashita ka?*
		'Oh. did you go to Japan?'
	37	S25: *oh hai. uh:* (1) *uh:* (1) ((giggles))
		'Oh yes. Uh: (1) uh:' (1) ((giggles))
	38	CP2: ((giggles))
	39	S25: °uh let's see. uh I went two years ago?
	40	CP2: *n?*
	41	S25: oh.

In CS2, the same student added more turn types in his conversation using follow-up questions and expansions more conducive to the use of *n desu*, and he produced *n desu* in those utterances. The following excerpt from the conversation in CS2 is at a similar juncture in the conversation from CS1, in which class standing, major and hobbies were discussed.

Excerpt 2. S25 (PFG) and CP2 in CS2

9	S25: *eeto: ima nannensei desu ka:*
	'uhm: What year are you?'
10	CP2: *ima yonensei desu.*
	'I'm a senior now.'
11	S25: *aa soo desu ka.*
	'Oh okay.'
12	CP3: ((nods))
13	S25: *to:* ((point to his chest)) *uh: sannensei* [*desu.*
	'and: ((point to his chest)) uh: I'm a [third-year student.'
14	CP2: [*sasaki san sannensei desu ka. hee.*
	[you're a third-year student. Oh:. okay.
15	S25: *eto: senkoo wa nan desu ka?*
	'U:m what is your major?'

	16	CP3:	*senkoo wa shakaigaku desu.*
			'My major is sociology.'
	17	S25:	*ee shakai-gaku tte eigo de nan desu ka?*
			'Uh what is shakaigaku in English?'
	18	CP2:	*sociology.*
	19	S25:	*aa soo desu ka.* <hai> *omoshiroi desu ka?*
			'Oh okay. <yes> is that interesting?'
	20	CP3:	*omoshiroi desu.*
			'It's interesting.'
	21	S25:	*uh: watashi no senkoo wa bijinesu desu*
			'Uh: my major is business'
	22	CP2:	*hee.*
			'Ohh'
	23	S25:	*maneejimento* ((nodding))(*desu*)
			'management ((nodding))(*desu*)'
	24	CP3:	*maneejimento: soo desu ka: omoshiroi desu kaa?*
			'mangement: I see: is it interesting?'
	25	S25:	*a hai ee* ((giggles)) *maa maa* [*omoshiroi.*
			'A yes yeah ((giggles)) so-so [interesting.'
	26	CP3:	[*maa maa* ((laughs))
			['so so ((laughs))'
	27	S25:	*eeto: ano: uh shumi wa nan desu ka?*
			'U:m: uh: uh what are your hobbies?'
	28	CP2:	*shumi wa eeto: nan da roo. Umi ni ittari*
			'My hobbies are uhm: what are they? Going to the beach'
	29	S25:	*a soo desu ka.*
			'Oh I see.'
	30	CP3:	*ongaku o kiitari* ((nods))
			'Listening to music ((nods))'
→	31	S25:	*aa donna ongaku ga suki na n desu ka?*
			'Oh what kind of music do you like?'
	32	CP2:	*eeto: chotto: souru de: chotto rokku na:*
			'Eeto: a little: soul and: a little rock'
	33		((giggles)) (.) *eto: Uua tte iu nihon no kashu ga suki desu.*
			((giggles)) (.) eto: I like the singer called Uua in Japan.'
	34	S25:	((nods))
	35	CP3:	*ato (.) indo no dagakki* ((hits her lap)) *taiko*
			'and (.) Indian drums ((hits her lap)) taiko'
→	36	S25:	*a taiko. A watashi: aa uh: taiko o suru n desu.*
			'Oh taiko. A I: uh uh: do taiko.'
	37	CP2:	*e: soo desu ka. donna taiko desu ka?*
			'Oh really? What kind of taiko is it?'
	38	S25:	*ee uh Suwa sutairu taiko?*
			'uh uh Suwa style taiko?'
	39	CP3:	*Suwa?*
			'Suwa?'
	40	S25:	*Shinnyoen*
			'Shinnyoen'

S25's participation here is quite different from his participation in CS1, where he mainly answered questions and relied on CP2 to keep the talk going. He uses a variety of turn types in CS2, e.g., new-topic initiating turns, follow-up questions, and expansions, where he offers related information about himself in addition to answering the CP's questions. In CS2, S25's question in line 9 is the first topic-initiating move after the initial greeting where they exchanged names. S25 starts the first topic by asking CP3 what her class standing is (line 9). After acknowledging CP's answer, he expands the topic and offers information about his own class standing (line 13). He follows up by asking another question about CP's major (line 15). He asks two more follow up questions, *omoshiroi desu ka* "Is it interesting?" in line 19, and *donna ongaku o kiku n desu ka?* "What kind of music do you listen to?" in line 31 demonstrating the appropriate use of *n desu*. The follow-up question in line 31 is pivotal in the exchange because it elicits more information about CP's interest, and provides another opportunity for S25 to follow up in line 36 and say, *a watashi: uh uh taiko o suru n desu* "Oh, I play taiko" using *n desu*. This use of *n desu* is very effective in showing the connectedness of his remark to that of CP that she likes Indian taiko music. Thus, S25 capitalized on the opportunity to use *n desu* again in a pragmatically relevant point in the talk and co-constructed a moment of alignment to the interlocutor. The alignment he displays with this turn and other co-occurring pragmatic resources such as various conversational moves make this exchange much more involved than the one in CS1 where his participation was limited to a smaller repertoire of pragmatic resources.

Pedagogical implications

The results of this study have important pedagogical implications. First, the study suggests that the use of a discourse-based curriculum using activity as a target of instruction is a viable approach to foreign language instruction. Studies have shown that teaching grammatical structures without context, as is often seen in language textbooks, leads to students' inability to use grammatical structures appropriately (Iwai, 2007; Jones & Ono, 2005a, 2005b; Mori, 2005). The lack of understanding of an ongoing activity can lead to a participation that is inconsistent with how the activity is to be co-constructed (Mori, 2002). Teaching *n desu* as part of a larger activity of small talk provided opportunities for students to learn how to engage in small talk rather than how to use *n desu* in discrete sentences. As a result, the students' use of *n desu* was appropriate to the context and it contributed to the co-construction of involved small talk with the use of other relevant pragmatic resources.

The construct of conversational competence featuring co-occurring pragmatic resources to help co-construct small talk proved to be useful for instruction, as effective use of these resources led to the co-construction of rapport and sociability between the students and their interlocutors. Use of multiple pragmatic resources as part of conversational competence is especially useful for instruction when the individual differences of the students are considered. Students come with different kinds of pragmatic competence requiring an instructor to address different resources for different students. Having a construct with multiple resources offers flexibility in instruction as different students can focus on their respective areas of weakness.

Lastly, this study suggests that pragmatics-focused instruction as the mainstay of instruction is an effective approach to language instruction. If we see language use as a process of accomplishing actions situated in particular contexts, language instruction must help learners develop such competence. Sustained, long term pragmatics-focused instruction has been shown to be beneficial for the learners' development of pragmatic competence in participating in small talk in this study. The study showed that this approach facilitated beneficial and productive changes in the learners' participation and made their participation more consistent with the everyday practice in the target language.

Conclusion

This study demonstrated that the extended predicate *n desu* in small talk is teachable, and that PF instruction resulted in the increased use of *n desu*.. The study also showed that the time spent on pragmatics learning has an impact on the learners' pragmatic development, thus calling for a curriculum with long-term, sustained instruction of pragmatics. The data analysis showed that the use of *n desu* was tied to other co-occurring features of small talk, and the use of *n desu* by the learners contributed to the co-construction of involvement in small talk with a native speaker peer. The data showed the use of a combination of the co-occurring pragmatic resources contributed to enhanced engagement and coherence of small talk. The results strongly support the effectiveness of sustained pragmatics-focused instruction featuring the instruction of co-occurring pragmatic features that co-construct the activity of small talk.

Future research should explore what can be added to the list of resources of conversational competence at different levels of instruction. As students' competence increases, more resources can be added that would contribute to the co-construction of more sophisticated small talk. Another area for future research would be a further comparison between the GFG and the PFG over a longer period and in a more advanced level of study. Will a GFG eventually catch up with the PFG as they increase fluency in the use of grammatical structures? There is an implicit expectation among many language-teaching practitioners that students will learn how to speak once they learn enough vocabulary and grammar. At a more advanced level, will a PFG still hold an advantage in the use of pragmatic resources? These issues will hopefully be addressed in future studies to improve the instruction of pragmatics in the foreign language classroom.

References

Alfonso, A. (1980). *Japanese language patterns*. Tokyo, Japan: Sophia University.

Aoki, H. (1986). Evidentials in Japanese. In W. Chafe & J. Nichols (Eds.), *Evidentiality: The linguistic coding of epistemology* (pp. 223–238). Norwood, NJ: Ablex.

Clancy, P. M. (1982). Written and spoken style in Japanese narratives. In D. Tannen (Ed.) *Spoken and written language: Exploring orality and literacy* (pp. 55–76). Norwood, NJ: Ablex.

Cook, H. M. (1990). An indexical account of the Japanese sentence-final particle *no*. *Discourse Processes, 13*, 401–439.

Coulmas, F. (1981). Introduction: Conversational routine. In F. Coulmas (Ed.), *Conversational routine* (pp. 1–17). The Hague, The Netherlands: Mouton de Gruyter.

House, J. (1996). Developing pragmatic fluency in English as a foreign language: Routines and metapragmatic awareness. *Studies in Second Language Acquisition, 18*, 225–252.

Hymes, D. (1972). On communicative competence. In J. B. Pride & J. Holes (Eds.), *Sociolinguistics: Selected readings* (pp. 269–293). Harmondsworth, United Kingdom: Penguin.

Ishida, K. (2009). *Indexing stance in interaction: A pedagogical approach to teaching the pragmatic use of the Japanese plain and desu/masu forms* (Unpublished doctoral dissertation). University of Hawai'i at Mānoa, Honolulu.

Iwai, T. (2000, February). *Acquisition of the discourse marker n desu by JFL learners*. Paper presented at the annual meeting of the American Association of Applied Linguistics, Vancouver, Canada.

Iwai, T. (2005, May). *The development of conversational competence among L2 Japanese learners*. Paper presented at the Association of Japanese Teachers Seminar, Chicago, IL.

Iwai, T. (2007). Becoming a good conversationalist: Pragmatic development of JFL learners. In D. R. Yoshimi & H. Wang (Eds.), *Selected papers from the conference on pragmatics in the CJK classroom: The state of the art* (pp. 121–140). Honolulu, HI: NFLRC. Available online at http://nflrc.hawaii.edu/CJKProceedings.

Iwasaki, S. (1992). *Subjectivity in grammar and discourse: Theoretical considerations and a case study of Japanese spoken discourse*. Amsterdam, The Netherlands: Benjamins.

Jones, K., & Ono, T. (2005a). Discourse-centered approaches to Japanese language pedagogy. *Japanese Language and Literature, 39*(2), 237–254.

Jones, K., & Ono, T. (2005b). Special Issue: Discourse and language pedagogy. *Japanese Language and Literature, 39*(2).

Kasper, G. (2004). Participant orientation in German conversation-for-learning. *The Modern Language Journal, 88*(4), 551–567.

Kasper, G., & Rose, K. R. (2002). *Pragmatic development in a second language*. Oxford, United Kingdom: Blackwell Publishing.

Kuno, S. (1973). *The structure of the Japanese language*. Cambridge, MA: MIT Press.

Makino, S., & Tsutsui, M. (1986). *A dictionary of basic Japanese grammar*. Tokyo, Japan: The Japan Times.

Mori, J. (2002). Task design, plan, and development of talk-in-interaction: An analysis of a small group activity in a Japanese language classroom. *Applied Linguistics, 12*(3), 323–347.

Mori, J. (2005). Why not why? The teaching of grammar, discourse, and sociolinguistic and cross-cultural perspectives. *Japanese Language and Literature, 39*(2), 255–290.

Rose, K. R., & Kasper, G. (2001). Pragmatics in language teaching. In K. R. Rose & G. Kasper (Eds.), *Pragmatics in language teaching* (pp. 1–9). Cambridge, United Kingdom: Cambridge University Press.

Tateyama, Y. (2001). Explicit and implicit teaching of pragmatic routines: Japanese sumimasen. In K. R. Rose & G. Kasper (Eds.), *Pragmatics in language teaching* (pp. 200–222). Cambridge, United Kingdom: Cambridge University Press.

Wang, Y. (2009). *A cross-linguistic study of yes-no questions in Japanese and Chinese conversational discourse* (Unpublished doctoral dissertation). University of Wisconsin-Madison, Madison.

Yoshimi, D. R. (2001a). Lesson 2 Culture/Usage Notes. In T. Iwai, Y. Wada, J. Haig, & D. R. Yoshimi (Eds.), *Japanese for oral communication: A new approach to Japanese language and culture* (pp. 9–14). (Available from the Department of East Asian Languages and Literatures, University of Hawai'i at Mānoa, 1890 East-West Road, Honolulu, HI 96822)

Yoshimi, D. R. (2001b). Explicit instruction and JFL learner's use of interactional discourse markers. In K. R. Rose & G. Kasper (Eds.), *Pragmatics in language teaching* (pp. 223–244). Cambridge, United Kingdom: Cambridge University Press.

Yoshimi, D. R. (2003, August). *Steps in pragmatics-oriented approach to JFL instruction*. Lecture presented in the 2003 Japanese Summer Institute on "Pragmatics in the JFL classroom: Advanced training", University of Hawai'i at Mānoa, Honolulu.

Yoshimi, D. R. (2009). From *a!* to *zo*: Japanese pragmatics and its contribution to JSL/JFL pedagogy. In N. Taguchi (Ed.), *Pragmatic competence* (pp. 19–39). New York, NY: Mouton de Gruyter.

Yoshimi, D. R., & Iwai, T. (2001, March). *Tell me about it: Teaching extended discourse in Japanese*. Paper presented at the meeting of the Hawai'i Association of Language Teachers, Honolulu, HI.

Appendix A: Sample model dialog

Lesson 6

Example dialog 5: Talking about your siblings

a.

中野:そうですか。で、お兄さんはいくつなんですか。

ヒガ:兄ですか。今21歳です。ハワイ大学の3年生なんです。

中野:そうですか。何を勉強しているんですか。

ヒガ:コンピューターを勉強しているんです。

中野:コンピューターですか。へえ。

b.

リー:中野さんのお兄さんは何をしているんですか。

中野:うちの兄は普通の会社員なんですけど...

リー:へえ、どんな会社なんですか。

中野:ソフトウエアの会社で働いているんです。

リー:へえ、すごいですね。

Example dialog 6: Asking where your friend/teacher is from

a.

リー:中野さんのうちは日本のどこなんですか。

中野:千葉の浦安っていうところなんです。

リー:千葉の浦安ですか。

中野:ええ、東京ディズニーランドの近くなんです。

リー:あ、そうですか。いいですね。

b.

リー:先生のおたくは日本のどちらですか。

先生:うちは横浜なんです。

リー:横浜ですか。いいところですね。

c.

中野:リーさんのうちはどこなんですか。

リー:私は、マウイのパイアっていうところなんです。

中野:パイアっていうんですか。

リー:ええ。

中野：へえ、どんなところなんですか。

リー：小さい町なんですけど、ウインドサーフィンで有名なんですよ。

中野：リーさんのうちはどこなんですか。

リー：へえ、そうなんですか、すごいですねえ。

Example dialog 7: Paying and receiving compliments about personal possessions

a.

中野：ヒガさん、その携帯電話いいですね。

ヒガ：これですか。母に去年の誕生日にもらったんです。

中野：そうですか。小さくていいですよね。

ヒガ：ええ、便利なんですよ。

中野：いいですね。

b.

リー：このかばん、いいですね。

中野：それですか。姉がくれたんです。

リー：そうですか。いいお姉さんですね。

中野：え、まあ、ときどきは…

Appendix B: Sample activity sheet

Lesson 6   Talking about family

Activity 5

Goal: A: to be able to ask someone where he/she lives and comment on his/her answer in an appropriate manner.

B: to be able to talk about where you live with a brief explanation of what kind of place it is.

A: Who: You are a student who is studying Japanese at UH.

Situation: You have been talking about each other's family.

Task: Ask where B is lives (is from). Comment appropriately.

B: Who: You are a Japanese student who is studying at UH.

Situation: You have been talking about each other's family.

Task: Tell A where you live (you are from) with a brief description, if necessary.

Use: Example Dialog 6; Core Expressions: 8, 9

Linguistic Resources:

___さんのうちはにほんのどこなんですか。Where are your from in Japan?

___さんのうちはどこなんですか。Where do you live?

___さんは、しゅっしんはどちらなんですか。Where are you from?

___っていうところなんです。I'm from (I live in) a place called ___

___のちかくなんです。It's near ___

___ってしってますか？（はい）___のちかくなんです。

Do you know ___? (Yes) It's near ___
___って、どんなところなんですか。What kind of place is ___?
___で、ゆうめいなんです。 It's famous for ___.
___のひがしのほうにあるんです。It's in the east side of ___.
 (きた-north; みなみ-south; にし-west; まんなか-middle)

やまのむこう	the other side of the mountains
じゅうたくち	residential area
あめがおおい	has lots of rain
かぜがつよい	windy
べんりな	convenient
しずかな	quiet

Appendix C: Transcription symbols

The following symbols were used for the transcription.

.	falling intonation
?	rising intonation
,	continuative intonation
:	lengthening of sound
–	cut off word
↑	high pitch
°	attenuated speech
OH	loud speech
(.)	short pause
(2)	timed pause
(( ))	comment
[ ]	overlap
=	latching
(word)	uncertain word
( )	unintelligible portion
' '	English translation

Effects of Dynamic Written Corrective Feedback on JFL Students' Homework

JFL学習者の宿題へのDynamic Written Corrective Feedbackの効果

Yuka Akiyama
Massachusetts Institute of Technology

Mayumi Fleshler
Statistical Consultant

Abstract

This study investigates the efficacy of written corrective feedback on two groups of first-semester JFL students' homework. The treatment group was required to respond to "dynamic written corrective feedback (WCF)," which is modeled after a study by Hartshorn, K. J., Evans, W. N., Merrill, F. P., Sudweeks, R. R., Strong-Krause, D., and Anderson, J. N.. (2010), by continuously correcting/revising their homework by using metalinguistic error codes, answer keys, and maintaining an error log. In contrast, the control group was required to correct/revise the homework only once by looking at the answer keys. The research investigated dynamic/non-dynamic WCF in terms of (1) the accuracy rate of particles and predicates in grammar exercises and essay writing, (2) the overall quality of students' essay writing, and (3) students' perception of dynamic WCF. The Wilcoxon rank-sum test concluded that the median accuracy rate of the particle usage was significantly different (p<.05) in grammar tests, but not significant in essay writing. For accurate use of predicates, a significant difference was observed in essay writing, but not in grammar tests despite observable improvement in the latter. As for the overall quality of essay writing, the two groups did not differ significantly. The qualitative data, on the other hand, indicated the necessity to implement metalinguistic *error codes and the tally sheet with sufficient planning and caution to make best use of the practice.*

要旨

本研究はHartshorn, K. J., Evans, W. N., Merrill, F. P., Sudweeks, R. R., Strong-Krause, D., and Anderson, J. N. (2010) により定義されたdynamic written corrective feedbackを日本語初級学習者の宿題に一学期間応用し、そのエラー訂正プロセスが助詞と述語の正確さと作文全体の質にどのような影響を及ぼすのかを調べた。この研究ではdynamic WCFの (1) 文法問題と自由作文における助詞と述語の正確さへの効果、 (2) 作文全体の質への効果、そして (3) dynamic WCFプロセスへの学生の反応を調べた。Wilcoxon rank-sumテストの結果、文法問題での助詞の正確さはdynamic WCFがnon-dynamic WCFグループを有意に上回ったが、自由作文では有意差がなかった。一方、述語の正確さは文法問題と自由作文の両方でdynamic WCFがnon-dynamic WCFを上回ったが、文法問題での述語の正確さの向上は統計的に有意とは言えなかった。又、作文全体の質に有意差は見られなかった。アンケートの結果、dynamic WCFプロセスを効果的に行うためには、エラーコードやエラー記録表を使う際の注意点を認識し、長期的な授業計画を立てる必要があることがわかった。

Introduction

Written corrective feedback (WCF) in second language acquisition refers to written responses to a learner's non-target-like production with the intention of improving students' writing ability. WCF has been a topic of rigorous research for the last decade especially since Truscott (1996, 1999) suggested abandoning WCF by challenging the widespread assumption that corrective feedback helps learners improve the accuracy of their writing. Despite Truscott's argument, many practitioners still employ some form of WCF because they believe that students' "cognitive investment of editing text after receiving error feedback is likely a necessary, or at least helpful, step on the road to longer term improvement in accuracy" (Ferris, 2004, p. 54) or because they are ethically concerned that students are in need of WCF. In fact, Ferris (1999) investigated the belief of students with regards to error correction and claimed that most students regarded WCF as valuable and would feel frustrated if it was not provided (Komura, 1999; Leki, 1991). Thus, the effectiveness of WCF is still under intense debate, and many practitioners seem to wonder if they are using its potential to the full extent (Hyland & Hyland, 2006). This is primarily because contradictions in research findings and inconsistencies in research designs, data interpretation, and sample populations have not supported an effective method to students with a particular linguistic focus (Bitchener, 2008; Ferris, 2004, 2006; Guenette, 2007).

For instance, some research studies evaluate the efficacy of WCF by how successfully students revise text, while others measure the effects by having students work on new pieces of writing. Truscott and Hsu (2008) claimed that improvements made during revision do not provide evidence for the effectiveness of grammar correction to improve a learner's writing ability, citing that the "indication and location feedback" group and the "no feedback" group were practically identical two weeks after the intervention, when they worked on a new piece of writing, although the former was significantly more successful in the revision.

Another problem in WCF research design is whether or not to employ a control group that does not receive any WCF. Practitioners have been hesitant to assign a control group for the ethical concern that it is unfair not to provide any WCF to one group of students (Ferris, 2004, 2006). However, a true control group needs to be employed if the efficacy of WCF is to be investigated accurately, as many researchers have come to agree (Bitchener, 2008).

It is also problematic that some studies provide unfocused WCF, while other studies provide focused WCF. The former marks all non-target-like errors, whereas the latter provides WCF only to specific error categories, such as articles and idiosyncratic errors. Although focused WCF is considered more effective in the field of *oral* corrective feedback to cope with information overload (Doughty & Varela, 1998; Han, 2002; Lyster, 2004), no conclusive evidence has been found in the field of *written* corrective feedback.

In addition, research design needs to address the number of target error categories. Most published research studies have provided WCF on 15 or more error categories (Bitchener, 2008). However, Ferris (1999) and Ferris and Roberts (2001) broadly categorized the errors into two (treatable and untreatable errors), and five categories (verbs, noun endings, articles, word choice, and sentence structure), respectively.

In summary, these differences in research design have led to contradictory research findings, and thus prevented practitioners from making the best use of WCF. Future WCF research needs to address this pivotal issue of research design for its development and for its contribution to the field of SLA (Bitchener, 2008; Ellis, 2009; Ferris, 2004, 2006; Truscott, 1996).

Review of literature

Types of written corrective feedback

The three most commonly observed practices that many teachers adopt are direct, indirect, and metalinguistic corrective feedback. First, direct WCF is a way for teachers to explicitly guide students by directly correcting errors that students have made. Errors can be directly corrected by crossing out, inserting, or supplying a phoneme, morpheme, word, or phrase, by writing metalinguistic explanations at the end of students' writing with references to where the errors are made, or by providing oral metalinguistic explanation individually or in small groups (Bitchener, 2008).

Second, indirect WCF guides students by indirectly indicating students' errors but provides no correction. It can be done through either "indication only" or "indication plus locating the error" (Ellis, 2009, p. 98). The former can be done either by indicating the existence of errors with check marks or by recording the number of errors in the margin. The latter, on the other hand, underlines or circles the errors to indicate where the errors exist (Bitcherner, 2008). Among the studies that compare the two ways of indirectly indicating errors, Ferris and Roberts (2001) claim that the "indication only" method is more effective than the "indication plus locating the error" method because students engage in deeper processing with the former WCF. On the other hand, Lee (1997) argues that learners correct errors better when the errors are pointed out both by indication and location than when they are indicated simply by a check mark in the margin.

Most studies that compare the efficacy of direct vs. indirect WCF have come to the conclusion that indirect WCF is more effective than direct WCF although it may not be as effective for students at lower levels of L2 proficiency (Ferris & Roberts, 2001). These studies argue that indirect WCF promotes guided learning and problem solving (Lalande, 1982) and forces the students to "do something with the error correction besides simply receiving it" (Chandler, 2003, p. 293). Moreover, indirect WCF may help students "notice" (Schmidt, 1990) an error and engage in hypothesis testing, which may activate deeper internal processing (Doughty & Williams, 1998; Ferris, 2002). For example, Ellis (2009) claims that indirect WCF, which requires more cognitive processing than direct WCF, may lead to students' long-term learning. Ferris (2002), in fact, reported a study where indirect WCF over the course of a semester significantly reduced students' error frequency when working on new pieces of writing even though direct WCF was more effective for text revisions.

Third, metalinguistic WCF indicates the nature of errors explicitly either by the use of error codes or by describing errors grammatically. Some studies found the use of error codes more helpful than direct or indirect WCF (Lalande, 1982) while other studies (Ferris, D., Chaney, S., Komura, K., Roberts, B., & McKee, S., 2000; Ferris & Helt, 2000; Robb, T., Ross, S., & Shortreed, I., 1986; Semeke, 1984) found no statistical differences between the three. Ferris and Roberts (2001) showed in their longitudinal study that metalinguistic WCF treatment may work only with certain types of errors (i.e., "treatable errors" such as verbs, noun endings, and articles) and that, despite both students' and teachers' clear preference of more explicit coding approach over less explicit indication approach, it may be adequate and more efficient to merely indicate the location of errors without labeling them with error types.

In sum, practitioners have been and probably will keep wondering which type of WCF is "less time-consuming" but "directs student attention to surface errors" and helps students to become better writers (Robb et al., 1986, p. 91). In order for practitioners to use WCF with empirical research evidence and confidence, structured research design, systematic definition of terminology, and more consideration into both students' and practitioners' perception of WCF are essential. However, it may take some time before WCF researchers come to a consensus on how to solve these inconsistencies. Hence, the most urgent question in the interim for which practitioners need an answer seems to be "What should we do with WCF when there is not enough research evidence to support the practice?"

Skill acquisition theory and dynamic written corrective feedback

In an attempt to suggest practical steps to use WCF, Hartshorn et al. (2010) conducted an alternative instructional methodology called "dynamic WCF" with 47 advanced-low to advanced-mid ESL students and compared it with the traditional process writing. The researchers developed the methodology based on Skill Acquisition Theory (SAT), which asserts that declarative knowledge (what one knows) and extensive practice with repeated examples help one acquire procedural knowledge (what one can produce), which ultimately leads to automatization. In other words, the methodology relies on students' cognitive ability to process what they know into what they produce through explicit instruction and intensive practice through authentic tasks and activities.

The researchers defined "dynamic" as feedback that "reflects what the individual learner needs most as demonstrated by what he/she produces" and that adopts "a principled approach to pedagogy that ensures that writing tasks and feedback are 'meaningful, timely, constant, and manageable' for both students and teachers" (Hartshorn, 2010, p. 87). First, in order for WCF to reflect learners' dynamic and diverse needs, the practice provided unfocused WCF and utilized an error tally sheet. The tally sheet asked students to count the number of errors for each error category, so that instructors would be able to identify students' high-frequency errors and address them in explicit classroom instruction. Second, for the WCF to be "meaningful," the methodology used metalinguistic error codes which identified error types and their locations. For the WCF to be "timely and constant," the instructors returned the feedback in the following classes until no errors were observed. For the WCF to be "manageable," dynamic WCF limited the length of the students' writing instead of limiting the focus of the corrective feedback. This practice helped avoid "information overload" on the students' part (Bitchener, 2008, p. 109) and helped give high-quality, authentic and constant feedback on the instructors' part.

The study investigated the effect of dynamic WCF in contrast to traditional process writing in terms of accuracy, fluency, complexity, and rhetorical competence. Accuracy was measured by the "error-free T-unit ratio (EFT/T)" that is recommended by Wolfe-Quintero, K., Inagaki, S., and Kim, H. (1998). Fluency was simply defined as the number of words that a student can produce in a particular period of time. Complexity was measured by the mean length of a T-unit, namely "the average number of words per T-unit" (Hartshorn, 2010, p. 91). Rhetorical competence was rated using a rubric that was adapted from the Test of English as a Foreign Language Internet-based Test (TOEFL iBT).

The study found that dynamic WCF significantly improved students' accuracy rate although the findings also indicate its possible negative effect on students' fluency and complexity. This result may be attributed to the possible reaction of students in the treatment group who paid more attention to accuracy and decreased their writing speed. In terms of rhetorical competence, no difference was observed between the mean scores of the treatment group and contrast group. Overall, although a slightly negative effect of dynamic WCF was observed in the study, the researchers argue for the efficacy of dynamic WCF as a significant improvement in students' accuracy rate in contrast to the "small but apparent negative effect on students' fluency and complexity rate" (Hartshorn, 2010, p. 101).

The researchers conclude the article by pointing out that their observation "underscores the notion that *how* one uses WCF might make a great difference in the outcome of students' writing and that a systematic approach to WCF could have a positive effect on the accuracy of ESL writing" (Hartshorn, 2010, p. 102). They also propose that practitioners use different approaches to WCF depending on what students need to improve in their writing: accuracy, rhetorical competence, complexity, or fluency.

Methodology

Purpose of the study and research questions

Most WCF research studies to this date take place in the ESL composition context and are conducted on students whose proficiency level is higher than intermediate (Furneaux, Paran, & Fairfax, 2007). Although some WCF studies have been published in Japanese pedagogy (Hirose, 2009; Ishihashi, 2002; Uehara, 1997), whether or not teachers' WCF has a positive effect on students' writing has not been discussed quite enough (Uehara, 1997). Thus, in an attempt to investigate the efficacy of WCF to elementary-level students in a non-composition-based classroom in a non-ESL context, the following research questions are addressed.

1. Does dynamic WCF on elementary-level JFL students' homework have a positive effect on their accurate use of particles and predicates in grammar exercises and spontaneous writing?
2. Does dynamic WCF improve the overall quality of students' essay writing that includes accuracy, fluency, and complexity?
3. What is students' perception of the dynamic WCF and its dynamic revision/correction?

Participants of the study

Thirty five college students who took first-semester Japanese in the JFL context at a university in the United States. participated in this study. Considering the low proficiency level of the sample population, this study is focused on improving the accuracy rate of discrete sentence-level writing rather than paragraph/discourse-level composing. Ultimately, the study aims to inform practitioners of a practical way to utilize WCF on students' homework in response to the immediate needs of practitioners who need empirical evidence to guarantee their WCF practice.

The experiment was conducted on two sections of first-semester Japanese students. The dynamic WCF treatment group (LJ111 Section A) consisted of 18 students who ranged from 18 to 23 years of age, and the non-dynamic WCF contrast group (LJ111 Section B) consisted of 17 students who ranged from 18 to 21 years of age. Table 1 summarizes the composition of the two groups in terms of their native language and gender. This breakdown of students' L1 is useful for examining the potential effect of language distance, namely the notion that differences between various L1s and the target language may account for some of the relative difficulty or speed with which a learner may acquire the language (Odlin, 1989). Ringbon (1987) claimed that the L1 influence shows up to a great extent in younger learners with lower L1 proficiency in highly communicative tasks.

Considering these L1-L2 distance factors, it is generally said that Korean speakers have advantages in acquiring Japanese particles and syntax since the language has a similar grammatical structure to Japanese. On the other hand, Chinese speakers have advantages in writing because Chinese and Japanese share a number of Chinese characters (*kanji*), and Chinese speakers tend to write Japanese faster than other language groups.

With this in mind, the percentage of native speakers of these two languages was calculated: 50% (11.11% Korean and 38.89% Chinese) in the treatment group and 52.93% (41.17% Korean and 11.76% Chinese) in the contrast group. These data imply an advantage in acquiring particles for the contrast group that has a much larger body of Korean speakers. In contrast, the advantage of fast writing and *kanji* use is implied in the treatment group that has a larger body of Chinese speakers. This configuration, however, is not considered much of an advantage because the analysis focuses on the accuracy rate of particle and predicate use. Lastly, a few students with prior knowledge of Japanese were placed into first-semester Japanese based on an in-house placement test. These students' Japanese proficiency level did not differ with others' in the least, especially after the first couple of weeks of the semester.

Table 1. Summary table of subjects' language and gender

1st language	treatment group			contrast group		
	male	female	total	male	female	total
Korean	0	2	2	1	6	7
Chinese	2	5	7	1	1	2
English	2	5	7	4	2	6
Filipino	0	0	0	0	1	1
Spanish	2	0	2	0	1	1
totals	6	12	18	6	11	17

General settings of instruction

The researcher herself gave both groups of students 50 minutes of Japanese instruction four days a week (50 min×4 times=200 min/week) for a semester of 15 weeks. *GENKI: An Integrated Course in Elementary Japanese* was used as the main textbook and its supplementary workbook (grammar exercises) and additional handouts (paragraph writing) were used as daily homework. The first-semester Japanese course covered chapters one to six of the textbook. The students learned the three Japanese writing systems: *hiragana* and *katakana* in chapters one and two, and *kanji* in chapters three through six. The class was conducted mainly in Japanese with English explanations and translations at times.

Procedure

The researcher/instructor taught the same course materials to two sections of first-semester Japanese students and provided dynamic WCF for the treatment group and non-dynamic WCF for the contrast group. The two groups were required to conduct different revision/correction procedures, but both groups received the same metalinguistic WCF (see metalinguistic error codes in Appendix 1).

The students in the treatment group were required to make corrections on their own using metalinguistic feedback for the first revision/correction, submit the revision/correction in the following class, revise/correct again the second time by looking at the answer keys posted online, and submit the final version in the following classes until no errors were observed. In addition, the students in the treatment group were asked to keep a log of their errors in a tally sheet (see sample error tally sheet in Appendix 2) and submit it on the last day of each chapter. The instructor taught the treatment group how to use the tally sheet and informed them that the sheet would be used for identifying their own weaknesses and for providing data for in-class explicit instruction on common errors.

On the contrary, the contrast group simply revised/corrected the homework once by looking at the answer keys and submitted the final version on the last day of each chapter. The explicit instruction was conducted in the form of a "common errors handout" a day before each chapter test, so that the two groups would differ only in the dynamicity of the WCF procedure and the use of the error tally sheet.

Lastly, in order to make sure that both groups of students would have sufficient opportunities to familiarize themselves with the metalinguistic error codes, the students received the codes on their homework for three weeks before the intervention, although they were not required to use them. The following Figure 1 shows the difference in the dynamic vs. non-dynamic WCF procedure.

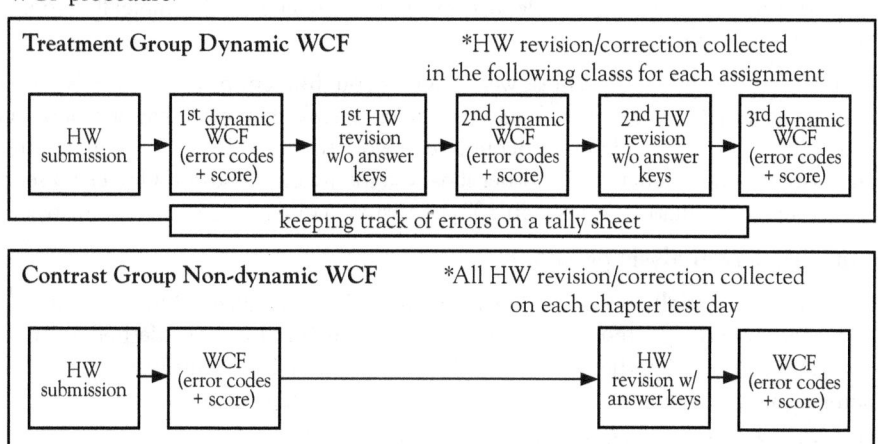

Figure 1. Dynamic WCF vs. non-dynamic WCF procedure on students' homework

Data collection

Quantitative data collection procedure

The first-semester Japanese covers Chapter 1 to 6 of the Genki textbook and the test that covered the material from Chapter 1 to Chapter 3 was conducted as a pre-test. Right before Chapter 3 was chosen to be the time to conduct the pre-test because it was assumed that many students, especially speakers of alphabetic languages, would have trouble learning the three Japanese writing systems in the first two chapters and that it would be difficult to measure students' grammatical ability in the early stage. In addition, Chapter 3 is a good indicator of particle use because students learn seven particles and 13 verbs in the chapter.

The pre-test was worth 28 points and was conducted in 30 minutes (see pre-test in Appendix 3). It consisted of three sections: (A) 30 fill-in-the-blank particle questions (0.4×30=12 points), (B) three word order questions where students added particles and conjugated predicates (2×3=6 points), and (C) a short essay (10 points).

The post-test (see post-test in Appendix 4) was worth 38 points and conducted in 50 minutes on the last day of the semester. It covered material from chapters one to six, and consisted of the same three sections as the pre-test: (A) 40 fill-in-the-blank particle questions (0.4×40=16 points), (B) six word order questions (2×6=12 points), and (C) a short essay (10 points).

Sections (A) and (B) were conducted to measure the accuracy rate in controlled grammar exercises whereas Section (C) was conducted to test students' accuracy rate and overall quality of writing in open-ended spontaneous writing.

The accuracy rate in the use of particles was calculated in percentages in Sections (A), (B), and (C). The accuracy rate in the use of predicates was calculated in Sections (B) and (C). To test whether dynamic WCF had a positive effect on the essay as a whole, the essay was additionally graded based on the overall accuracy (i.e., particles, predicates, spelling, *kanji*, and word choice) as well as on fluency and complexity. The fluency was graded simply by counting the number of morphemes. The complexity was measured by the average number of morphemes in one sentence. Both fluency and complexity were given scores on a scale of 0 to 5, and the whole essay score was calculated by subtracting points for accuracy errors (one error was worth a 0.5 point deduction) from the fluency and complexity score (with a maximum of 10 points).

Both the pre-test and the post-test were original and different from the exercises they engaged in for their homework. Thus, the students worked on grammar questions and essay topics that they had never encountered before the tests. In addition, in an attempt to establish inter-rater reliability, another Japanese instructor at Boston University scored 20% of the sample population to keep an 80% consistency rate between the two instructors.

Quantitative data analysis procedure

There were potentially two procedures to analyze the data collected in this study: the paired t-test matching the pre-test and post-test scores for each individual (Method 1), and the two-sample t-test using the post-test results only (Method 2). We ultimately decided to use a non-parametric version of Method 2 for the reasons explained below.

First, in order to utilize Method 1, for each matched i-th pair we would need to assume the pre-test score to be normally distributed with mean m_i and variance s^2 and the post-test score to be normally distributed with $m_i + \Delta$ and variance s^2. This means that the underlying mean difference in the test score between the two tests, Δ, must be solely due to either the intervention (dynamic WCF) or the conventional feedback method (non-dynamic

WCF). However, in contrast to a standardized test such as the TOEFL test, in which the level of difficulty is presumably consistent between each administered test, the pre-test and the post-test in our study were substantially different in terms of their level of difficulty, contents, and range of coverage of the material. Because this inconsistency between the two tests came into play, Δ most likely depended on i, in a manner that each student responded differently to the two tests based on his/her ability or tendency to respond to such a difference. Because of this violation of the assumption, Method 1 was not selected.

Second, although the random sampling criterion needed to be met to use Method 2, we relaxed the random sampling criterion to proceed with the analysis because the pre-test results did not show any significant difference between the two groups, whose members are all relatively new to the Japanese language.

Lastly, the normality assumption must be satisfied in order to proceed with Method 2. However, the preliminary examination of the post-test data showed that the normality assumption was largely violated partly because of the small sample size. Thus, we decided to apply a nonparametric procedure, the Wilcoxon rank-sum test, assuming two independent samples to test the central tendency comparing the median test scores between the two groups measured on the post-test. At this point, predicates in test (B) were eliminated for further analysis because the median scores were equal between the two groups.

Qualitative data collection procedure

In order to add student voice to the quantitative data, the study also qualitatively analyzed students' reaction to each type of WCF based on an anonymous questionnaire (see questionnaire in Appendix 5 and 6) which was conducted at the end of the semester. Although students' perception of WCF does not necessarily reflect how effective the WCF methods actually are (Ferris & Roberts, 2001), we believe that the practitioners need to understand students' possible frustration when dealing with different types of WCF procedures.

Results

Research question 1: Effects on accuracy rate in the use of particles and predicates

As Table 2 summarizes, the test results showed that the median scores of the particle usage measured on the two grammar tests (A) and (B) were significantly different between the two groups (p<.05) although no significant difference was observed in the essay test (C). For the predicate usage, a significant difference was observed only in the essay writing tests (C) (p<.05). However, we note that, although we did not proceed with testing for the usage of the predicates in the grammar test (B) as the two median values coincided, the mean values of the control group and the treatment group were 78.7 and 91.0, respectively. Thus, there was some observed higher achievement in the treatment group though its significance could not be tested statistically.

Table 2.   Summary table for the post-test scores comparing the two groups

	median scores (out of 100)		Wilcoxon rank-sum test
	non-dynamic WCF	dynamic WCF	p
(A) particles	80.0	87.5	0.045
(B) particles	90.9	95.4	0.013

continued...

Table 2. Summary table for the post-test scores comparing the two groups *(cont.)*

	median scores (out of 100)		Wilcoxon rank-sum test
	non-dynamic WCF	dynamic WCF	*p*
(C) particles	94.9	97.2	0.108
(C) predicates	89.7	95.1	0.045
(C) overall quality	65.0	67.5	0.464

We also would like to point out that the results for the particle usage in the grammar test (A) and the predicate usage in the essay writing (C) could be argued as borderline cases (*p*-values=.045, coincidentally for both variables). This was mainly because we used the two-sided test, not having known initially whether or not the dynamic WCF method would provide a positive effect in learning the Japanese language.

Earlier in this paper, we mentioned that the contrast group had more Korean students who have positive transfer from their L1 in their particle usage. Therefore, one might hypothesize that the contrast group would have an advantage in learning proper usage of particles. Nevertheless, the treatment group achieved a significantly higher accuracy rate in particle usage on the grammar tests (A) and (B). This implies that the significance level could only become higher if the random sampling criterion were met.

Research question 2: Effects on the overall quality of students' essay writing

As for the overall essay score in the essay writing test (C), which measured not only the accuracy rate but the fluency and complexity, no significant difference was observed between the two groups. This indicates that the treatment did not lead to significant improvement in the students' overall writing ability.

Research question 3: Students' perception of dynamic/non-dynamic WCF procedure

The qualitative, descriptive data on the intervention was analyzed to add student voice to the quantitative analysis. First, one of the questions asked the students to describe the overall dynamic/non-dynamic WCF procedure using three adjectives (see questionnaire in Appendix 3 and 4). Table 3 summarizes the adjectives the students used to describe the procedure. They are grouped into three categories: positive, neutral, and negative. The number in parenthesis shows how many students responded to the question in the same/similar manner.

Table 3: Students' description of the dynamic/non-dynamic WCF in three adjectives

	positive	neutral	negative
dynamic WCF (treatment group)	•helpful (9) •useful (3) •concise/efficient (2) •systematic/objective (2) •productive (2) •effective (1) etc.	•easy (2) •worthwhile (1)	•time-consuming (2) •repetitive (2) •tedious (1) •difficult (1)
non-dynamic WCF (contrast group)	•helpful (11) •useful (4) •necessary (3) •educational (3) •awesome (2)	•easy (6) •quick (2)	•time-consuming (2) •difficult (2) •unnecessary (1) •annoying (1)

Table 3 shows that most students from both groups considered WCF helpful although some thought it was time-consuming and difficult. The adjectives that only the students in the treatment group listed include "concise," "efficient," "systematic," and "objective." These adjectives in particular describe the nature of dynamic WCF, which stresses its consistency but manageability. On the other hand, it is noteworthy that many more students in the contrast group considered their WCF "easy" and "quick." This may be due to the fact that the students in the contrast group had direct access to answer keys and were less cognitively challenged in the revision/correction procedure.

The second question asked if error codes helped them figure out errors (see questionnaire in Appendix 3 and 4). Table 4 summarizes students' attitude toward the metalinguistic error codes after using them for a semester.

Table 4. Students' perception of metalinguistic error codes

	positive	neutral	negative
error codes used in dynamic WCF (treatment group)	•very helpful (11) •useful once you get used to the codes (3) •easy to understand (1) •better than being given just checks (1)	•easier if codes are in words instead of symbols (e.g., SP=spelling) (1)	•sometimes hard to understand (2) •sometimes hard to figure out similar codes (1)
error codes used in non-dynamic WCF (contrast group)	•helpful (5) •better than just checking the answers (2) •straightforward (1) •helpful if one remembers the codes (1)	•confusing at first but OK once one gets used to the codes (3) •OK (2)	•too complicated (2) •"I did not focus on the codes at all." (2)

It is notable that the students in the treatment group considered error codes very helpful and actually took advantage of them when making corrections. On the other hand, those in the contrast group paid much less attention to the codes. The codes were "just there." This result indicates that students will not make the best use of instructors' feedback unless they are somehow *forced* to use it and engage in its uptake. Just providing the feedback may not lead to students' autonomous learning especially for elementary-level students, who have yet to establish their way of learning a new target language. Subsequently, teachers' time and effort to label errors may end up being in vain if the students are not required to use the codes for revision/correction.

Another point to keep in mind is that the students in both groups thought of the error codes as confusing at first and then gradually realized their usefulness. The students in both groups were introduced to the error codes three weeks before the intervention, yet some of them expressed difficulty figuring out the codes and used them incorrectly. Therefore, the error codes need to be visually recognizable and memorable. In addition, it is crucial that instructors demonstrate how to use the error codes and give sufficient practice in class before they have students work with the codes on their own.

The third question asked students' overall opinions about the frequency of WCF: at least twice in the treatment group and once in the contrast group (see questionnaire in Appendix 3 and 4). Table 5 summarizes what each student liked and disliked about the frequency of WCF and its revision procedure.

Table 5. Students' perception of frequency of dynamic/non-dynamic WCF

	likes	dislikes
dynamic/constant HW correction (treatment group)	•one can recognize mistakes (7) •one has to process mistakes deeply; thus, helps with retention (5) •"love it!" (5) •one can get exposed to more Japanese (4) •it helps develop a studying habit (3) •one can learn from mistakes (3) •instant feedback stays in memory (2) •making corrections on one's own is better than just checking answers (2) •no correction=no HW=good motivation not to make mistakes (1)	•sometimes unclear why it's a mistake without answers (7) •uncertain what to do without the error codes (4) •time-consuming (3) •uncertain if the correction one makes is correct (2) •no easy credits (necessary to read the textbook over and over) (2) •confusing sometimes which page to submit in which class (1)
non-dynamic/ one-time HW correction (contrast group)	•one can learn from mistakes (4) •it helps recognize mistakes (3) •it gets exposed to more Japanese (2) •one can check answers promptly (2) •one can learn their weaknesses (2) •one can learn how to make corrections (2) etc.	•time-consuming (5) •submitting all corrections all at once is tough and does not help much (4) •pointless if just copying answers (3) •tedious (2) etc.

Despite the fact that it took twice as much time to get credit, the students in the treatment group appreciated making corrections on a regular basis and made it a habit to motivate themselves, to make fewer mistakes, and to retain what they had learned. On the other hand, the students in the contrast group did not perceive their non-dynamic WCF as a habit in order to improve their writing. Rather, they simply regarded the WCF as a way to notice errors. Thus, it seems that the non-dynamic WCF procedure did not help the contrast group develop "learner autonomy," the ability to "reflect on, experiment with, and interact with one's own learning" (Schwienhorst, 2007).

Another point to remember is that some students in the treatment group felt frustrated with the procedure because they did not know what to do with the error codes and/or because they were afraid of repeatedly making mistakes. This frustration perhaps resulted from their uncertainty regarding whether their own hypothesized revision/corrections were actually right or not.

Additional questions were asked of the treatment group about the error tally sheet (see questionnaire in Appendix 5 and 6). Table 6 summarizes the treatment group's perception of counting the number of errors and taking notes of the error frequency using the tally sheet. The results indicated that some students appreciated the practice while others were very negative about it. Approximately half the students followed the practice to motivate themselves, prepare for exams, and identify their weaknesses. On the contrary, the other half thought the practice was useless and "tedious" because counting the number of errors was too much to do. These results show that simply asking students to count the number of errors does not lead to their increased motivation, at least for some students who do not believe in the practice or do not understand the point of counting the frequency of errors.

Table 6.   Students' perception of the error tally sheet

	positive	neutral	negative
error tally sheet (treatment group)	•makes one see what to pay attention to (3) •good motivation to avoid same mistakes (2) •good for preparing for exams (1)	•embarrassing to see so many mistakes, but fine overall (2) •useful but not necessary (2)	•not useful (3) •tedious (2) •too much; merely correcting is enough (1) •didn't submit it (2)

Discussion

This mixed-method study investigated the use of dynamic WCF on the homework of 35 students who studied first-semester Japanese. The findings of this study are significant as they inform practitioners, who teach elementary-level students in a non-ESL-composition context, of a way to effectively utilize WCF with consideration into students' perception of the methods. Moreover, the study contributes to the field of WCF by addressing its effectiveness in a non-ESL foreign language setting. The quantitative method was used to examine how students' accuracy rate and overall quality of writing correlated with two types of WCF revision/correction procedures. Additionally, the qualitative analysis of the questionnaire data was incorporated to add student voice to the study. Once again, this study was conducted to inform practitioners of a way to maximize the WCF practice and to answer such naturally intriguing questions as: "Is it sufficient to simply let our students decide whether or not to use the error codes?" and "What should we ask our students to do with the errors they make on their homework?"

The results of this study support the findings by Hartshorn et al. (2010) in that the students who received dynamic WCF significantly improved their particle accuracy rate in grammar exercises and predicate accuracy rate in essay writing. As for the predicate accuracy rate in grammar exercises, its accuracy rate improved to a great extent although it could not be statistically tested. This study also supported the findings of Hartshorn et al. that dynamic WCF does not lead to a significant difference in the improvement of the overall quality of students' spontaneous writing that includes accuracy, fluency, and complexity.

From the qualitative measure, it was observed that some students who received dynamic WCF took advantage of dynamic WCF for test preparation and gradually developed good studying habits through the procedure. These students believed in the efficacy of dynamic WCF, accepted the challenge, and increased self-motivation despite the fact that twice as much time and energy was required to complete the procedure.

From the questionnaire data, it was observed that elementary-level students need some kind of guidance in correcting errors in the form of metalinguistic error codes that are instantaneously recognizable and easy to remember. Moreover, the data called attention to the pre-condition to use metalinguistic error codes, namely extensive in-class training of error correction using the codes.

As for the use of the error tally sheet, slightly more students were against the practice than for it because they did not see the point in simply counting the frequency of errors. Having students do something with the tally sheet may make the practice seem less "pointless." One way to effectively implement this practice would be for the instructor to set a maximum number of errors allowed for each error category and "penalize" those who go over the limit. For example, instructors can create an additional task sheet for each error category and have the students work on the errors of which they exceeded the limit. This will enable students to see the operationalized goal for each error category and utilize the tally sheet.

Implications of the study

The results of this study provide several implications for teaching. First, practitioners need to recognize the difference between "what is effective" and "what students like." The results of the study show that even those students who did not like the practice of dynamic WCF procedure overall improved the accuracy score and developed good studying habits by being required to identify their weaknesses and by repeatedly correcting their mistakes. It is sometimes necessary to require instruction that students often object to, so practitioners' energy would not go in vain.

Second, practitioners need to provide sufficient practice in using metalinguistic error codes. Simply asking students to look at the codes and figure out the errors on their own would not work especially with students who are elementary-level or who do not possess a high level of learner autonomy. It is the practitioners' responsibility to figure out students' level of learner autonomy and provide appropriate amount of guidance in helping students correct errors.

Potential limitations and future research

The study primarily includes six potential areas of limitation.

1. In terms of the sample population, although both groups had similar gender and ethnic configurations, the native languages of the students as well as their personality traits were not identical between the two groups for the lack of random sampling. Considering the fact that Japanese is a new language for most of the students, however, the analysis of the results can be considered fairly reliable. Also, the relatively small sample size did not allow the study to employ a control group. In order to truly investigate the efficacy of WCF and its types, however, future studies need to employ a control group.

2. In terms of assessing students' spontaneous writing in the essay section, it is very likely that some students avoided complicated forms and kept using simple forms to increase their accuracy rate. This may be why the treatment did not lead to significantly improving the particle accuracy rate in the essay writing. Thus, more controlled testing design might have produced different results for the essay section.

3. Although the data analysis revealed some advantages of the dynamic WCF, it is not clear which dynamic component(s) most contributed to the results (the amount of practice, the error tally sheet, metalinguistic awareness, being aware of one's own weaknesses, the timing of looking at answers, consistency in providing/receiving feedback, etc.). Future studies need to specifically address which dynamic constituent resulted in the improvement.

4. It is not certain whether the dynamic WCF treatment in this study, which was mainly concerned with the sentence-level accuracy of elementary-level students' writing, can be applied to more advanced JFL students' paragraph/discourse-level composing, let alone to the content of students' writing. Future studies need to examine the efficacy of dynamic WCF with students at different levels who have various writing goals (e.g., content, accuracy, fluency, complexity, and rhetorical competence).

5. Regarding the period of the experiment, the study conducted the writing post-test after only 12 weeks of the intervention and mainly assessed learners' explicit knowledge in exercises. In the future, it is suggested that researchers also employ a longitudinal

study to demonstrate the treatment's long-term effects and its impact on acquiring implicit knowledge.

6. Some may view this study as compromising objectivity since the instructor herself taught the two groups. The instructor/researcher addressed this issue by adopting the two-sided test for data analysis and by establishing inter-rater reliability to avoid any subjective judgment.

Conclusion

This mixed method research study looked at the effects of dynamic WCF on elementary-level JFL students' accuracy rate in particle and predicate usage and overall quality of writing. The quantitative results showed that the treatment significantly improved accuracy rate in particle usage in grammar exercises and predicate usage in essay writing. The accuracy rate in predicate usage in grammar exercises also improved to a great extent although it could not be tested statistically. On the other hand, the treatment did not result in any significant improvement in the overall quality of writing that included accuracy, fluency, and complexity. This analysis supports the findings by Hartshorn et al. (2010) that dynamic WCF results in improving accuracy but not fluency or complexity.

The qualitative data showed that some students appreciated the dynamic WCF procedure and used it to develop their learner autonomy. The use of metalinguistic codes was perceived rather favorably by the treatment group as they valued some scaffolding in error correction in the form of meaningful and constant WCF. However, it was also observed that students would need in-class training to accurately use metalinguistic codes. As for the error tally sheet, it did not strike the students as a useful tool. However, it can be used more effectively and perceived positively if instructors provide the students with practical goals with which to use the sheet.

References

Bitchener, J. (2008). Evidence in support of written corrective feedback. *Journal of Second Language Writing, 17,* 102–118.

Chandler, J. (2003). The efficacy of various kinds of error feedback for improvement in the accuracy and fluency of L2 student writing. *Journal of Second Language Writing, 12,* 267–296.

Doughty, C., & Varela, E. (1998). Communicative focus on form. In C. Doughty & J. Williams (Eds.), *Focus on form in classroom second language acquisition* (pp. 114–138). New York, NY: Cambridge University Press.

Doughty, C., & Williams, J. (Eds.) (1998). *Focus on form in classroom second language acquisition.* New York, NY: Cambridge University Press.

Ellis, R. (2009). A typology of written corrective feedback types. *ELT Jouranl, 63*(2).

Ferris, D. (1999). The case for grammar correction in L2 writing classes: A response to Truscott (1996). *Journal of Second language Writing, 8,* 1–11.

Ferris, D. (2002). *Treatment of error in second language student writing.* Ann Arbor: University of Michigan Press.

Ferris, D. (2004). The "grammar correction" debate in L2 writing: Where are we, and where do we go from here? (and what do we do in the meantime ...?). *Journal of Second Language Writing, 13,* 49–62.

Ferris, D. (2006). Does error feedback help student writers? New evidence on the short- and long-term effects of written error correction. In K. Hyland & F. Hyland (Eds.),

Feedback in second language writing: Contexts and issues (pp. 81–104). Cambridge, United Kingdom: Cambridge University Press.

Ferris, D., Chaney, S., Komura, K., Roberts, B., & McKee, S. (2000, March 14–18). *Perspectives, problems, and practices in treating written error.* Colloquium presented at the International TESOL Convention, Vancouver, British Columbia, Canada.

Ferris, D., & Helt, M. (2000, March). *Was Truscott right? New evidence on the effects of error correction in L2 writing classes.* Paper presented at the meeting of the American Association of Applied Linguistics, Vancouver, Canada.

Ferris, D., & Roberts, B. (2001). Error feedback in L2 writing classes: How explicit does it need to be? *Journal of Second Language Writing, 10,* 161–184.

Furneaux, C., Paran, A., & Fairfax, B. (2007). Teacher stance as reflected in feedback on student writing: An empirical study of secondary school teachers in five countries. *IRAL, 45*(1), 69–94.

Guenette, D. (2007). Is feedback pedagogically correct? Research design issues in studies of feedback on writing. *Journal of Second Language Writing, 16,* 40–53.

Han, Z. (2002). A study of the impact of recasts on tense consistency in L2 output. *TESOL Quarterly, 36,* 543–572.

Hartshorn, K. J., Evans, W. N., Merrill, F. P., Sudweeks, R. R., Strong-Krause, D., & Anderson, J. N. (2010). Effects of dynamic corrective feedback on ESL writing accuracy. *TESOL Quarterly, 44*(1), 84–109.

Hirose, W. (2009). The effect of teacher feedback on writing in Japanese as a second language: A comparison of students' revisions after written comments and writing conferences. *Bulletin of the Center for Japanese Language, Waseda University, 20,* 137–155.

Hyland, K., & Hyland, F. (2006). Feedback on second language students' writing. *Language Teaching, 39,* 83–101.

Ishibashi, R. (2002). Teachers' corrections and non-corrections on JSL learners' writing. *Gengobunka to Nihongo Kyoiku, 23,* 1–12.

Komura, K. (1999). *Student response to error correction in ESL classrooms* (Unpublished master's thesis). California State University, Sacramento.

Lalande, J. F. (1982). Reducing composition errors: An experiment. *Modern Language Journal, 66,* 140–149.

Lee, I. (1997). ESL learners' performance in error correction in writing. *System, 25,* 465–477.

Leki, I. (1991). The preferences of ESL students for error correction in college-level writing classes. *Foreign Language Annals, 24,* 203–218.

Lyster, R. (2004). Differential effects of prompts and recasts in form-focused instruction. *Studies in Second Language Acquisition, 26,* 399–432.

Odlin, T. (1989). *Language transfer: Cross-linguistic influence in language learning.* New York, NY: Cambridge University Press.

Ringbon, H. (1987). *The role of the first language in foreign language learning.* Clevedon, United Kingdom: Multilingual Matters.

Robb, T., Ross, S., & Shortreed, I. (1986). Salience of feedback on error and its effect on EFL writing quality. *TESOL Quarterly, 20,* 83–93.

Schwienhorst, K. (2007). *Learner autonomy and CALL environments.* London, United Kingdom: Routledge.

Schmidt, R. (1990). The role of consciousness in SLL. *Applied Linguistics, 11,* 129–158.

Semke, H. (1984). The effects of the red pen. *Foreign Language Annals, 17,* 195–202.

Truscott, J. (1996). The case against grammar correction in L2 writing classes. *Language Learning 46*(2), 327–369.

Truscott, J. (1999). The case for "the case for grammar correction in L2 writing classes": A response to Ferris. *Journal of Second Language Writing, 8,* 111–122.

Truscott, J., & Hsu, A. Y. (2008). Error correction, revision, and learning. *Journal of Second Language Writing, 17,* 292–305.

Uehara, K. (1997). Nihongo kyoiku ni okeru sakubun no "kijutsu feedback" ni tsuite: 'Code' ni yoru bunseki no kokoromi. [Written feedback in Japanese education: Experimental study using "codes"]. *Nanzan Nihongo Kyoiku, 4,* 135–161.

Wolfe-Quintero, K., Inagaki, S., & Kim, H. (1998). *Second language development in writing: Measures of fluency, accuracy, and complexity.* Honolulu, HI: University of Hawai'i Press.

Appendix 1: Metalinguistic error codes

○: particles   □: *kanji*   SP: Spelling   ⁀: conjugation   WC: Word Choice

WO↙: Word Order   ∧: something is missing   IS: Incomplete Sentence

⌒: redundant   ?: unclear meaning   HKK: *hiragana, katakana, kanji* usage

e.g. えんぴつとの─とⒷはつくえの上があいます。
　　　　　　　HKK　　　　　　　　SP

e.g. 私はキムさん。　日本で行きました。元気はいいでした。
　　　　WC　　IS

Appendix 2: Sample error tally sheet

	p. 49–50	p. 50–51	p. 53–34	p. 55–56	essay	total
particles ○	3					
kana, kanji (HKK)	2					
kanji □	1					
spelling (SP)	0					
word choice (WC)	2					
word order (WO)	0					
something missing ∧	2					
meaning not clear ?	0					
incomplete sentence (IS)	0					
omit/redundancy ⌒	2					

Appendix 3: Pre-test sample questions and essay prompt

A. Fill in the blanks with appropriate particles. If particles are not necessary, put X.

If particles are optional, put an appropriate particle in parentheses like (を).

- たなかさん＿＿＿よく＿＿＿にほん＿＿＿えいが＿＿＿みます。
- あした＿＿＿なんじ＿＿＿がっこう＿＿＿いきますか。
- どこ＿＿＿あさごはん＿＿＿たべますか。
- これ＿＿＿ゆうびんきょくです。あれ＿＿＿ゆうびんきょくです。

B. Make the following cluster of words into a sentence by changing the **word order** and adding appropriate **particles**. Also, **conjugate** the predicates.

〈メアリーさん　きっさてん　いく　よく　その〉

C. You are looking for a Japanese roommate for your apartment and would like to post an ad on BICS (the website for Japanese people in Boston). First, introduce yourself. Then, explain your daily schedule. Use as many grammar structures and expressions as possible that you learned from Chapter 1 to 3.

Appendix 4: Post-test sample questions and essay prompt

A. Fill in the blanks with appropriate particles. If particles are not necessary, put X. If particles are optional, put an appropriate particle in parentheses like (を).

- おかあさんはにく＿＿＿きらいです。
- 私はまい日＿＿＿二時かん＿＿＿えいご＿＿＿テープ＿＿＿ききます。
- 私はたけしさん＿＿＿いっしょ＿＿＿うみ＿＿＿およぎませんでした。
- 昨日＿＿＿おかあさん＿＿＿でんわ＿＿＿かけました。
- ゆっくり＿＿＿おふろ＿＿＿はいってください。

B. Make the following cluster of words into a sentence by changing the **word order** and adding appropriate **particles**. Also, **conjugate** the predicates.

〈コンピューター　きょねん　かう　たかい　五月〉

C. Your summer vacation is over. Now, you need to submit an essay about your summer. Write about "when you did what with whom at where" and how it was. Use as many grammar structures and expressions as possible that you learned from Chapter 1 to 6.

Appendix 5: Treatment group questionnaire sample questions

1. Describe the homework revision/correction procedure in three adjectives.
2. What was the hardest part of making corrections on your own?
3. What did you like/dislike the most about making corrections on your own?
4. What did you like/dislike the most about making corrections twice/constantly?
5. Did the error codes help you figure out your errors? Or, were they confusing?
6. What did you think of the use of error codes?

7. Do you think making corrections helped you to prepare for the tests and writingprojects? If you think so, why? If you do not think so, why not?
8. What did you think of keeping the error log? Did it help you figure out what kind of mistakes you often make? Was it too much of a hassle?

Appendix 6: Contrast group questionnaire sample questions
1. Describe the homework correction procedure in three adjectives.
2. What did you like/dislike the most about making corrections?
3. Did the error codes help you figure out your errors? Or, were they confusing?
4. What did you think of the use of error codes?
5. Do you think making corrections helped you to prepare for the tests and writing projects? If you think so, why? If you do not think so, why not?

内容重視の言語教育の理論と実践:「批判的」日本語教育に向けて

Theories and Practices of Content-based Language Instruction: Toward "Critical" Japanese Language Education

佐藤慎司 (Shinji Sato)
プリンストン大学 (Princeton University)

長谷川敦志 (Atsushi Hasegawa)
ニューヨーク大学 (New York University)

熊谷由理 (Yuri Kumagai)
スミス大学 (Smith College)

神吉宇一 (Uichi Kamiyoshi)
財団法人海外産業人材育成協会 (The Overseas Human Resources and Industry Development Association)

要旨

内容重視の言語教育(Content-Based Language Instruction, 以下 CBI)が唱えられて久しい。現在までにCBIに関する実践報告は数多くなされており、CBIの言語学習上の有効性に関しても第二言語習得研究などの分野で検証されてきている(Dupuy, 2000; Krashen, 1985; Rodgers, 2006)。しかし、「内容」の定義を確認し、CBIを教育の一分野として位置づけ検討し直している研究報告は少ない。本章では、まず、教育の持つ使命の一つが、現今のコミュニティをよりよく発展させつつ、そのコミュニティの未来を担って行く次世代の育成であることを確認し、その使命

とCBIとの関連性について考察する。次に，現行のCBIの様々な形態をより深く理解するために，CBIが唱えられるようになった背景，そして，「内容」という概念の捉えられ方を振り返った後，CBIの現状を概観する。そして最後に，CBIの取り組みに必要なものは，クリティカルな姿勢・視点をはぐくむような教育理念と，その理念に基づいたカリキュラムおよびプログラム開発であることを唱える。

Abstract

The importance of Content-Based Instruction (CBI) has long been recognized in the field of second/foreign language education. Many researchers have reported actual practices and the effectiveness of CBI, especially in the field of second language acquisition (Dupuy, 2000; Krashen, 1985; Rodgers, 2006). However, the definition of the content and the role of CBI within the broader field of education are two areas that need more research and discussion. In this chapter we first state that one of the missions in education is to help learners become important members of the community who take responsibility for the community's future. We then examine the relationship between that mission and CBI. Next, in order to understand different types of CBI, we review definitions of "content" as well as the history and the current state of CBI. Finally we discuss what is missing in the current CBI is the principles that foster critical attitudes and perspectives and call for developing a curriculum that is designed based on such principles.

はじめに

内容重視の言語教育(Content-Based Language Instruction, 以下 CBI)が唱えられて久しい。現在までにCBIに関する実践報告は数多くなされており，CBIの言語学習上の有効性に関してもKrashen(1985)をはじめとする第二言語習得研究において検証されてきている。しかし，「内容」の定義を確認し，CBIを教育の一分野として位置づけ検討し直している研究報告は少ない。本章では，まず，教育の持つ使命の一つが，現今のコミュニティをよりよく発展させつつ，そのコミュニティの未来を担って行く次世代の育成(佐藤・熊谷 2011; 文部科学省 2006; Partnership for 21st Century Skills, 2002)であることを確認し，その使命とCBIとの関連性について考察する。次に，現行のCBIの様々な形態をより深く理解するために，CBIが唱えられるようになった背景および「内容」という概念の捉えられ方を振り返った後，CBIの現状を概観する。最後に，CBIの取り組みに必要なものはクリティカルな姿勢・視点をはぐくむような教育理念とその理念に基づいたカリキュラムおよびプログラム開発であることを唱える。そして，その教育理念やプログラム開発の必要性を強調する内容重視の言語教育を内容重視の批判的言語教育(Critical Content-Based Language Instruction, CCBI)と呼ぶことも併せて提案したい。

内容重視の言語教育

内容重視の言語教育(CBI)が生まれた背景

内容重視という考え自体は言語教育に古くから存在していたが(Brinton, Snow, & Wesche, 1989)，教授法の大きな動きとして注目を集めるようになったのは1970年代に入ってからであった(Richards & Rodgers, 2001)。当時，カナダでは多くの学校でフランス語のイマージョンプログラムが開設され，第二言語学習と教科学習を同時に進める必要性が生じていた。また，同じ頃イギリスでも全ての教科において言語(英語)を重視しようとする動きが起こり，これもCBIの発展に寄与した。つまり，CBIは学校における教科教育と言語教育の統合から始まったわけである。そして，その後，言語と内容の統合という考えは一般的な第二言語・外国語教授法のアプローチとして定着していった(Richards & Rodgers, 2001)。1970年代はコミュニカティブアプローチが台頭し始めた頃で，意味のあ

る言語使用，言語使用場面の重要性，コミュニケーションの手段としての言語という考えが受け入れられ始めた時期であった。その大きな流れの中で，CBIも広く認められるようになったのである。その後，学習ニーズの多様化，第二言語・外国語教授法自体の変化に対応するために，CBIの形も変容してきた。現在でもCBIは社会的・個人的ニーズに合うように，さらに変化を続けている。つまり，現在に至るまでのCBIの発展にはそれぞれの時代や学習者のおかれる環境に即した実用性への志向が大きく関与していると言える。

内容重視の言語教育 (CBI)の定義

　CBIの定義は言語の授業と(言語以外の)教科内容の授業を統合するという比較的わかりやすいものである。Brinton, Snow, & Wesche(1989)は，高等教育を例に挙げ「大学の科目と第二言語・外国語のスキルを同時に教えること」と説明している(p. 3)。また，大学の外国語教育の大きな目標として「第二言語・外国語を使って情報を得る過程を通してアカデミックな言語スキルを伸ばすこと」とし，最終的には，「学生がそれらのスキルを特定の第二言語・外国語で他の科目にも応用できるようになること」としている(Brinton, Snow, & Wesche, 1989, p. 3)。一方で，Stryker & Leaver(1997)では外国語教育の究極の目的を比喩的に「学習者が羽を広げ，巣を離れ，地平線に向かって高く舞っていくこと」とし，授業の初日から，コミュニケーションの手段として，その言語を学ぶことを学生に奨励している(p. 27)。このような理念には，学生が自律的な学習者になるためのエンパワーメントの意味合いがあり，後述するクリティカルな姿勢・視点とも通じる点がある。

　CBIの定義自体はシンプルであるのに対し，実際にCBIにおける「内容」が何を指すのかという議論になると学校の教科(academic subject)(Crandall & Tucker, 1990)，学校の教科に限らず，様々なトピックやテーマ，学習者にとって興味のある，あるいは重要な事柄(言語でなくてもよい)(Genesee, 1994)，一般のことばに関する，とりわけ学習言語の理解に寄与する知的なトピック(Chaput, 1993)，外国語を通して，学習者の学年に相応で，適切に教えられる概念のこと(Curtain & Pesola, 1994)といったようにその範囲はかなり広い。

　上述のような内容の捉え方の違いはプログラムの特色によるところが大きい。つまり，対象とするカリキュラムが「内容と言語の連続体」(Met, 1991, p. 283)のどこに位置するか，何を目標として位置づけるかによって，「内容」が指すものが異なってくる。それに伴い，CBIのアプローチも異なる。大別すると，「テーマベースモデル」(テーマを扱いながら言語学習が中心となる)，「シェルターモデル」(内容の学習が中心で言語学習は内容の理解をサポートするのみ)，「アジャンクトモデル」(母語話者とともに講義科目を履修し，さらに言語面を補うために講義科目と直接関係するように設置された言語コースを同時に履修し，内容と言語の両方を学習する)の三つに分けられ(村田・原田 2008)，関係者はこの中から適当なものを選ぶということになる。

　このように，内容の捉え方，CBIのアプローチは様々であるが，どのように「内容」を捉え，どのようなアプローチで教えるかに関しては，それぞれのプログラム，教師の置かれた立場，環境，目的やニーズによって慎重に選ばれるべきであろう。

教育活動としての内容重視の言語教育 (CBI)：日本語教育全体への提言

　言語教育は教育の一分野であり，CBIは言語教育における一つのアプローチ・教育理念である。したがって，ここでは教育の使命とCBIの関係について考えてみたい。教育の大切な使命の一つとして，現今のコミュニティをよりよく発展させつつ，そのコミュニティ

の将来を担う人材の育成が挙げられる(甲斐 2011; 佐藤・熊谷 2011; 文部科学省 2006; Partnership for 21st century Skills, 2002)。そのような人材にはコミュニティのメンバーとやりとりをする力, 相手を説得する力や相手の話に耳を傾けたりする態度などが必要とされる。しかし, その根本には, コミュニティのどの側面を現状維持すべきで, どこは改善すべきなのかという分析的視点をもつことが必須である。そのためにはまず, 現状だけでなく, 人の意見や価値観, ひいては自分の意見や価値観をいろいろな側面から捉えることのできる力が必要である(佐藤・熊谷 2011; 鈴木・大井・竹前 2006)。このような力を, 我々はここで「クリティカルな姿勢・視点」と呼ぶことにする。

一般的に, 批判的思考力(critical thinking)というとき, それは論理的に物事を分析する能力として理解されることが多い。実際, 多くの高等教育機関では批判的思考力の育成が強調されている(鈴木・大井・竹前 2006)。例えば, アメリカでは各州と産業界が「21世紀スキル」の構想を開発し, その育成を目指しており, その中の重要項目として批判的思考力(critical thinking)が含まれている(Partnership for 21st Century Skills, 2002)。また, ほとんどのアメリカの大学のホームページには, 大学の綱領(mission statement)に, 「批判的思考力(critical thinking)」, 「将来のコミュニティを担っていく人材の育成」といったような事柄が記載されている[1]。

多くの高等教育機関が批判的思考力(critical thinking)の育成を重視しているということは, この能力の育成が教育の大きな使命であるということの裏付けでもある。しかし, 一般的に用いられる批判的思考力(critical thinking)という用語には問題が二点ある。一つは批判的思考力の定義自体が極めて曖昧であることである。この点について, 我々は「クリティカルな姿勢・視点」という言い方で再定義を試みる。我々の言う「クリティカルな姿勢・視点」とは, 物事を論理的に分析するだけに留まらず, 自分の置かれた現状や社会[2]に内在する社会的・慣習的な前提を問い直し, その維持や変革に能動的に関わっていこうとする姿勢・視点である。批判的思考力(critical thinking)に関するもう一つの問題は, 批判的思考力を育成することが前面に出ることにより, そもそも何のために批判的思考をしなければならないのかという肝心の問いが抜け落ちてしまう場合が多いことである。それは批判的思考力の育成が, たとえばスキルトレーニングの一環として行われるようなことに起因すると我々は考えている。そのことを解決するためには, 内容を重視した教育を行うことが求められる。この内容を重視した批判的教育は, 言語教育だけにおいて実践されるものではなく, 他の教科・科目を含むすべての教育活動において行われるべきものであり, そこでは, コミュニティの未来を担っていくために必要な「クリティカルな姿勢・視点」も重要な教育目標として捉えられる必要がある。

では, 日本語教育という文脈で内容重視の教育を考える時, そこで教師はどのような存在になるのだろうか。まず, 教師自身がクリティカルな姿勢・視点をもって教育活動に携わる必要があることは言うまでもない。また, 単に学習者と一緒に物事を深く分析するだけではなく, 学習者がなぜ物事を深く分析しなければならないのかという問いを考え

---

[1] 例えば, プリンストン大学の場合, 「to further develop a humane and collaborative environment that serves the educational mission of the University by encouraging, supporting and celebrating intellectual curiosity, active citizenship, ethical leadership and respect for our diverse community.」といった記述がある。(http://www.princeton.edu/campuslife/mission/)

[2] ここで「社会」とは「日本社会, 国際社会といった包括的な全体社会を始め, もっと小さなコミュニティ, あるいはグループといった自然発生的, および人為的な集団や仲間」と定義する(佐藤・熊谷 2011, p. vii)

られるような学習の場を提供し支援することも重要である。そこでは,日本語教師は日本語学習者を,日本語の語彙,表現,文法や様々な内容に関して知識が不十分な者・知識やスキルを与えられるべき存在というように捉えるのではなく,内容に関してはもちろん,言語の使われ方に関しても疑問を持ち,必要があれば改善していくことのできる者として捉えることが求められる。そのように,教師が学習者を能動的な存在と捉え,学習者自身が自らを能動的な存在と感じることによって,まさに教室というコミュニティに存在するすべての人の能動的な関わりを生み出し,カリキュラムや教授法の維持と変革を考えていくことができる。

それでは,日本語教師は,具体的にどのようなクリティカルな姿勢・視点をもった日本語話者を育てることを目指したらよいのだろうか。例えば,言語使用の形式や慣習を習得することにのみ囚われるのではなく,自分自身の目的や用途にあった日本語を学び,自らの(体現したい,あるいは,理想の)アイデンティティを日本語で表現し,交渉できるような日本語話者。また,「ノンネイティブ」という立場から(日本語教師も含む)「ネイティブ」との関係に対して受け身的になるのではなく,マルチリンガル話者としての立場から自信をもって自己実現していけるような日本語話者。さらには,「日本人」「日本文化／社会」の枠に囚われすぎず,その流動性,多様性を認識した上で,状況に適した言語使用ができる日本語話者などがあげられる。そのような日本語話者になることで,学習者が自分の所属する(あるいは,所属したい)様々なコミュニティとの関わりの中で自己実現できるようになるだけでなく,日本語コミュニティをもよりよく発展させることに貢献することが可能になる。昨今の「ノンネイティブ」作家による越境文学の隆盛,そして,彼らの作品に対する高い評価は,その好例であるとも言えよう。

次節では外国語教育,日本語教育のCBIの実践を概観するとともに,筆者らの提言するようなクリティカルな姿勢・視点が,どの程度意識され,実践されているのかを検討する。

外国語教育における最近の動向

北米におけるCBIは,70年代初頭から様々な状況で実践が始められるが,80年代後半になってその数が劇的に増えたという(Grabe & Stoller, 1997)。本節では,1)分野別言語教育(discipline-based language instruction)[3]・プロジェクト型言語教育(project-based language education), 2)教科カリキュラム横断型外国語教育(Foreign Language Across the Curriculum; FLAC), 3)目的別言語教育・専門外国語(Language for Specific/Special Purpose; LSP)の3つに分け,最近の動向を概観する。

分野別言語教育・プロジェクト型言語教育

分野別言語教育は,いわゆる「外国語クラス」に「内容」を上乗せする形で取り込もうとする試みであり,前節で触れたテーマベースモデルを基本としている。次節で説明するFLACモデルは複数の分野の教師が協働で言語／内容コースをデザインするのに対し,分野別言語教育は言語コースに内容要素を追加する形を取っている。最近の実践・研究報告の例を表1にまとめた。

---

[3] Grabe & Stoller (1997)は,「content-based」という用語が,「form-based」との対比として用いられていることを問題視し,あえて「discipline-based」という用語を使っている。

表1　最近のCBI実践・研究報告例　報告者

報告者	レベル	言語	内容
Caldwell (2001)	全レベル	フランス語	世界文学
Hoechel-Alden (2006)	中級	ドイツ語	文学
McGee (2001)	中級／上級	ドイツ語	文化／シビリゼーション
Brown, Bown, & Eggett (2009)	中級／上級	ロシア語	ライティング
Berho & Defferding (2005)	中級	フランス語　スペイン語	美術
Byrnes & Sprang (2003)	上級	ドイツ語	リテラシー

表1から分かるように，初級レベルでの実践は限られており，中上級レベルに達した学生を対象にしたコースがほとんどである。また，分野別言語教育で取り入れられる内容は，文学，リテラシーなど，いわゆる人文系分野に焦点がおかれているものが多い。これは言語プログラムが人文系学部の一部であるという学問分野の分類上の制約，および言語教師のトレーニングの背景からしても，当然の状況かもしれない。

分野別言語教育の一つの形態として，プロジェクト型言語教育・問題提起型言語教育が挙げられる。プロジェクト型言語教育の多くは，その背景にDewey(1962)の教育哲学をもち，言語学習に対する配慮だけでなく，言語と学習科目内容の連結や統合に焦点をおいている(Beckett, 2006)。プロジェクト型言語教育とは，一言で言うと，「何らかのトピックについて言語を用いて学習する場を作ること」である(Beckett, 2006, p. 6)。しかし，それはただ単にカリキュラムにプロジェクトを組み込めばよいというのではなく，プロジェクトの過程において，経験を通しての学習(experiential learning)，トピックについての研究・調査，そして，問題解決(problem solving)といった要素を併せ持たなければならない(Stoller, 2006)。

この種の活動として，2年目後半のスペイン語の授業で行われたLuke(2006)の例が挙げられる。このプロジェクトでは，各学生がスペイン語圏に関係のあるトピックを選び，インターネット上で色々な情報を集め，相互自己評価で互いのプロジェクトの批評を行い，最終的には作品(パワーポイント，旅行のパンフレット，ポスターなど)を発表するという活動が，学期を通して行われた。当該のプロジェクトとそこで行われる種々の活動は，学習者の自律性を伸ばすことを第一の目的としており，その過程において学習者自身が興味のある内容を学習するという手法をとっている。また，このようなプロジェクトが教室内だけでなく教室外で行われている事例もある。Moreno-Lopez, Saenz-de-Tejada, & Smith(2008)で報告されたスペイン語圏留学先の地元の小中学校でのサービス活動のように，教室外での活動は，学習者の周りに存在するコミュニティを言語学習の場と設定し，学習者が実際の体験を通して学習すること(サービスラーニングとも呼ばれる)を目指した試みである。

上述のように、プロジェクト型言語教育のCBI実践はジョン・デューイの理念を基盤にしているため、その実践の背景には、批判的思考力(critical thinking)の考え方が存在する(Dewey, 1910参照)。また、教師対学生という固定的・一方向的な役割を離れ、学習者間で学びあう機会を提供するという点においても、クリティカルな姿勢・視点を養うのには適したモデルだと言えるだろう。しかしながら、現在までに報告されているCBI実践を概観する限り、クリティカルな姿勢・視点は学習の過程における偶発的産物ではあっても、意図された目標にはなっていない。教育デザイン・カリキュラム開発の段階からクリティカルな姿勢・視点の育成をも目指している報告はなされていないのが実情である。

教科カリキュラム横断型外国語教育 (Foreign Language Across the Curriculum: FLAC)

アメリカにおけるCBIへの関心の高まりと同時に、イギリスでは教科カリキュラム横断型言語教育(Language Across the Curriculum, LAC)という教育アプローチへの人気が高まっていた。LACは、全学年を通して全ての科目で読み書きの指導を主眼においた教育をすることを目指していた。そのような動きが、後の北米の中等教育での教科科目における読み書き教育(Writing/Reading in the Content Areas)、そして、高等教育での教科カリキュラム横断型ライティング教育(Writing Across the Curriculum)というモデルの開発へと繋がっていった(Grabe & Stoller, 1997)。これらの教育アプローチに共通するのは、言語・リテラシー(読み書き)の指導が、全ての科目においてもっとも重要な目標として据えられている点である。それは、内容とは言語を通して学習されるものであり、言語・リテラシーのスキルに注意を払うことで内容学習の向上につながるという考えに基づいている。このような教育アプローチの特徴として、1)学習者の内容学習への積極的な取り組みを促す、2)学習者が言語学習と内容学習の両側面に対して自分の中でバランスを取りながらタスクを遂行する機会を与える、3)協働学習を促す、4)分野によってディスコース(分野独特なルールや約束事)が異なることを意識化するよう促す、5)学習者のモチベーションが高まるような内容教材を用いるといったことが挙げられる。

このようなLACの考え方を外国語教育に応用したのがFLACである。FLACは、CBIのひとつのモデルであるとされているが、その目標とメソッドは、分野別言語教育とは異なる。もっとも大きな違いは、FLACは大学の複数の分野が協働でカリキュラムを組むという点である(Caldwell, 2001; Jurasek, 1993)。つまり、「アジャンクトモデル」に近い形がとられる場合が多い。また、FLACの主目的は外国語習得自体ではなく、科目分野での学びを豊かにすることであるとされている。その場合、外国語は研究のための道具と見なされ、文献をオリジナルの言語で読むことによって、その分野や異文化に対する知識を豊かにし(Caldwell, 2001)、批判的思考力(critical thinking)を培うことができる(Jurasek, 1993)と考えられている。

FLACの実践例としては80年代にアメリカで一早くその実践を開始したアーラム大学(Jurasek, 1993)が有名である。アーラム大学では、フランス語やドイツ語などの言語と、歴史や哲学などのクラスを統合した様々なカリキュラムが開発、実施されている。また、セントオラフ大学(Anderson, Allen, & Narvaez, 1993)は、アーラム大学のモデルを基に、2年間外国語を学習した者を対象に、コースの読み物の半分を外国語で読み、通常のクラスとは別に1時間外国語でのディスカッションに参加することで特別に単位を与えるというカリキュラムを実施している。ミネソタ大学(Metcalf, 1993)でも、同様の試みが1990年より行われている。しかしながら、FLACはプログラム開発、継続の経費の問題を抱えており、安定したプログラム運営を行うのが難しいことでも知られている。政府や教育財団からの助成金を受けてFLACを開発する大学が多い中、助成期間が切れるとともにプログラムが消滅するというケースも多いようである。

FLACにおいては, 外国語が研究のための単なる道具とみなされている限り, 言語教師は学習者が情報を収集・解読するための道具としての言語に関するルールを教える者, コンテント教師(言語以外の科目の教師)は内容に関して学習者に知識を提供する者という役割分担を課せられ, その協働は表面的な, いわば棲み分けのようなものになってしまうであろう。今後, 大学で複数の分野の教師が協働でクリティカルな姿勢・視点の育成を目指した内容重視の言語教育(CBI)を立ち上げていくためには, コンテント教師と言語教師が, クリティカルな姿勢・視点に対する意識はもちろんのこと, 学習目標, 教材, 学習過程, 評価に対する考え方に関しても意識の擦り合わせを行うことが必要になってくる。

目的別言語教育/専門外国語 (Language for Specific/Special Purposes; LSP)

目的別言語教育(LSP)とは, 学習者の言語学習の目的に直結した言語の教育を行うことを目指したアプローチである。その中でも, 第二言語としての英語教育の分野における専門英語(English for Specific Purposes: ESP)は, 1960年代からいちはやくその必要性が訴えられるようになり, 現在では確固たる分野として確立され, 研究・実践ともに進んでいる[4]。しかし, 何をもってESPとするのか, ESPと一般英語教育の違いは何なのかといった議論になると, 研究者の間でも統一された見解がないのが現状である。ESP分野の第一人者であるJohns & Dudley-Evans(1991)によると, ESPの目的は特定の学習状況・環境におかれた成人英語学習者のニーズ分析をした上で学習教材やアクティビティーを設計する教育アプローチであると説明している。

外国語教育での試みについての報告は, 大きく2つのタイプに分けることができる。まず一つ目は, 大学の授業で学習者が身につけた外国語能力を卒業後のキャリアで活かすことを目指したカリキュラム開発, あるいは実践についての報告, そして, 二つ目は, 既に仕事に従事している学習者を対象に実際の現場で必要とされる能力を伸ばすことを目的とした報告である。

一つ目の大学の外国語の授業からの報告としては, 技術者のためのドイツ語(Neville & Britt, 2007; Grosseck, 2010), ビジネスドイツ語(Weigert, 2004), スペイン語で学ぶ刑事司法制度(Crank & Loughrin-Sacco, 2001)などがある。その中で, Weigert(2004)は, ビジネスドイツ語という分野には既に国際的に公認されている試験(Prufung Wirtschaftsdeutsch international)があるという状況の中, 一般的にカリキュラムがその試験に合格することにのみ焦点をおき, 事実的な情報やテクニカルな語彙を学生に教えこむという傾向が強いことを問題視している。そして, 学生のリテラシーやディスコースの能力を伸ばすという考え方への転換を訴え, ジャンルに基づいたビジネス上必要とされるディスコース(例えば, プレゼンテーションやクライアントとの交渉)を学ぶことを目指したカリキュラムを紹介している。

二つ目の既に仕事に従事している学習者を対象とする報告としては, Lear(2005)の医療関係者のためのスペイン語のニーズ分析がある。その論文の中で, Learは, 看護師, 助産師, 栄養士などが働く産科医院でのフィールド調査の結果をもとに, 医療関係者が患者との意思疎通を図るために, 患者の話すスペイン語を身につけることを必要としている

---

[4] ESPでは, English for science and technology, English for occupational/professional purposes, English for business and economics, English for medical purposes, English for academic legal purposes, English for the arts/art and design, English for sociocultural purposes, vocational ESL, workplace literacy programs, English for Academic Purposes (EAP), academic literacy といった職業的, 学問的な状況での様々なニーズに応えるためのプログラムが試行されている。

現状を明らかにした。そして，時間的にも経済的にも学校に行って外国語(この場合は，スペイン語)を勉強する余裕のない人のために，職場で仕事をしながら現場のニーズに直結した言語教育を受ける機会を提供する必要性を訴えている。

以上からも明らかなように，LSPは専門性，実用性，そして実践力に焦点をおいた言語教育のアプローチである。しかし，プログラムによっては狭い範囲の専門分野に焦点を置きすぎるために，それ以外の一般的な場でコミュニケーションを行う能力が育たないという批判も受けている(Stryker & Leaver, 1997)。また，LSPでは，学習者が場ごとで期待されていることを理解し，うまく対応していくための教育を目指す傾向が強いため，学習者の主体的な意思を無視し，ルールや慣習への順応や同化を求めるという問題も指摘されている。

LSPの1つの形態であるESPが，研究・実践において既に確立されていることは先に述べた通りである。ESPの中でも特に，アカデミック英語(English for Academic Purposes: EAP)の領域では，実用性(pragmatism)と批判性(criticality)との関係において激しい議論がもちあがっている。Benesch(2001)は，EAPで主流をしめる実用性のみを強調したアプローチは，現実性(realism)や真正性(authenticity)を理由に，ある学問分野で要求される知識やスキルをゆるぎなく変化しないものとして捉えていると批判している。さらに，現行のEAPでは，英語を第一言語としない学習者は専門の学問分野での未熟者，あるいは新参者という立場に置かれ，ゆくゆくメンバーとして受け入れてもらうことを目的に与えられる知識や技能を受動的に学び，自らの言語や考え方をそのコミュニティの規範や要求に合わせることを強要されていると議論している(Benesch, 2001, 2009)。

そのようなアプローチに対し，クリティカルなアプローチを提唱する研究者らは，EAPが目指すニーズ分析は，単に専門科目分野でどのような能力が要求されるのかを分析するだけではなく，次のような点についても深く分析・検討する必要があるとしている。

- 誰がそのような能力やゴールの設定をしているのか
- なぜそのような能力，ゴールが必要とされるのか
- そのようなゴール設定をすることで誰が有利な立場におかれるのか
- そのようなゴールに対して異議を唱えるべきなのかどうか

つまり，現状を明らかにするだけでなく，よりよい状況をも検討していく必要性を謳っているのである。そして，そこでの知見をもとに開発されたクリティカルなEAP(Critical EAP)は，実用性のみを重視したEAPには欠けている「現状を疑問視・問題視する場」を学習者に提供することができるとしている(Benesch, 2001, 2009; Canagarajah, 2002; Harwood & Hadley, 2004; Morgan, 2009a, 2009b; Pennycook, 1997; Starfield, 2004など)。さらに，クリティカルなEAPを実践する教師自身は，学習者が必要とする専門分野に対応するための能力を伸ばすと同時に，専門教育・職業の現場，そして，それをとりまく社会の状況を改善するために必要な変革にも注意を払うべきであるとも主張している(Benesch, 2009; Chun, 2009; Morgan, 2009a, 2009b; Pennycook, 1997)。

以上のように，EAPの分野では，クリティカルな姿勢・視点を育むという批判的なアプローチの必要性が唱えられはじめている。しかし，英語以外のLSPにおいては，同様の問題提起や議論はまだ行われていないようである。

通常のLSP(英語教育も含む)においては，言語がその分野(コミュニティ)での規則や慣習どおりに使えるかどうかのみが学習者を判断するものさしとなり，それぞれの学習者が持つ様々な知識や能力は有効に活用されていない(あるいは，無視されている)という

問題点が挙げられる。そのような現状は，上で述べたように，あるコミュニティにおいて学習者が未熟者，あるいは新参者という扱いを受けることからも明らかである。これは，言語教育が「内容」と分離されて考えられていることの表れだと言えるのではないだろうか。

クリティカルな姿勢・視点をLSPに取り入れる際，EAPの分野で議論されているように，実用性と批判性のせめぎ合いが一番の難点となることは明らかである。職場で専門職に従事しつつ実際に必要な言語能力を身につけていくという実践の場合は，コストや効率化の面からみて批判的なアプローチの有効性・必要性が受け入れられにくいだろう。しかし，学習者(外国語使用者)が社会的な文脈において弱者の立場にあるような場合は特に，批判性の育成を怠るべきではない。批判的な視点から自らがおかれる現状を分析できてはじめて，自分が果たすべき役割や行使すべき権利が把握できるからである。したがって，LSPでは，様々な学習者が置かれるローカルな状況に即して，実用性と批判性のバランスを考えていくことが必要であろう。

日本語教育における最近の動向

1990年代より日本語教育においてもCBIの意義が唱えられ(岡崎 2002)，様々な取り組みが報告されている。本節ではまず，(1)プロジェクト型教育・分野別教育，(2)教科カリキュラム横断型言語教育(Foreign Language Across the Curriculum, FLAC)，(3)日本における目的別日本語・専門日本語(JSP)の順にそれぞれの分野の動向を紹介する。

プロジェクト型日本語教育・分野別日本語教育

プロジェクト型日本語教育：大学における初級レベルの内容重視の言語教育実践

大学における初級レベルでのCBI実践報告は多くない(佐藤・ロチャー 2011; 佐藤・ナズキアン・浜田 2010; チャン・チェ 2004; 西口 1998; 纐纈・長谷川・安田・松本 2008)。その取り組みの一つとしては，佐藤・ナズキアン・浜田(2010)によるアメリカにおける活動が挙げられる。コミュニティ・ブログプロジェクトと呼ばれるブログを利用したその実践では，1)学生自身が選んだテーマに関してできるだけ多くの情報を集め，その情報を自分の意見と共に発信すること，2)グループメンバー，クラスメート，提携校や他の日本語話者と情報・意見交換をすること，という二つの目的を設定している。そして，学習者が興味のあるテーマごとにグループを作り，そのテーマに関する情報を集め，ブログ上で発信したり，意見を交換したりしている。また，纐纈・長谷川・安田・松本(2008)でもプロジェクト型の実践を行い，学習の早い段階(初級クラス)からCBIの理念を基にした活動を取り入れることにより，大学における教養教育としてのニーズを満たせるのではないかという問題提起している。日本の大学においては，チャン・チェ(2004)が総合型日本語教育の実践の一部として，初級を対象にしたCBI的な活動を実施している。これらの取り組みに共通するのは，教師が内容を選んで学習者に提供するのではなく，学習者自らが学習したい内容を選ぶという点であり，どの実践でも，既にベースとして通常のカリキュラムがあり，その範囲内でCBIプロジェクトを実施しているという特徴がある。

初級レベルでは，言語的な制約が多いためか，扱うテーマ(内容)についてどこまで深めていくかという点に十分な注意が払われていないというのが全体的な傾向であろう。上述した纐纈ら(2008)は，大学教育としての知的レベルを満たすことの必要性を説いた数少ない論文の一つであるが，それでも，クリティカルな姿勢・視点は学習目標の一部として設定されてはいない。クリティカルな姿勢・視点の育成を目標に据えた実践としては，佐藤・ロチャー(2011)による「日本語の文字プロジェクト」が挙げられる。このプロジェク

トは, 学習者がカタカナの使用実態を調査・分析・考察し, 最終的にはそこで得た知識を利用して俳句・川柳・ショートストーリーなどの創作作品を作るというものであった。初級学習者にとって身近な「カタカナ」というテーマを題材にしているものの, 内容的には深い分析・考察の必要なプロジェクトであった。また, 学習者がカタカナに関する教科書の記述と実際の使用方法を比較することによって, 教科書の記述の限界を理解するとともに, 教科書を能動的に使用することの大切さを話し合うなど, 批判的な姿勢・視点育成のための活動(熊谷 2007, 2011)も行われた。しかし, このような実践はまだほとんど報告されていないという状況である。大学での日本語教育は, たとえ初級レベルといえども, 知的レベルの向上を目指すとともに, クリティカルな姿勢・視点の育成を目標の一つとして掲げていくべきであろう。

分野別日本語教育:日本研究・日本事情と中上級レベルの内容重視の言語教育実践

中上級レベルになると, プロジェクト型よりも, 日本研究・日本事情といったテーマを基にカリキュラム全体が組まれる傾向が日本においてもアメリカにおいても見られる。日本研究と日本語教育の現状は「諸外国における『日本事情』教育についての基礎的調査研究」(長谷川 1998)で報告されている。世界中の機関からの回答の集計結果によると, 日本文化・社会のクラスの目的に関して, 「日本語の運用能力を高めること」と同時に「日本文化, 社会や現代日本社会についての一般的興味を触発すること」「日本人との直接的交流を念頭において, 日本人の日常的・具体的な行動様式や考え方への理解を深めること」と答えた回答者が, 「日本研究の専門的知識を与えること」「専門的日本研究への入門的知識を与えること」と回答した者より多かった(p. 54–55)。つまり, 日本事情教育の現状は「内容教育」への指向ではないことがここから窺える。しかし, この傾向は日本文化・社会のクラスが各国内や各大学においてどう位置づけられているかにより異なるだろう。また, 担当教員の専門や学習者のレベルなどによっても, 日本文化・社会のクラスは非常に多様である。

また, 最近では, アメリカにおいて様々なCBIの実践報告がなされている(近松 2008, 2009, 2011; Chikamatsu & Matsugu, 2009; Morioka, 2007)。2010年には「高等教育における日本語と日本研究の橋渡し」というフォーラムがデュポール大学で開催され, その報告書では, 日本研究と日本語教育の関係について次のような問題が提起された。1)初級レベルへの橋渡しはどうするか, 2)知的, 批判的思考能力をどう推進していくか, 3)言語教師とコンテント教師(言語以外の科目の教師)の連携をどうするか, 4)知識提供者としての役割だけでなく, 仲介者, 一参加者としての教師の役割を再考する, 5)クラス外での文化的活動を促進する, などが挙げられた。また, これらの問題への取り組みのきっかけとして, この報告書では, 言語教師による日本文化・日本史・国際関係クラスの実践, また, コンテント教師による言語にも焦点を当てた文学・アジア研究・国際研究のクラスの実践, さらに, コンテント教師と言語教師が協力して行った授業の実践や地域の様々な団体との交流をはかった実践などが報告された。

上記のようにクリティカルな姿勢・視点の育成(「批判的思考能力をどう推進していくか」)が将来的な課題の一つとして取り上げられていることからも分かるように, 現時点ではクリティカルな姿勢・視点を目指した実践の報告はあまり見られない。そのような状況の中で, クリティカルな姿勢・視点を目指した数少ない実践のひとつとして, 近松(2011)の報告が興味深い。コースのテーマとして「戦争と日本人」「シカゴ日系人史」などが選ばれ, 学生は様々な読み物, 視聴覚教材, ゲストスピーカーの話, 教室内外の活動を通して, テーマについて考察していく構成となっている。批判的思考を育てるような活動としては, 読み物の記述における言語使用(例えば, 原爆投下に関する「落とす」「

落ちる」「落とされる」)の例を挙げ,学習者が今まで学習してきた言語規則(自動詞・他動詞・受け身など)を批判的に捉え直すきっかけになったエピソードなどを説明している。また,近松(2009)では,日英両言語における読み物教材を利用し,比較を通して批判的思考の育成を促す活動も報告している。今後はこのような報告に併せて,より具体的かつ包括的なカリキュラムの構築が必要になっていくだろう。したがって,次節では,実際にクリティカルな視点・姿勢を育成するためのカリキュラムを構築する際,注意すべき点に関してまとめる。

教科カリキュラム横断型日本語教育の実践

日本語教育におけるFLACの実践は少ない。全米の中でもいち早くFLACを導入したことで知られるセントオラフ大学では,2008年から「Asian Conversations」という日本語のFLACが行われている。「Asian Conversations」は二年目(または三年目)に履修できる通年プログラムで,三つのコンテントコースと二つの言語コースで構成されている。学生はプログラムを通して,言語・コンテントを繋がりのある「一つ」として学習できるようにカリキュラムが組まれている。プログラムの中間にあたる一月期には一ヶ月間の短期留学が組み込まれ,日本で実際に日本語を使って実習(民族誌的な調査など)が行えるようになっている。Larson(2011)によると,このプログラムの原型は1999年に始まったが,アメリカ政府からの助成金により2008年に大幅に改善され,現在の形になったということである。

また,オレゴン大学では,2010年より「Global Scholars Program」というFLACプログラムが始められた(Idemaru, Nakadate, O'Brien, 2011)。日本語五年目レベルを「Academic CBI Prep」「Partial Academic CBI」「Full Academic CBI」の三段階に分割し,その最終段階にあたる「Full Academic CBI」は日本語のみを使用した通常の学部レベルのコンテントコースになっており,イマージョン的な要素も強い。

ノートルダム大学では,上記のようにプログラム全体をFLACのコースにするのではなく,プログラム内で部分的にFLACの取り組みを2009年より行っている(縮緬・シャムーン 2011)。英語で行われる既存のコンテントコース(Introduction to Japanese Pop Culture)に付随する形で,一単位のFLACコースが開講され,FLACコースは言語教師とコンテント教師のチームティーチングで行われている。FLACを実施する上の問題は,先にも述べたように言語教師とコンテント教師の連携をどう推進していくかかが重要な鍵になるが,その際,言語教師とコンテント教師の大学での地位の格差が一つの問題となっている。

目的別日本語教育／専門日本語 (JSP)の実践

近年日本国内においては,以前にもまして目的別・対象別日本語教育,専門日本語(JSP)教育に対する関心が高まっている。その背景には二つの要因がある。一つは,一般的な言語知識や言語技能の習得から,文脈に沿った言語使用とそれを通した社会化を重視するという言語学習観への変化である(Firth & Wagner, 1997; Kramsch, 2002)。もう一つは,医療・福祉関係者やIT技術者,理系の大学院を修了した高度な専門性を持った研究者など,専門特化した外国人人材を就労者として受け入れようとする日本社会の変化が関係している。また,その状況変化によって,今まで顕在化していなかった日本語教育の社会的課題も浮き彫りになりつつある。本節では,日本国内における目的別・対象別日本語教育の中から,アカデミックジャパニーズ,ビジネス日本語教育,看護・介護の日本語教育,技術研修生に対する日本語教育についてその現状をまとめ,そこでの課題を述べる。そして,これらの現状と課題を,CBIの再考という視点から改めて捉え直す。

アカデミックジャパニーズ

日本語教育においてアカデミックジャパニーズが注目されたのは，2002年の日本留学試験開始の影響が大きい(門倉 2009; 三宅 2003; 森 2005)。アカデミックジャパニーズで育成すべき能力は，専門的研究を下支えする問題提起力や思考力，探究力，発信力などである。具体的には，膨大な情報を受動的に受け取るだけでなく，自分自身の興味関心はもちろんのこと，研究活動に求められる学問的・社会的意義なども踏まえた上でそれらの情報を検討し，主体的・批判的に物事を捉え直し，その内容や価値を適切に発信する力である(門倉 2009)。

アカデミックジャパニーズに関する具体的な実践報告では，作文・論文などのライティング指導や読解指導など，書き言葉を中心とした言語スキルの育成を扱ったものが多い(例えば，石毛 2009; 二通 2009)。スキル育成重視のアプローチが多い背景には，アカデミックジャパニーズにおける「内容」は，各学生が研究テーマとする専門的内容であると考えられていることにある。理系から文系まで，多様な学生が集う日本語教室で，それぞれの専門的な内容に踏み込んだ日本語教育を言語教師が担うことには，自ずと限界がある。また，学習者が多様であるがゆえに，共通の興味関心を持つ「内容」を設定することが難しい。そこで教師は，以後役に立つであろう基礎的な言語知識やスキルを教授しようとし，学習者もまた日本語教室には「効率的」な言語知識とスキルの提供を期待する。その結果，教師も学習者も日本語の教室では教師から知識やスキルが伝達され，それを受け取ればいいのだと考えてしまう。教師・学習者ともに，日本語教育に対するこのような意識を変革させる必要がある。現状を批判的に捉えること，知識の伝達ではなく，そこで改めて考えるというクリティカルな姿勢・視点を盛り込むことで，「専門的な内容は専門家でないと教えられないから言語学習では言語知識だけを扱う」という言語教育が置かれている社会的な構造自体を再考する必要がある。

ビジネス日本語[5]

日本において，ビジネス日本語教育が注目を集めている要因は大きく二点ある。一点目は，日本の留学生受け入れ政策の変化である。現在の留学生政策では，留学期間終了後も日本に残り，日本企業で働くことが求められるようになっている(文部科学省・外務省・法務省・厚生労働省・経済産業省・国土交通省 2008)。二点目は，日本企業が留学生の雇用に積極的になってきたことである[6]。このような状況変化により，ビジネス日本語教育が対象とする学習者にも大きな変化が見られる。従来，ビジネス日本語教育の主たる学習者は，既に企業に勤めている外国人社員であった。彼らは，社会人・ビジネスマンとしての経験を積んでおり，英語やその他の言語でできる活動を，日本語を使ってもできるように，想定される場面での日本語による会話や言語表現を習得することを学習の目的としていた。一方，現在では，日本企業への就職を見据えて，大学や日本語学校におけるビジネス日本語教育が求められるようになってきた。また，海外の大学を卒業して，現地で直接雇用された外国人新入社員に対する日本語教育ニーズも増加している。このような学習者に対するビジネス日本語教育は，職業人・社会人としての基礎的な能力育成を目的とする必要がある。具体的には，就労のための基礎的な日本語力，日本の雇用慣行に対する理解，日本の企業文化や社会保障システムの理解，専門分野に関す

5　アメリカにおけるビジネス日本語の現状はTakami (2010)を参照。

6　アジア人財資金構想プロジェクトサポートセンターHPに企業の具体的な声が掲載されている。(http://www.ajinzai-sc.jp/kkoe.html)

る言語知識や,チームを動かしていくためのコミュニケーション力など,求められる内容は多岐にわたる(海外技術者研修協会 2007)。

企業が外国人社員の採用に積極的になったのは,少子高齢化対策による労働力確保,サービスの質の向上,コスト削減,組織の適切な人材配置,産業の維持など様々な要因がある(安里 2011)。特に高度外国人人材の受け入れという側面には,グローバル化する市場に対応するための企業活動の変化,つまり,今までのやり方を踏襲するだけでなく,新たな価値観のもとに事業を創造していく人材の確保を求めているという側面もある(谷口 2011; 塚﨑2008)。大学教育で対象となるのは,ここで言われる高度外国人人材である。近年のビジネス日本語教育では,高度人材育成という観点から,業務で求められる日本語力を高めることを念頭に置きつつも,より幅広い職業人・社会人として求められる能力を包括的に育成するために,プロジェクト型言語教育やビジネス場面における異文化接触のケーススタディを用いた教育,「ケースメソッド」の応用などが提案されている(海外技術者研修協会2007; 近藤・金 2010; 堀井 2010)。しかしこれらの取り組みは,教育・学習の方法論の改善としては評価できるが,現在の社会構造を批判的に捉え再検討するための教育を志向する上では,十分にその役割を果たしているとは言えない。

留学生が日本的な就職活動を乗り切るための「就職予備校」的なビジネス日本語教育であったり,「企業が求める人材像」を鵜呑みにしたビジネス日本語教育であったりすることは,現状を追認してそこに適応する人材を育てるような教育を再生産しているだけである。そういった意味で,現状を批判的に捉え,新たな社会を構築するというクリティカルな姿勢・視点を持ったCBIによるビジネス日本語教育を構想することは重要である。

看護・介護の日本語

日本とフィリピンおよび日本とインドネシア間で締結された経済連携協定(EPA)によって,2008年以降両国から看護師・介護福祉士候補者[7]が来日するようになった。これが,看護・介護の日本語が注目を浴びるようになった直接的な背景である。EPA候補者たちは,まず基礎的な日本語教育や,日本の生活理解,日本の看護・介護事情などの研修を受ける[8]。内容を意識した基礎日本語教育の実践事例として,看護や介護の事例を通した日本語教育(布尾 2011; 羽澤・神吉・布尾 2009),プロジェクトワークを通した日本語学習(春原 2009),看護・介護用語の学習や就労場面ロールプレイの実施(登里・石井・今井・栗原 2010)など,いくつかの事例が挙げられる。しかし,これらの取り組みは,あくまで日本語学習であり,看護や介護の専門的な内容を学ぶことを目的としているわけではない。それは日本語教師が看護や介護について,不十分な知識をもとに取り扱うことを避けるために,あくまで守備範囲が「日本語とその周辺」に絞られているからである。

EPA候補者たちは,導入研修終了後,それぞれの病院・施設で働きながら国家試験合格を目指す。病院・施設における日本語学習については,国家試験受験のための具体的な学習支援の方法について(池田・深谷・堀場 2011)や,日本語学習を通した学習者の社会化について(嶋 2011)明らかにされているが,まだ研究の数は多くない。候補者は国家試験に合格しなければ帰国を余儀なくされるため,就労現場ではいかに効率よく知識を習得するかという学習を行っているケースが多い[9]。看護・介護の日本語教育の今後

7　日本の国家試験に合格して,看護師・介護福祉士の資格を取得するまでは候補者と呼ばれる。

8　2011年3月以降,日本国内だけでなく,海外で3〜6か月の渡航前研修も実施されている。

9　最初の合格者を輩出したとしてメディアで紹介された足利赤十字病院の取り組みをはじめとした

を考えるには,国家試験受験という制度的障壁を再考するために日本語教育がどのような貢献ができるかを考えると同時に,日本語さえできれば問題が解決できるというナイーブな言語中心主義に陥らないことが必要であろう。そのためには,日本語教育がどこまでのことを担いうるのかという専門性の議論と,専門知識(内容)と日本語(言語)を学ぶ際にこの両者の関係をどのように考えるかという議論が必須である。

技術研修における日本語

技術研修制度とは,コロンボ・プラン[10]への加盟とアジア諸国に対する日本の戦後補償の一環として,1950年代に設置されたものである。この制度は,最新の技術を学び技術革新を担う人材を育成することで,開発途上国の経済発展や社会発展を促進するという国際協力事業として位置づけられる。研修生に対する日本語教育の歴史は,この制度とともに始まり,現在では50年以上の歴史がある。技術研修制度,もしくはそこから派生した技能実習制度においては,導入研修といわれる基礎教育期間があり,その後,実地にて技術研修を行うという手法が主流である。つまり,研修生が主として実地で学ぶ技術・技能と日本語が切り離され,基礎教育期間に基礎的な言語知識と,技術研修を意識した一般的な語彙習得を促すような設計がなされることが多い[11]。

その理由として,大多数の学習者は日本語学習歴がほとんどないことや,日本語教育期間が数週間から数カ月程度しかないことが挙げられる。つまり,短期間で効率的に日本語学習を進めることが求められるのである。また,研修目的・研修項目の多様性をはじめとして様々な学習者が存在する(鶴尾 1988)。研修生に対する日本語教育は,入門初期レベルのものがほとんどであり,かつ短期間に学習目的,専門,日本語の必要性,母語による学習経験等が多様である研修生を対象とすることから,研修生に対する日本語教育においてCBIの実践を行っている事例はほとんどない。わずかに春原(1992)で報告されているように,技術研修生の日本語教室と地域の様々な機関が交流の場のネットワークを組織していくような取り組みが見られるだけである。しかし,経済発展が先行した日本が途上国の人材に対して技術などを「たまたま提供する側にいるが,それは恒常的な状況ではなく,いずれ立場は変わる」(春原1997)ことを考えると,今までは受動的に物事を受け取っていた研修生たちも,今後の新たな社会を構築していく上で,先進国で先行的に行われている事柄を能動的に取捨選択し,よりよい社会を作っていくことが求められる。そのような状況において,クリティカルな姿勢・視点を持ったCBIを技術研修制度における日本語教育でも実施していくことが重要ではないだろうか。

以上,目的別日本語教育/JSPについて概観したが,これらの取り組みには言語教育が持つ本質的な二つのジレンマが顕著に表れる。一つは言語教育の守備範囲はどこまでかという問題,もう一つは実用性・効率化とのせめぎ合いという問題である。

学習者の専門やニーズを考慮した内容を言語と切り離さずに扱おうとすればするほど,言語教師(日本語教師)は多様な専門性に精通していることが求められるようになる。しかし,現在の専門分化した学問世界で,ありとあらゆる内容に言語教師が精通することはほとんど不可能に近い。一方,学習者の専門分野やニーズをいったん「脇に置いて」,

---

就労先の病院関係者の話から。

10　コロンボ・プランとはアジア太平洋地域の国々の経済発展・社会開発を促進するために1950年に発足した国際機関のことである。日本は1954年に加盟。『新版日本語教育事典』を参照。

11　AOTSの技術研修生向け日本語教育(http://nihongo.aots.or.jp/j_aots.jp.edu.html)や,新たな技能実習制度での日本語研修の位置づけ(http://www.moj.go.jp/content/000023246.pdf)を参照。

教師が得意なテーマ・内容で学習を進めると，学習者の学習ニーズと合致しない。特に目的別日本語教育といわれるものは，学習者の学習目的が明確であり，ニーズも絞られている。また，職業人に対する専門日本語教育の場合でも，大学における教育の場合でも，市場原理によって効率的に目に見える成果(投資したコストと結果としての点数や学習到達点)を挙げることが求められる。その結果，断片化された知識の習得のように，数値化しやすいものが学習目標とされ，言語学習だけが「内容」から切り離されて扱われる。

一方で，内容を中心とした学習は，語学とは別に専門分野で実施される。言語と内容は切り離せないにも関わらず，語学と専門教育が切り離され，専門教育部分をある特定の言語を用いて専門分野の教師が担うことになる。結果として，語学教師は，専門教育を円滑に行うための予備教育的な言語教育にのみ従事することになる。内容を学ぶために言語は必要ではあるが，それは内容の学習の準備段階としての必要性でしかないと考えられているゆえんである。しかしながら，クリティカルな姿勢・視点を持ってよりよい社会の構築を志向した場合，内容を学ぶために基礎的な言語が必要であると同時に，内容を学んだ上で，その内容を検討し，思考をまとめ，発信する際にも言語が必要となる。そして，そのような批判的な言語活動がさらに内容についての深まりをもたらす可能性がある。「言語」「内容」にクリティカルな姿勢・視点というもう一つの軸を導入することで，言語か内容かという二項対立的な議論ではなく，言語と内容を包含しつつ，言語や内容の学びが社会変革へとつながっていくような学習活動を構想できるのではないだろうか。

内容重視の批判的言語教育 (CCBI)に向けて

これまでの部分では，ここ10年間に報告されたCBI実践を概観した。概ね「内容」と「言語」をどのようにバランスよく統合して教育を行うか，という点に主眼を置いた報告が多く，学びの過程におけるクリティカルな姿勢・視点の育成を目指した報告は少ないようである。本節では，内容重視の言語教育(CBI)の中でも，特に「クリティカルな姿勢・視点」，つまり，物事を論理的に分析するだけに留まらず，自分の置かれた現状や社会に内在する社会的・慣習的な前提を問い直し，その維持や変革に能動的に関わっていこうとする姿勢・視点の育成に重きを置くCBIを内容重視の批判的言語教育(Critical Content-based Instruction: CCBI)と呼び，我々が今後CCBIを目指す上で，どのような課題を解決していかなければならないのかについて，考察したい。

内容重視の批判的言語教育 (CCBI)を実施するにあたっての課題

制度上・構造上の力関係の不均衡の解消

どの機関においても制度上・構造上の力関係の不均衡は存在する。そのような不均衡は，CBIのように分野間の協力が必要な教育モデルにおいては，より大きな障壁となる。例えば，Byrnes(2001, 2006)は，アメリカの大学における外国語コース(特に初・中級)と英語で行われるコンテントコースの制度上・構造上の分裂に言及し，言語教師(多くは非テニュア)とコンテント教師(多くはテニュア)の地位の違いによる力関係の不均衡の現状を問題視している(Benesch, 2001参照)。一般的に言語教師はコンテント教師よりも地位が低いと見なされ，その結果，学部内協力やリソース(物的・知的)の共有化などの面で大きな障害が生じる。実際，前節で紹介した多くの実践も，FLACモデルを除いては，基本的に言語教師主導のCBIであり，利用可能なリソースを活用しきれていない，もしくは活用したくても協力関係ができていないため利用できない，といった現状が存在するようである。

FLACにおいては, 日頃「ゲットー化」[12]されている外国語学部の教員が他の学部の教員と密接な接触を持つ場を必須にすることで, その地位の改善を目指すという政治的ともいえる重要な目標が挙げられている(Jurasek, 1993)。しかし, その一方で, FLACの唱える「外国語教育と学問分野を統合する」という目標の提示自体が, 外国語を教えることは技術を提供することであってアカデミックな(学問)分野ではないという見方を暗に認め, 言語教師はあくまでも言語技術を教える者であり, コンテント教師は内容に関する専門家であるという力関係の図式を維持, 継続させているという批判もある(Sudermann & Cisar, 1992)。

　上記のような状況は簡単に改善され得るものではないが, 今後もこのような議論を活発化させ, 不均衡・不平等をなくすように働きかけていく必要があるだろう。学習者のクリティカルな姿勢・視点の育成を目指すCCBIにおいては, 教師自身がクリティカルな姿勢・視点を持つことが重要なのである。

教師, 機関のビリーフの変革

　構造の不均衡は, 人的協力関係やリソースの共有化の困難といった目に見える問題だけではなく, なかなか表面化されない学生・教師・機関のビリーフや一般通念といったものにも影響を及ぼしている。それと同時にそれらのビリーフや一般通念がさらなる構造の不均衡を生み出したり, 維持したりしているという相互関係にあるということも言える。そのような状況の中, これまででまとめた様々な教育・非教育機関におけるCBI実践報告に関して共通して言えることは, 「実用性」を批判的視点から見直すという観点が欠けているという点である(Pennycook, 1997参照)。

　上述のように, CBIの発展の背景には社会・個人のニーズの多様化といった側面があり, 効率的で実用的な目標を目指した実践が多いのが現状である。例えば, ビジネス日本語は実際にビジネスで役立つ言語使用・知識を教えるという目的があり, アカデミックジャパニーズでも大学の授業で役に立つ言語を教えるといった実践的なスキルの習得を目標に掲げている。そのような背景のためか, 固定的で慣習的な既存知識や規範をそのまま学習させようとする傾向が強い。しかし, 社会, 産業界, そして, 資格試験のニーズにのみ応えるような人材だけを育成していては, その社会, 産業界, 資格試験の現状を検討し改善していけるような人材は育たない。

　多くの高等教育機関では, 批判的思考力(critical thinking)という形で, 既に物事を深く分析的に考察する教育は強調されてはいる。しかしながら, 多くの場合において批判的思考の定義, 批判的思考を行う目的がはっきり提示されていない。本論の冒頭で説明したように, 我々が目指すクリティカルな姿勢・視点は, 物事を分析的に深く考察した上で, さらに自分の置かれた現状を振り返ることができる力であり, 「当たり前」の現状に内在する社会的・慣習的な前提を問い直し, 能動的に関わっていこうとする姿勢・視点である。そのような理念は効率性や実用性といったニーズが最優先される環境では相反する概念として捉えられがちである。そんな中, Pennycook(1997)が説いている「批判的実用性(critical pragmatism)」[13]という概念は, 効率性や実用性という概念を批判

---

[12] ゲットー化("ghettoize")」というのは, 外国語教員が学内において最も低い地位におかれ, 短期契約, あるいは非常勤(パートタイム)という不安定, 且つ, 不平等な労働条件を強いられているような状況を指す(Jurasek, 1993)。

[13] 「批判的実用性(critical pragmatism)」という用語は, Cherryholmes が1988年に「一般の実用性(vulgar pragmatism)」に対抗する概念として初めて提唱したもので, 現状維持を目的に規範や通例を闇雲に受け入れるのではなく, 常に認識論的, 倫理的, 審美的な選択を考慮にいれた実用性

的に捉え，なおかつ未来への変革を指向しているという点で非常に示唆に富んでいる (Benesch, 2001, 2009; Canagarajah, 2002; Harwood & Hadley, 2004; Morgan, 2009a, 2009b; Pennycook, 1997; Singh & Doherty, 2004; Starfield, 2004)。実用性と批判性を対抗概念として捉えるのではなく，そのせめぎあいをしっかり踏まえた上で，学習者が必要とする短期的，そしてより長期的な学習目的を打ち立てていくことが必要なのである。

内容重視の批判的言語教育 (CCBI)を目指したカリキュラム：学習目標，教材，学習過程，評価

上述のように，CCBIを行うには制度的・構造的な問題，さらには通念的な障害も存在するが，実際にCCBIを実践する上で考えるべき重要な課題は，どのようにカリキュラムを構築していったらよいのかということではないだろうか。今後，議論を進めていく上で考察すべき点を，学習目標，教材，学習過程，評価の順に以下列挙したい。

CCBIの活動をデザインする際には，まず言語，内容，クリティカルな姿勢・視点を，それぞれ独立したものとして切り離して考えるのではなく，クリティカルな姿勢・視点の育成を教育目標の根底に据え，言語，内容の学習目標を設定することが大切である。さらに，学期，学年といった短期的な枠組みではなく，初級レベルから中級，さらには上級へと長期的な学習過程の一環としてCCBIをデザイン，開発していくことが理想である。現段階では，初級レベルでクリティカルな姿勢・視点を取り入れた実践報告はごくわずかであったが，今後は初級レベルでの活動を言語教育における長期的なクリティカルな姿勢・視点育成の第一段階として位置づけ，活動のデザインを行っていく必要がある。

次に，どんな教材を用いるかという点に関してであるが，既存の市販教科書は概して固定知識を定着させることに特化している場合が多い。例えば，前節で紹介したJSPで用いられるような教科書・教材は，ビジネス場面の言語使用や技術関連用語など，特化した状況での言語能力や付随的内容をいかに学習させるかという視点で作られている。そのような教材をそのままの形で使用するだけでは，クリティカルな姿勢・視点を育成していくことは難しい。しかし，逆にそれらの教材が固定的な知識を定着させることに焦点をおいている点に着目し，学習者が批判的に検討・分析できるような機会を設ければ，そのような教科書はクリティカルな姿勢・視点を育成するには格好の教材であるとも言える(熊谷 2008)。その例としては，熊谷・深井(2009)で報告されている「教科書書きかえプロジェクト」がある。その活動では，教科書に提示される紋切り型の言語使用の規範や社会文化的な習慣などについて，学習者自身の経験・知識や様々なリソースを基に検討，分析し，テキストを書きかえるという教室実践を行った。そして，実践を通して，言語そのものの多様性(地域差，性差，階級差など)，様々な価値観，考え方，意見，視点が存在することを確認することで，既存の教科書をより有効に使用することが十分に可能であることを示している。

また，批判性の育成を念頭に置いた教材開発も必要である。例えば，Iwasaki & Kumagai(forthcoming)は，様々な社会文化的テーマに関する新聞・雑誌記事，随筆を教材とし，テキストを作成する上での筆者の意図的な言語の選択を批判的な視点から分析しながら読むことで，学習者の批判性の育成を目指した読みの教科書を作成している。学習者を対象に作られた教材だけでなく，母語話者対象に書かれた「生教材」を活用することで，実際に用いられている言語，内容などを，筆者，対象読者の位置する社会的な背景状況やテキストの果たす目的や役割などに注意して分析し，その解釈について

が教育活動には必須であるという立場をとるものである(Pennycook, 1997, p. 256)。

様々な人と意見交換をすることによって，多様な理解や解釈が存在することを確認できる(Iwasaki & Kumagai, 2008; Kumagai & Iwasaki, 2011)。そして，規範と実際の言語使用を比べることで，規範の恣意性・信憑性などについて批判的に考えると同時に，実際に学習者が学習言語を使って創造的に社会，コミュニティに関わっていくような活動を設計し，カリキュラムの中に組み込んでいけば，CCBIは十分実現可能である(佐藤・熊谷2011)。

カリキュラムを設計するにあたり，学習目標，教材，学習過程の他に欠かせない要素は，評価/アセスメントの方法である。従来のような「言語」の育成にのみ焦点を当てたカリキュラムではなく，内容に関する学習，批判的思考力(critical thinking)の育成を目指すにあたり，何を学習の成果として判断するのか，学習の過程はどう捉えるのか，どうすれば学習過程が評価できるのか，誰が評価をするのか(従来通り教師だけが評価するのか，学習者同士，学習者自身も評価するのか)など，CCBIにおけるアセスメントのありかたについても考えていかなければならない。これらのアセスメントに関する議論は，そもそもクリティカルな姿勢・視点を評価するべきなのか，するのであれば何を基準とし，何をもってクリティカルな姿勢・視点の表れとするのかといった根本的な問題も含んでいる。そして，学習の短期的な過程や成果だけではなく，長期的な視野に立ったアセスメントを行うことも必要である。さらに，その評価法は，CCBIの活動やカリキュラムの目標と常に合致していなければならない(佐藤・熊谷2010)。そして，学習者の学習成果についての評価だけでなく，活動自体の有効性や意義に関しても，教師自身の振り返り・内省や学習者からのフィードバックをもとに評価を繰り返し改善していくことが必要である。

以上，本節ではCCBIを目指すにあたって遭遇する困難な点や課題について考察した。上述の点以外にも，それぞれのプログラムの状況や事情に応じた様々な問題が存在するであろう。次節では，そのような多くの問題を乗り越えてでもCCBIを目指すべき理由についてもう一度振り返り，本論のまとめとしたい。

おわりに

最後に，これまで我々が述べてきたクリティカルな姿勢・視点の育成を特に強調するCCBIがなぜ必要なのか確認したい。CCBIは学習者がある特化した状況で必要とされる言語・知識を身につけることを否定するものではない。当然のことながら，その言語・知識がなければ，学習者が社会的に不利益を被る可能性が高くなることは想像できる。しかし，教育に携わる者が忘れてはならないのは，教育の根本的な目的とは，我々とともにこれからの世界，社会，コミュニティの未来を担っていく人々を育成していくことだということである。そのために必須であるクリティカルな姿勢・視点とは，ある「言語」や「内容」を完全に習得した後に育成すべきようなものではなく，学習の段階や進捗に関わらず「言語」「内容」を学ぶ過程において相伴って培っていくべき大切な姿勢・視点であると考える。

現在の日本語教育に必要なことは，日本語教育自体を「語学」の枠を越えた教育の営みの中に位置づけることである。そもそも教育とはいったいどんな営みを指すのか，大学教育と社会人教育との繋がり(アーティキュレーション)はどこにあるのか，言語教育，外国語教育は何を目指すのかといった教育一般，大学教育，社会人教育，言語教育，外国語教育という何層もの大きな枠組みの中に日本語教育をしっかりと位置づけ，日本語教育のあるべき姿を考えていくための機会を持つことである。そして，そこで話し合われたビジョンを教育に携わる他者と共有していくことの大切さである。その際，日本語教育(を含む言語教育)をほかの分野の動向によって，そのあり方を左右される受身的

な末端分野, あるいは, ほかの分野での実践をサポートするための従属的, 道具的な分野として考えるべきではない。日本語教育のあり方を真摯に見つめ直し, 世の中をよりよくするために日本語教育が果たしうる役割を教師・研究者自身の批判的・積極的な姿勢によって実現していこうとすることが必要であろう。そして, それこそが内容重視の批判的言語教育の理念を実現していること, 今後実現していくことになるのではないかと筆者らは考える。

引用文献

安里和晃 (2011)「人口減少社会における社会の再生産と移民」安里和晃 (編著)『労働鎖国ニッポンの崩壊: 人口減少社会の担い手はだれか』第1章, ダイヤモンド社, pp. 16–28.

池田敦史・深谷計子・堀場裕紀江 (2011)「インドネシア人看護師候補者への日本語指導―ある病院での実践から―」『聖路加看護大学紀要』37, 15–18.

石毛順子 (2009)「第二言語の作文に対する学習者の意識」『アカデミック・ジャパニーズ・ジャーナル』1, 17–24.

岡崎眸 (2002)「内容重視の日本語教育」細川英雄(編)『ことばと文化を結ぶ日本語教育』第4章, 凡人社, pp. 49–66.

甲斐雄一郎 (2011)「国語教育における「国語力」の捉え方」田尻英三・大津由紀雄(編)『言語政策を問う!』第7章, ひつじ書房, pp. 165–178.

海外技術者研修協会 (2007)『平成18年度　構造変化に対応した雇用システムに関する調査研究: 日本企業における外国人留学生の就業促進に関する調査研究　報告書』<http://www.aots.or.jp/asia/r_info/pdf/press070514_2.pdf> (2011年11月30日)

門倉正美 (2009)「日本留学試験のプロフィシェンシー―『複テキスト性』という観点の提案―」『アカデミック・ジャパニーズ・ジャーナル』1, 1–16.

久保田竜子 (2008)「日本文化を批判的に教える」佐藤慎司・ドーア根理子(編)『文化, ことば, 教育』第7章, 明石書店, pp. 151–173.

熊谷由理 (2007)「日本語教室でのクリティカル・リテラシーの実践へ向けて」『WEB版リテラシーズ』, 4(2), 1–9. http://literacies.9640.jp/vol04.html (2008年1月1日)

熊谷由理 (2008)「日本語を学ぶということ: 日本語の教科書を批判的に読む」佐藤慎司・ドーア根理子(編)『文化, ことば, 教育』第6章, 明石書店, pp. 130–150.

熊谷由理 (2011)「クリティカル・リテラシーの育成に向けて: カタカナ・プロジェクト実践概要」佐藤慎司・熊谷由理(編)『社会参加を目指す日本語教育: 社会に関わる, つながる, 働きかける』第1章, ひつじ書房, pp. 3–18.

熊谷由理・深井美由紀 (2009)「日本語学習における批判性, 創造性の育成への試み:「教科書書きかえ」プロジェクト」『世界の日本語教育』19, 181–202.

近藤彩・金孝卿 (2010)「『ケース活動』における学びの実態 - ビジネス上のコンフリクトの教材化に向けて」『日本言語文化研究会論集』6, 15–31.

佐藤慎司・熊谷由理 (編) (2010)『アセスメントと日本語教育: 新しい評価の理論と実践』くろしお出版

佐藤慎司・熊谷由理(編) (2011)『社会参加を目指す日本語教育: 社会に関わる, つながる, 働きかける』ひつじ書房

佐藤慎司・ナズキアン富美子・浜田英紀 (2010)「初級レベルにおける内容重視の言語教育(CBI)の可能性: コミュニティブログプロジェクト」アメリカ日本語教師会文化SIG発表原稿, フィラデルフィア

佐藤慎司・ロチャー松井恭子 (2011) 「内容重視の批判的言語教育(CCBI)の理論と実践」Conference Proceedings. The 18th Princeton Japanese Pedagogy Forum. <http://www.princeton.edu/pjpf/past/18th-pjpf/04_PJPFSatoMatsuiMojiProject.pdf> (2011年11月30日)

嶋ちはる (2011) 「EPA外国人看護師候補生の国家試験学習プロセスに関する縦断的研究」『2011年度日本語教育学会春季大会予稿集』, 135–140.

鈴木健・竹前文夫・大井恭子(編) (2006) 『クリティカル・シンキングと教育—日本の教育を再構築する』世界思想社

谷口真美 (2011) 『ダイバシティ・マネジメント：多様性をいかす組織』白桃書房

近松暢子 (2008) 「日本研究と言語教育の狭間で—上級日本語コンテント・ベース・コース　戦争と日本人の考察—」畑佐由紀子(編)『外国語としての日本語教育』第7章, くろしお出版, pp. 119–134.

近松暢子 (2009) 「米国におけるコンテント・コミュニティベース授業の試み—米国シカゴ日系人史—」『世界の日本語教育』19, 141–156.

近松暢子 (2011) 「ツールを超えた思考プロセスとしての日本語へ：コンテントベースにおける批判的・創造的思考活動の可能性」ジャーナルCAJLE, 12, 1–22.

チャンジンハ・チェユンソク (2004) 「ゼロビギナーへの試み」細川英雄(編)『考えるための日本語』, 明石書店, pp. 192–216.

塚﨑裕子 (2008) 『外国人専門職・技術職の雇用問題：職業キャリアの観点から』明石書店

鶴尾能子 (1988) 「学習者の多様性の実態と対応—(財)海外技術者研修協会の産業技術研修生受入れの場合—」『日本語教育』66, 76–90.

西口光一 (1998) 「自己表現中心の日本語教育」『大阪大学留学センター研究論文集多文化社会と留学生交流』3, 29–44.

二通信子 (2009) 「論文引用に関する基礎的調査と引用モデルの試案」『アカデミック・ジャパニーズ・ジャーナル』1, 65–74.

布尾勝一郎 (2011) 「海外からの看護師候補者に対する日本語教育」『日本語学』Vol. 30–2, 18–28.

登里民子・石井容子・今井寿枝・栗原幸則 (2010) 「インドネシア人介護福祉士候補者を対象とする日本語研修のコースデザイン—医療・看護・介護分野の専門日本語教育と, 関西国際センターの教育理念との関係において—」『国際交流基金日本語教育紀要』6, 41–56.

羽澤志穂・神吉宇一・布尾勝一郎 (2009) 「EPAによるインドネシア看護師・介護福祉士候補者受入研修の現状と課題」『2009年度日本語教育学会春季大会予稿集』, 182–187.

長谷川恒雄 (1998) 「諸外国における『日本事情』教育についての基礎的調査研究」科研報告書

纐纈憲子・シャムーンデボラ (2011) 「ポップカルチャークラスにおけるチームティーチングの試み」アメリカ日本語教師会発表原稿, University of Hawai'i, Mānoa.

纐纈憲子・長谷川敦志・安田真乃・松本一美 (2008) 「初級レベルにおける「内容重視教育」を目指して」畑佐由紀子(編)『外国語としての日本語教育』第8章, くろしお出版, pp. 135–150.

春原憲一郎 (1992) 「ネットワーキング・ストラテジー：交流の戦略に関する基礎研究」『日本語学』11, 17–26.

春原憲一郎 (1997) 「技術研修生と日本語教育の連携」『日本語学』17, 169–175.

春原憲一郎 (2009)「インドネシアEPA看護師・介護福祉士候補者受入研修のコンセプトと実際」笹川平和財団(編)『始動する外国人財による看護・介護―受け入れ国と送り出し国の対話―』, 56–59.

堀井惠子 (2010)「プロジェクト型ビジネス日本語教育の意義と課題」『武蔵野大学文学部紀要』11, 86–96.

三宅和子 (2003)「留学生・日本人大学生のアカデミック・ジャパニーズとは」『日本留学試験とアカデミック・ジャパニーズ:日本留学試験が日本語教育に及ぼす影響に関する調査・研究―国内外の大学入学前日本語予備教育と大学日本語教育の連携のもとに―』平成14~16年度科学研究費補助金基盤研究費(A) (1)中間報告書

村田久美子・原田哲男 (2008)『コミュニケーション能力育成再考』ひつじ書房

森朋子 (2005)「大学教育における「アカデミック・ジャパニーズ」を考える」『東京家政学院大学紀要』45, 117–122.

文部科学省 (2006)「教育基本法(平成十八年十二月二十二日法律第百二十号)」Retrieved from <http://law.e-gov.go.jp/htmldata/H18/H18HO120.html> (2011年11月30日)

文部科学省・外務省・法務省・厚生労働省・経済産業省・国土交通省 (2008)「『留学生30万人計画』骨子」<http://www.kantei.go.jp/jp/tyoukanpress/rireki/2008/07/29kossi.pdf> (2011年11月30日)

Anderson, K. O., Allen, W., & Narvaez, L. (1993). The applied foreign language component in the humanities and the sciences. In M. Krueger & F. Ryan (Eds.), *Language and content: Discipline- and content-based approaches to language study* (pp. 103–113). Lexington, MA: D. C. Heath.

Beckett, G. H. (2006). Project-based second and foreign language education: Theory, research, and practice. In G. H. Beckett & P. C. Miller (Eds.), *Project-based second and foreign language education: Past, present, and future* (pp 3–40). Greenwich, CT: Information Age Publishing.

Benesch, S. (2001). *Critical English for academic purposes: Theory, politics, and practice.* Mahwah, NJ: Erlbaum.

Benesch, S. (2009). Theorizing and practicing critical English for academic purposes. *Journal of English for Academic Purposes, 8,* 81–85.

Berho, D. L., & Defferding, V. (2005). Communication, culture, and curiosity: Using target-culture and student-generated art in the second language classroom. *Foreign Language Annals, 38*(2), 271–276.

Brinton, D., Snow, M., & Wesche, M. (1989). *Content-based second language instruction.* New York, NY: Harper & Row.

Brown, N. A., Bown, J., & Eggett, D. L. (2009). Making rapid gains in second language writing: A case study of a third-year Russian language course. *Foreign Language Annals, 42*(3), 424–452.

Byrnes, H. (2001). Reconsidering graduate students' education as teachers: "It takes a department!" *The Modern Language Journal, 85,* 512–530.

Byrnes, H. (2006). Perspectives: Interrogating communicative competence as a framework for collegiate foreign language study. *The Modern Language Journal, 90,* 244–266.

Byrnes, H., & Sprang, K. A. (2003). Fostering advanced L2 literacy: A genre-based, cognitive approach. In H. Byrnes & H. H. Maxim (Eds.), *Advanced foreign language learning: A challenge to college programs* (pp. 47–85). Boston, MA: Heinle & Heinle.

Caldwell, A. M. (2001). A FLAC model for increasing enrollment in foreign language classes. *The French Review, 74*(6), 1125–1137.

Canagarajah, S. (2002). Multilingual writers and the academic community: Towards a critical relationship. *Journal of English for Academic Purposes, 1*, 29–44.

Chaput, P. (1993). Revitalizing the traditional program. In M. Krueger & F. Ryan (Eds.), *Language and content: Discipline- and content-based approaches to language study* (pp. 148–157). Lexington, MA: D. C. Heath.

Chikamatsu, N., & Matsugu, M. (Eds.). (2009). Bridging Japanese language and Japanese studies in higher education: Report from the forum on integrative curriculum and program development. *Association of Teachers of Japanese Occasional Papers, 9*.

Chun, C. W. (2009). Contesting neoliberal discourses in EAP: Critical praxis in an IEP classroom. *Journal of English for Academic Purposes, 8*, 111–120.

Crandall, J., & Tucker, G. (1990). Content-based language instruction in second and foreign languages. In S. Anivan (Ed.), *Language teaching methodology for the Nineties* (pp. 83–96). Singapore: SEAMEO Regional Language Centre.

Crank, J. P., & Loughrin-Sacco, S. J. (2001). Foreign language across the curriculum: A model for the delivery of professional language training. *Journal of Criminal Justice Education, 12*(1), 193–211.

Curtain, H., & Pesola, C. (1994). *Languages and children: Making the match*. New York, NY: Longman.

Dewey, J. (1910). *How we think*. Boston, MA: D. C. Heath.

Dewey, J. (1962). *Democracy and education. An introduction to the philosophy of education*. New York, NY: Macmillan.

Dupuy, B. C. (2000). Content-based instruction: Can it help ease the transition from beginning to advanced foreign language classes? *Foreign Language Annals, 33*, 205–223.

Firth, A., & Wagner, J. (1997). On discourse, communication, and (some) fundamental concepts in SLA research. *The Modern Language Journal, 81*, 285–300.

Genesee, F. (1994). *Integrating language and content: Lessons from immersion*. Santa Cruz, CA: National Center for Research on Cultural Diversity and Second Language Learning.

Grabe, W., & Stoller, F. L. (1997). Content-based instruction: Research foundations. In M. A. Snow & D. M. Brinton (Eds.), *The content-based classroom: Perspectives on integrating language and content* (pp. 5–21). New York, NY: Longman.

Grosseck, M-D. (2010). German not only a foreign language but also a language for special purposes. *Procedia-Social and Behavioral Sciences, 2*, 3363–3367.

Harwood, N., & Hadley, G. (2004). Demystifying institutional practices: Critical pragmatism and the teaching of academic writing. *English for Specific Purposes, 23*, 355–377.

Hoechel-Alden, G. (2006). Connecting language to content: Second language literature instruction at the intermediate level. *Foreign Language Annals, 39*(2), 244–254.

Idemaru, K., Nakadate, N., & O'Brien, Y. (2011). Global scholars program at the University of Oregon. In Y. Tokumasu (Ed.), *Proceedings of the 18th Princeton Japanese pedagogy forum* (pp. 117–126). Princeton, NJ. Retrieved from http://www.princeton.edu/pjpf/past/18th-pjpf/10_Idemasu_Nakadate_OBrien.pdf

Iwasaki, N., & Kumagai, Y. (2008). Towards critical approaches in an advanced level Japanese course: Theory and practice through reflection and dialogues. *Japanese Language and Literature, 42*, 123–156.

Iwasaki, N., & Kumagai, Y. (Forthcoming). *The Routledge Japanese reader: A genre-based approach to reading as a social practice.* London, United Kingdom: Routledge.

Johns, A. M., & Dudley-Evans, A. (1991). English for specific purposes: International in scope, specific in purpose. *TESOL Quarterly, 25,* 297–314.

Jurasek, R. (1993). Foreign languages across the curriculum: A case history from Earlham College and a generic rationale. In M. Krueger & F. Ryan (Eds.), *Language and content: Discipline- and content-based approaches to language study* (pp. 85–102). Lexington, MA: D. C. Heath.

Kramsch, C. (2002). *Language acquisition and language socialization: Ecological perspectives.* London, United Kingdom: Continuum.

Krashen, S. (1985). *The input hypothesis.* London, United Kingdom: Longman.

Kumagai, Y., & Iwasaki, N. (2011). What it means to read "critically" in a Japanese language classroom: Students' perspectives. *Critical Inquiry in Language Studies, 8*(2), 125–152.

Larson, P. (2011). *CBI: A catalyst not a panacea.* Conference Proceedings. In Y. Tokumasu (Ed.), *Proceedings of the 18th Princeton Japanese pedagogy forum* (pp. 1–13). Princeton, NJ. Retrieved from http://www.princeton.edu/pjpf/past/18th-pjpf/01_PJPF2011keynote.pdf

Lear, D. W. (2005). Spanish for working medical professionals: Linguistic needs. *Foreign Language Annals, 38*(2), 223–232.

Luke, C. L. (2006). Fostering learner autonomy in a technology-enhanced, inquiry-based foreign language classroom. *Foreign Language Annals, 39*(1), 71–86.

McGee, L. G. (2001). Building community and posting projects: Creating "student pages" in web-based and web-enhanced courses. *Foreign Language Annals, 34*(6), 534–549.

Met, M. (1991). Learning language through content: Learning content through language. *Foreign Language Annals, 24,* 281–295.

Metcalf, M. F. (1993). Foreign languages across the curriculum from a social science perspective: The Minnesota model. In M. Krueger & F. Ryan (Eds.), *Language and content: Discipline- and content-based approaches to language study* (pp. 114–119). Lexington, MA: D. C. Heath.

Moreno-Lopez, I., Saenz-de-Tejada, C., & Smith, T. K. (2008). Language and study abroad across the curriculum: An analysis of course development. *Foreign Language Annals, 41*(4), 674–686.

Morgan, B. (2009a). Fostering transformative practitioners for critical EAP: Possibilities and challenges. *Journal of English for Academic Purposes, 8,* 86–99.

Morgan, B. (2009b). Revitalising the essay in an English for academic purposes course: Critical engagement, multiliteracies and the internet. *International Journal of Bilingual Education and Bilingualism, 12*(3), 309–324.

Morioka, A. (2007). *Teaching Japanese with content-based instruction.* (Doctoral dissertation). Retrieved from ProQuest. (UMI: 3295261)

Neville, D. O., & Britt, D. W. (2007). A problem-based learning approach to integrating foreign language into engineering. *Foreign Language Annals, 40*(2), 226–245.

Partnership for 21st Century Skills (2002). *Framework for 21st century learning.* Retrieved from http://www.p21.org/storage/documents/1.__p21_framework_2-pager.pdf

Pennycook, A. (1997). Vulgar pragmatism, critical pragmatism, and EAP. *English for Specific Purposes, 16,* 253–269.

Richards, J. C., & Rodgers, T. S. (2001). *Approaches and methods in language teaching* (2nd ed.). Cambridge, United Kingdom: Cambridge University Press.

Rodgers, D. M. (2006). Developing content and form: Encouraging evidence from Italian content-based instruction. *The Modern Language Journal, 90,* 373–386.

Singh, P., & Doherty, C. (2004). Global cultural flows and pedagogic dilemmas: Teaching in the global university contact zone. *TESOL Quarterly, 38*(1), 9–42.

Starfield, S. (2004). "Why does this feel empowering"? Thesis writing, concordancing and the corporatizing university. In B. Norton & K. Toohey (Eds.), *Critical pedagogies and language learning* (pp. 138–157). Cambridge, United Kingdom: Cambridge University Press.

Stoller, F. (2006). Establishing a theoretical foundation for project-based learning in second and foreign language contexts. In G. H. Beckett & P. C. Miller (Eds.), *Project-based second and foreign language education: Past, present, and future* (pp. 19–40). Greenwich, CT: Information Age Publishing.

Stryker, S., & Leaver, B. (Eds.). (1997). *Content-based instruction in foreign language education: Methods and models.* Washington, DC: Georgetown University Press.

Sudermann, D. P., & Cisar, M. A. (1992). Foreign language across the curriculum: A critical appraisal. *The Modern Language Journal, 76*(3), 295–308.

Takami, T. (Ed.). (2010). Meeting student needs: Perspectives on teaching Japanese for professional purposes. *Association of Teachers of Japanese Occasional Papers 10,* (pp. 1–23).

Weigert, A. (2004). "What's business got to do with it?" The unexplored potential of business language courses for advanced foreign language learning. In H. Byrnes & H. H. Maxim (Eds.), *Advanced foreign language learning: A challenge to college programs* (pp. 131–150). Boston, MA: Heinle.

Social Network Development During Study Abroad in Japan
日本での留学期間中の社会的ネットワーク形成

Spencer A. Ring
Daniel Gardner
Dan P. Dewey
Brigham Young University

Abstract

In this chapter, we investigate how students studying abroad in Japan form social networks. As Whitworth (2006) and Fraser (2002) have found, social networks can play an integral role in language proficiency development and language gains during study abroad (SA). However, much is yet to be understood regarding the processes by which SA students form social networks. The present study addresses this issue. Using the Study Abroad Social Interaction Questionnaire (SASIQ), we collected data regarding the social network formation of 204 students who studied abroad in Japan. Sample trends include students' participation in school and community clubs and social circles, as well as taking advantage of opportunities to get to know new friends and acquaintances through existing friends. Students praised programs for providing tutors or study buddies, organizing social activities with native students, and facilitating interaction in a number of other ways, and often requested that programs carry out more such interventions. These and other findings are reported herein.

要旨

Whitworth (2006)やFraser (2002)の研究から、留学期間中の社会的ネットワーク形成が言語能力の発達や習得に不可欠な役割を果たしていることが分かっている。しかし、留学生の社会的ネットワークを形成するプロセスについては、まだあまり知られていない。日本に留学した大学生がどのように社会的ネットワークを形成するのかを考察するために、本章ではStudy Abroad Social Interaction

Questionnaire (SASIQ)を用い, 日本に留学した学生204人の社会的ネットワーク形成プロセスについての調査を行った。その結果, 学校や公共のクラブやサークルへの参加, 既存の友人を介して新しい友人と知り合う機会の有効的な利用の仕方の重要性などがあげられた。留学プログラムが提供するチューターや会話パートナー, また日本語のネイティブスピーカーとの社交活動や, その他数々の交流活動も社会的ネットワーク形成には重要であることが分かった。

Introduction

It is commonly believed that one of the most effective ways to learn a second language (L2) is to study abroad (SA). Learners are expected to naturally make friends with local native speakers and therefore have many opportunities to use and acquire the language as a result. Research has shown, however, that they often struggle to build friendships with native speakers (Isabelli-Garcia, 2006; Pellegrino-Aveni, 2005; Wilkinson, 1998a, 1998b). In fact, as Wilkinson (1998a, 1998b) has depicted, they often form islands with their fellow program participants, primarily associating and using their native language with these participants during their time abroad. In spite of these documented struggles to keep company with local native speakers, little research has been done to establish how learners make friends with natives during SA, what challenges they face in doing so, and what SA programs do to facilitate this process. This study is an attempt to fill this gap by assessing this aspect of SA in Japan.

Highlighting the challenges learners face when choosing and acquiring polite and informal forms during SA in Japan, Iwasaki (2011) emphasizes the importance of L2 learners fitting in to a group of friends, noting that in regards to one group of students who went abroad, "it may have been their desire to fit in and make friends that contributed to their learning and choice of language . . ." (p. 87). The connection between social relationships and language use and acquisition has been addressed in the body of research and is typically recognized as being an important aspect of SA (Dewey, Belnap, & Hillstrom, in press; Dewey, Bown, & Eggett 2012; Milroy, 1987; Wang, 2010). This fitting in and making friends can be seen as a process of social network formation.

While the term "social network" is currently commonly used to refer to the connections/relationships individuals build via on-line communication tools, such as Facebook, Twitter, and LinkedIn, our focus in this study is on face-to-face relationships made by students while living in Japan. Xu, Wang, and Li define a social network as "the web-like pattern of relationships among individuals." (2008, p. 263). In social science research on social networks, these networks are seen as a compilation of social ties that often "acts as a mechanism both for exchanging goods and services, and for imposing obligations and conferring corresponding rights upon its members." (Milroy, 1987, p. 47). In the case of L2 learners studying abroad, this network can be the means of accessing language and learning about the L2 culture and can also bring with it commitments to various L2 communities. The concept of a social network goes beyond associations based simply on common status, location, or economic activities and instead involves interpersonal relationships varying in degree of closeness from acquaintance to close confidant (Milroy, 1987; Scott, 2000). In this study, we focus specifically on L2 social networks—networks (web-like patterns of relationships) built with native speakers of Japanese while studying abroad in Japan. Learners not only receive the typical benefits of friendships/relationships through these networks, but they also benefit linguistically by being able to use Japanese with these speakers and by often being coached in the language and culture by these social network members. In this study, we investigate how SA participants develop social networks while abroad, what factors can assist or inhibit the development of these networks, and how SA programs can facilitate social network development between SA students and native speakers.

Although a number of studies address social networking during SA (Dewey, Belnap, & Hillstrom, in press; Dewey, Bown, & Eggett 2012; Isabelli-García, 2006; Kurata, 2004; Levin, 2001; Tanaka, Takai, Kohyama, Fujihara, & Minami 1997; Whitworth, 2006), a need exists to better understand the types of factors, activities, and program interventions that lead to successful social network formation. By observing trends in free-response data collected from students who went to Japan on SA, we aim to gain insight into what works and what does not work for students trying to expand their networks in the SA setting. Results from this research will contribute meaningfully to the existing knowledge base of social network formation during SA and should prove useful to program administrators and teachers as they help students become integrated into viable network communities.

Review of literature

Research in second language acquisition during SA has investigated issues such as language proficiency development (Brecht & Robinson, 1995; Díaz-Campos, 2004; Freed, 1995; Magnan & Back, 2007; Segalowitz & Freed, 2004), language use (Badstübner & Ecke, 2009; Brecht, Davidson, & Ginsberg, 1995; Freed, 1990; Freed, Segalowitz, & Dewey, 2004; Hernández, 2010; Magnan & Back, 2007; Pellegrino-Aveni, 2005; Taguchi, 2008; Wilkinson, 2002), and the roles of gender (Brecht et al., 1995; Kinginger & Whitworth, 2005; Mathews, 2000; Polanyi, 1995; Talburt & Stewart, 1999; Twombly, 1995), attitudes (Isabelli-García, 2006; Yager, 1998), and identity (Kinginger, 2009; Kinginger & Whitworth, 2005; Kurata, 2007; Talburt & Stewart, 1999; Wang, 2010; Whitworth, 2006) in language use and acquisition. One additional topic addressed is that of social network formation (Burns, 1996; Dewey, Belnap, & Hillstrom, in press; Dewey, Bown, & Eggett, 2012; Isabelli, 2001; Isabelli-García, 2006; Kurata, 2004, 2007; Tanaka et al., 1997).

In this review of literature, we discuss the research and theory related to social network formation during SA. We begin by giving an overview of research on SA in Japan. We then address the relationship between social networking and L2 development and review research addressing factors that influence social network formation, looking particularly at how motivation, acculturation, identity, attitudes, and gender relate to SA participants' ability to form social networks. Finally, we describe how this study will add to the existing body of research and present our specific research questions.

Study abroad in Japan

Nearly 6,000 students from the U.S., study in Japan each year (Institute of International Education, 2010). As these numbers have steadily increased, interest in the impact that the SA experience has on language gains, intercultural competence, and others areas has grown accordingly. The publication of special issues of *Japanese Language and Literature* (Marcus, 2007) and of *The Occasional Papers of the Association of Teachers of Japanese* (Noda, Yuasa, & Quinn, 2005) devoted to this topic is evidence of this increasing interest. Although we still have much to learn about the benefits of SA, research in Japan suggests that it can lead to increased motivation (Huebner, 1995), vocabulary knowledge (Dewey, 2008), knowledge of *kana* and *kanji* (Huebner, 1995), oral fluency (Hashimoto, 1994; Marriott & Enomoto, 1995), pragmatic competence (Iwasaki, 2008; Marriott, 1995), and global proficiency and oral proficiency (Iwasaki, 2007). Students can also develop greater confidence in their ability to produce informal speech patterns (Makino, 1996), to engage in a variety of types of speech tasks (Dewey, Bown, & Eggett, 2012), and to read a variety of genres for multiple purposes (Dewey, 2004). There are some indications that the social networks learners form can influence their language acquisition (Dewey, Bown, & Eggett, 2012; Noda, 2005), but there is still little documentation of what it is that learners do to form social networks or of the challenges they face in attempting to do so.

Social networking and L2 development

A fairly sizable body of research has investigated the impact of out-of-classroom language use on language gains. While some of this research suggests connections between the amount of out-of-class language use within one's social network and language gains (Dewey, 2004; Dewey, Belnap, & Hillstrom, in press; Dewey, Bown, & Eggett 2012; Ginsberg & Miller, 2000; Hernández, 2010; Miller & Ginsberg, 1995; Taguchi, 2008), others (Freed, 1990; Mendelson, 2004; Segalowitz & Freed, 2004) show less evidence of extensive connections. Differences in findings may be attributed to differences in length of time abroad, target cultures, learner proficiency level, methods of measuring language use and language gains, etc. However, even among those studies failing to find comprehensive connections between language use and language gains, some evidence of relationships typically exists. For example, Mendelson (2004) evaluated connections between speaking proficiency development and language use for SA students on a 14-week program in Salamanca and an 18-week program in Granada. Though she found no obvious connections between language use and proficiency gains for either group, she did find that on self-assessments the 18-week group reported more gains in speaking proficiency and more interactive conversations than the their counterparts, who spent four fewer weeks abroad. This suggests the need to consider both country/location and length of time in country in investigations of patterns of language use and acquisition. Freed (1990) found no universal connection but discovered that lower-level learners in France appeared to benefit more from interaction with native speakers than advanced learners, who seemed to benefit more from non-interactive exposure to the language, such as reading and listening.

Beyond merely looking at amount of out-of-class language use, certain studies have investigated the nature of program participants' involvement in social networks and how this involvement affects language use and development (Whitworth, 2006; Fraser, 2002; Levin, 2001; Campbell, 1996). Fraser (2002) found that: "Students who followed less traditional study plans, including joining a football team, playing with an orchestra and serving as intern in a theatre made impressive progress compared with their peers enrolled in regular university courses" (p. 45). Results from Whitworth's (2006) study of these issues with SA students in France also suggest that participating in social activities where one must interact in the L2 augments language gains. Additionally, in a study that followed four L2 learners of Spanish during their sojourn abroad in Argentina, Isabelli-García (2006) found a distinct relationship between language gains and language socialization. In this study, Stan, the participant who achieved the highest level of linguistic competence out of four, also exhibited more growth in his social network than the other three students. Not surprisingly, the lowest gainer, Jennifer, nearly withdrew herself from socializing in the L2 by the end of her time in Argentina. Factors such as intimidating interactions with the opposite sex appear to have made an impact on Jennifer's motivation to engage in social networking during her time in Argentina.

Two studies in Japanese highlight the importance of social networks for language development. Dewey, Bown, and Eggett (2012) determined that students who engaged in a broader variety of social groups became more confident in their speaking abilities than those who experienced narrower involvement. Noda (2005) found that learners who showed greater evidence of Japanese language gains tended to be more involved in clubs, internships, part-time employment, and other group activities that extended their personal social networks substantially.

Factors affecting social network development

In addition to language gains, Isabelli-García's (2006) study discusses various factors linked to social network formation. One key factor is motivation. Her data, largely journal entries, clearly suggest that participants with higher levels of motivation tend to develop larger and more complex L2 social networks. Like Wilkinson (1998a, 2002), Isabelli-García (2006) found that participants' motivation to engage with social networks was influenced by the nature of their interactions within these networks: "changes in motivation among students occur as a result of interaction or lack thereof" (p. 254). Furthermore, she notes that motivation to interact is "most likely to be mediated by [students'] various stages of acculturation" (p. 234). She discusses Bennett's model of acculturation, which places individuals in a sequence of six stages ranging from ethnocentrism to ethnorelativism (Bennett, 1986, as cited in Isabelli-García, 2006, p. 234). Isabelli-García suggests that as students progress from ethnocentrism to ethnorelativism they become more willing to engage in social networking with native speakers and are likely to have larger, denser networks.

Participants' identities and, in particular, the way students view themselves as individuals in the target language community, can also be related to their social network formation (Alred & Byram, 2002; Isabelli-García, 2006; Pellegrino-Aveni, 2002; Siegal, 1995; Wang, 2010; Whitworth, 2006). As Young (1992) observes, when students believe themselves to be potential members of the L2 culture, they often subconsciously take on identity traits that will mark them as a member of that culture. Two students in Whitworth's (2006) study contrastingly illustrate how identity relates to social network formation. One student readily incorporated the norms of the host culture into her identity, which enhanced her language socialization, while a different student rejected those norms, which hindered her ability to build social networks (Whitworth, 2006). In this example, both students consciously accepted or rejected the identity they felt was imposed by the L2 culture.

Participant attitudes also contribute to the development of social networks during SA. Papatsiba (2006) shows how French students from the Erasmus program studying in other European countries established varying attitudes towards the host country and its natives. Initially these attitudes were characterized by both positive and negative generalization of the people. Once the students had established their initial attitudes toward the natives they analyzed the natives' attitudes towards them. In this second stage, the majority of the students considered the *natives*' attitude towards them to be the main reason why networking attempts either failed or were successful. Many students did not move beyond this stage and reevaluate these attitudes, while others did. In contrast, Isabelli-García's (2006) findings suggest that the students' own attitudes towards the host culture were to credit or blame for the level of social network development achieved, not the host culture's attitudes nor the perceived attitude towards the foreign students.

The role of gender in the SA experience has been investigated by several scholars. American women studying abroad in France (Kline, 1993), Russia (Polanyi, 1995), Argentina (Isabelli-García, 2006), Spain (Talburt & Stewart, 1999), Costa Rica (Twombly, 1995), Jordan (Hillstrom, 2011), and Egypt (Shelley, 2011) have complained of sexual harassment and related behavior that can inhibit social opportunities and negatively affect motivation to build social networks. On the other hand, Kinginger (2009) cites a 2007 study by Patron of "French students in Austria, where the absence of 'sexual harassment' provoked negative reactions from female students" (p. 184). One student complained that there must be something wrong with her because the males weren't paying sufficient attention to her. In both cases where females are distressed by specific types of attention or in cases where inattention from males is bothersome, it appears that expectations for socialized expectations of cross-gender interactions can affect students' self-perceptions, motivation, views of the L2 culture, etc.

Gender has stood out as a particularly salient aspect of identity. For example, Whitworth (2006) found that learners' genders and gender identities influenced their development of social networks during study abroad in France. One female student refused to conform to what she saw as social norms for French females, withdrawing from social circles where French women followed these norms, thereby limiting her interactions with native speakers. Another American woman, on the other hand, followed the stereotypes for French women as closely as she could and used these stereotyped roles to gain access to French social circles including both men and women. Siegal (1995) found similar patterns in terms of identity for female learners of Japanese as a second language in Japan. Specifically, some women conformed readily to typical Japanese female behavior, in particular regarding the use of feminine speech patterns, whereas others vehemently resisted.

In summary, issues such as motivation, acculturation, identity, attitudes, and gender have been addressed in the present body of literature regarding social network formation during SA. Nevertheless, an understanding of the activities SA students engage in to meet people, the factors which these students feel facilitate or inhibit social bonding, and the program interventions which they believe to be helpful or hurtful to making friends is not afforded by the current body of literature. In this study, we seek to address these issues in the context of SA in Japan. We attempt to do so by investigating the following research questions:

1. How do students form social networks in which they can use the L2?
2. What factors facilitate or inhibit students' ability to form strong friendships?
3. What program interventions facilitate or inhibit social network formation?

Methodology

Participants

Participants in this study were former recipients of Bridging Scholarships (scholarships ranging between $2,500 and $4,000) given to approximately one hundred undergraduate students annually through the Association of Teachers of Japanese to support study abroad in Japan by U.S., citizens. Initially, all past scholarship recipients whose current contact information was available (1,084 individuals) were asked to participate in the research by email invitation. Ultimately, 254 former students responded, and 204 of these (101 male and 103 female) completed all portions of the on-line survey relevant to the current research.

The 204 participants came from 98 universities or colleges and studied in 38 different SA programs in Japan. While abroad, they lived in 22 cities located from Hokkaido to Okinawa. Students' average age was 21.3 years ($SD=2.90$) at the time of departure for their study in Japan and 24.8 ($SD=4.62$) at the time they took the survey. Before participating in their SA programs, participants received an average of 2.07 years of Japanese instruction ($SD=1.87$). Average time spent in Japan was 8.4 months ($SD=3.70$). Participants received 13.2 hours ($SD=5.27$) of Japanese language instruction per week on average during their SA programs and had 5.8 hours ($SD=4.91$) per week of content classes (culture, history, arts, political science, etc.) in English. The strength of this sample is that students came from a broad range of SA programs and had a variety of backgrounds prior to going to Japan. While having a diverse sample can make it difficult to isolate variables, it also prevents any one program or background from having excessive influence on the results.

Instrument and data collection procedures

Data regarding participants' social networks was collected by means of the Study Abroad Social Interaction Questionnaire (SASIQ; see Appendix), a tool developed by Dewey (Dewey, Belnap, & Hillstrom, in press; Dewey, Bown, & Eggett 2012), based largely on the Montréal Index of Linguistic Integration (Segalowitz & Ryder, 2006). The SASIQ contains thirteen questions, which are used to generate quantitative metrics of participant social networks and to gather qualitative information to describe learners' network development. In the SASIQ, participants were asked to list up to twenty names of people they spoke Japanese with or native Japanese speakers with whom they spoke English on a regular basis while in Japan. They were then asked to elaborate on how they met each person. Other questions asked them to explain what they did to make native-speaker friends, how they strengthened these friendships, etc. Individual SASIQ questions relevant to each of our research questions will be listed in the Results section below. For each question, responses were categorized using a grounded theory framework (Glaser & Strauss, 1967; Strauss & Corbin, 1998), with categories being revised and solidified based on a cyclical process. Once categories were generated, all responses were coded by two raters. When raters did not agree on a category, a third rater examined responses. When two of the three raters agreed, this category was used. When none of the three raters could agree, responses were excluded from analysis.

Results

Social network formation

Data collected from the following two survey questions demonstrate how participants formed their social networks: (1) "Please elaborate how you met." (2) "What sorts of things did *you* do to make friends with native Japanese speakers?" Table 1 displays results for the first question. Table 1, as with all other Tables, includes data for the categories with the ten highest percentages. While our analysis generated more categories than these, space does not permit us to list all categories.

Table 1. Please elaborate how you met.

percentage per average number of friends (12.3)	category	example
14.1%	Met at school/ in classes/ on campus	Met her in the international students' room on campus.
12.1%	Introduced by another student/friend/coworker	Met her through my friend Yuri
9.6%	Host family, met through host family	She was my host mother.
7.6%	School clubs or other extracurricular activities	Met through the Hot Air Balloon Club
5.8%	Teachers, tutors, faculty	She was my AM teacher.

continued...

Table 1. Please elaborate how you met *(cont.)*

percentage per average number of friends (12.3)	category	example
4.8%	Lived together as dorm mates/roommates	We lived in the same dorm room.
4.4%	Knew prior to study abroad/introduced before study abroad/introduction arranged (i.e., by family) prior to study abroad. (i.e., "a friend of my mother")	She was my mother's friend in the U.S., years ago.
2.2%	Worked together/ met at internship/met through part time job	Boss at work.
2.1%	Study Abroad Program staff	Study abroad program manager
2.1%	Met in a public place, business, etc. (i.e., a nightclub, restaurant, park)	We met at a nightclub.

Nearly 30% of the students' social network members were met via campus-based activities (meeting on campus in general, being taught or tutored by teachers, tutors, etc. who were part of their networks, and participating in extracurricular activities on campus). Students met a substantial portion of their friends through living arrangements (homestay families, roommates, or dorm mates).

In response to the question regarding what strategies SA participants used to make native speaker friends, the most frequent response (nearly 40%) was joining clubs or teams, as shown in Table 2. Other campus-based strategies were also common, including attending formal and informal functions arranged at school and speaking Japanese with native students encountered on campus.

Table 2. What kinds of things did you do to make native speaker friends?

percentage per number of participants	category	example
39.6%	Joined school clubs or teams	I joined circles…
26.6%	Participated in social events or gatherings (outside of school)	Attended group parties
17.4%	Attended school or program events	Attended school social functions
14.9%	Spoke with people at school	We were in the same class
14.5%	Approached potential friends; initiated contact with potential friends (not at school)	Walked up to many random natives to talk to them
13.5%	Networked (made contacts with friends of friends, host family's friends, etc.)	I was lucky enough to know some Americans already living in Japan so I was able to make friends through them

13.0%	Frequented public places (parks, clubs, bars, karaokes, etc.)	The gym was a great opportunity…
10.1%	Spent time with or got to know the people they lived with	Participated in the…host family program
8.7%	Traveled to/visited other places	I traveled around and got to lots of different places.

Facilitating factors and inhibiting factors

Data from two questions show what factors facilitated or inhibited social network formation: (1) "Choose three people from your list above that you marked as being the closest of friends (highest scores). Please tell why you think you were able to develop good friendships with these people." (2) "Choose three people from your list above that you marked as being the lowest in terms of friendship level. Please tell why you think you were unable to develop good friendships with these people." Table 3 shows that for the first question, the category most frequently observed was the amount time spent with the interlocutor (31%). Since participants answered this question in terms of 3 friends, percentages in these tables represent the number of times a category was mentioned divided by the total number of friends reported. Table 6 shows categories and percentages for the second question under this heading. Just as with Table 3, percentages here were calculated according to the number of friends reported. The most frequently observed category was lack of time spent together (34%).

Table 3. What helped you develop strong relationships with your three closest friends?

percent per number of "closest friend"	category	example
31%	SA student and contact spent a lot of time together	I think the amount of time spent together…really helped the friendship.
22%	Similar interests	I was able to build close friendships with these people because we had like interests.
11%	Contact's being helpful, friendly, or kind to student	He was very engaged in helping the students find their way around Japan.
9%	Contact and SA student went on trips/ travelled together	We traveled together a lot.
9%	Personality	They were open to new people and ideas… and very interesting to talk to.
9%	Contact and SA student attended the same classes, had frequent interactions at school/school functions	The interactions in this class helped make everyone grow closer.
9%	Contact and SA student lived together/ close to each other	We were roommates, so were together a lot.

continued…

Table 3. What helped you develop strong relationships with your three closest friends? *(cont.)*

percent per number of "closest friend"	category	example
8%	Social affinity (i.e., "fun to be around")/ similar or compatible personality (i.e., "we just clicked together.")	We met and really hit it off becuase of our similar personality traits…We are both very outgoing, excited people
8%	Supportive host family interaction	My host mom and host sister and I grew very close because we talked and watched TV together every night.
7%	NS's willingness to use Japanese with the student; helped student with the language or culture	She was willing to work with me on my Japanese and to figure out what I was trying to day.

Three factors were commonly mentioned in the questions regarding facilitating and inhibiting factors as contributing to social network formation: time, similar interests, and personality. Learners felt that spending more time with friends allowed them to grow closer and also that not being able to spend time with friends kept them from developing better relationships. Similarly, when students shared similar interests with the NS, they felt they were more able to build strong relationships, whereas the opposite was true when they shared few common interests. Finally, the NS's personality tended to both facilitate and inhibit relationship development, with learners making comments like "She had the kind of personality that just made you feel comfortable being around her," (facilitating) or "He was just kind of strange and was sometime impatient and unkind" (inhibiting).

Living together (in a dorm or host family) seems to have contributed to the development of stronger social relationships, whereas differing social status (e.g., faculty vs. student, older vs. younger, supervisor vs. supervisee) tended to inhibit deeper relationship development for some students.

Program interventions

Data from the following two questions was used to describe helpful program interventions in addition to areas in which students reported improvements could be made: (1) "What did your study abroad program do to help you make native speaking friends or acquaintances while in Japan." (2) "What more could your study abroad program have done to help you make native speaking friends or acquaintances while in Japan?" Table 4 gives data for the first question under this heading. The most frequently observed categories were: 1) the study abroad program organized activities/events where SA students could meet native speakers, and 2) SA programs assigned tutors or study buddies. As seen in Table 5, many students felt that the program did enough or could do no more to facilitate social network development. Other frequently observed categories include providing more opportunities to meet native speakers, offering more classes that could be taken with native speakers, and implementing a speaking partner program. These suggestions largely mirror what students found to be effective in the first question regarding program interventions.

Table 4.	What did your study abroad program do to help you make native speaking friends or acquaintances while in Japan?	
percentage per number of participants	category	example
30%	Organized activities where students could meet NS	We had conversation days, twice a week and every so often we had parties where all of the members of the school would get together and chat or go out and eat.
30%	Assigned a tutor/buddy/volunteer	They had a program called "Nihongo Partners" where they would pair you up with one or two Japanese university students to meet with to talk to once a week.
17%	Introduced the students to clubs/circles	We were encouraged to join university clubs.
16%	Integrated classes—study abroad and Japanese students/allowed students to enroll in NS universities	They encouraged us to take classes with native speakers during our second semester…
14%	Provided/ assigned students to a host family	We had host families…
9%	Provided frequent speaking opportunities (generally)	There were many opportunities to interact and work with people who natively spoke Japanese.
9%	Arranged trips with Japanese students	Took us on many school trips.
7%	Arranged for the students to live/dorm with Japanese students	I was placed in a dormitory my first semester where I got to meet many Japanese students.
6%	Nothing/not much	Not a lot directly
5%	Provided a place where students could meet Japanese students (e.g., an international lounge, etc.)	They had a common room where natives would come over.
4%	Met arriving students/showed them around/helped them to adjust to Japan life	Assigned a tutor (native-Japanese) to make sure that you were all moved in and comfortable.

Table 5. What more could your study abroad program have done to help you make native speaking friends or acquaintances while in Japan?

percent per number of participants	category	example
34.3%	Nothing/other	I don't really know.
18.6%	Provide more opportunities for SA students to meet native Japanese students	Have more opportunities for exchanges with Japanese students.
13.7%	More classes integrated with native Japanese students	Courses taken together with other native Japanese people would have helped.
11.3%	Implement a speaking partner, mentor program, or structured conversation program; Improve or expand the existing program	Have a Japanese-English partner speaking system of some sort.
9.3%	More help to find or emphasis on joining clubs or student groups	The program should emphasize the need to join a club, one that you're interested in, and try not to join the same one so they don't create a "gaijin" club.
4.9%	Place students in same buildings as NS (facilities integrated) for classes	I wished that the classes had more native students. I also wish the classes were at least in the same building. At the university I was at, we were in a completely separate building on campus.
4.4%	Allow native Japanese students to live with SA students (in dorms)	More opportunities to live with Japanese people (outside of homestays)…
3.4%	Encourage/require home stay. Discourage dorm stay	More host family opportunities…
3.4%	More interaction or coordination with local universities	Maybe offer closer links with Kyoto Daigaku. It would have been nice to meet people our age, without making them come all the way out to our center.
3.4%	Provide a variety of housing options	If there was more homestay options I think that would have been very helpful.
3.4%	Organize more trips with Japanese students	I believe they could have arranged trips together with Japanese students…

Three things that stand out both in the list of useful program interventions and in the list of suggestions for additional interventions are: 1) providing various opportunities to interact with native speakers outside of class; 2) having students take courses with native speakers (cross-enrollment/integrated instruction; and 3) assigning native speakers as speaking partners, study buddies, guides, etc.

Discussion

Overall, school appears to be the setting where most relationships are initiated. Students reported meeting a large percentage of friends and acquaintances on campus and through school clubs and circles. They also listed teachers, tutors, or program staff among the acquaintances and friends in their social networks. The strategies they listed for expanding their social networks (see Table 2) often involved campus-based activities, including joining clubs, going to social gatherings, and talking to people at school. Also, many participants of this study found that taking classes with native speakers was a valuable avenue for building social relationships. While these results in no way suggest that programs not held on or near a university campus are not conducive to social networking, they do suggest that there are definite benefits of being close to other university students and having opportunities to take classes with native speakers and to meet via clubs, social activities, etc. held on campus. The importance of proximity to NS students on campus is illustrated by the following comments:

It was nice to be taken to campus, since we were off campus. I met lots of good people there that I wouldn't have met otherwise. Being separated makes it hard to get to know people our age.

[I]t would have been better to not be [sic] isolate us so much from the Japanese students. The fact that the foreign students had their own dorms and their own building where all their classes would take place and were far from all of us in our center often made it feel like even though our program was associated with the university, we were in a different school dissected from the rest of the campus.

In some cases, students lived close to native speakers, but the nature of their programs required little interaction. The following quote illustrates one student's desire to integrate more with native speaker students:

We were basically living in an English bubble at school and our dorms were all international students with only a handful of Japanese students. They could have integrated us more.

Meeting friends through other friends or acquaintances also seems to be a common way of building social networks. While this may be a common-sense solution, a large number of students didn't report using this strategy at all. Training in culturally appropriate ways of making friends through other friends during pre-departure orientations and in-country seminars could help students take greater advantage of this option.

Time was both an important facilitating and inhibiting factor. In terms of percentages, the amount of time spent together was the top factor that facilitated the development of close friendships, and inability to spend time together was the most frequent response in terms of factors inhibiting the formation of close friendships. In many cases students' schedules either matched well with or did not match well with those of their friends. In some cases students felt their acquaintances were unwilling to take time for them. In other cases they felt the need to spend more time on their own studies and therefore spent less time with friends. Some students complained of having too much homework to have time to socialize. As one student noted, "We had so much homework I didn't have time to see [my Japanese friends]." To help with this difficulty, students could be reminded of good time management strategies to help them prioritize activities and make adequate time for both homework and socializing. It might also be beneficial to give students more preparation time prior to study abroad so they are more linguistically ready to interact and can spend more time polishing their social skills and less time learning lower-level communication skills.

On a related note, students occasionally mentioned that the language barrier kept them from becoming close to NS friends. One student commented, "I didn't have enough Japanese to really get beyond the surface stuff. I wish I had prepared better before coming to Japan." If additional time was spent learning the language prior to study abroad, it is possible that this obstacle could be lessened. Davidson's research in Russian (Brecht et al., 1995;

Davidson, 2010) suggests that this may be the case. He recommends that students have two or more years of language prior to leaving for study abroad. Additional research is needed to determine the optimal amount of pre-departure instruction.

In terms of program interventions, students commonly mentioned that programs helped by organizing activities to meet native speakers. However, as Table 5 shows, providing opportunities to meet native speakers (i.e., organizing social activities, etc.) was also an item that students frequently stated that programs could improve in. Both responses indicate the value that learners place on program efforts to connect students with NSs. One student remarked, "I wasn't sure how to get to know Japanese people. It was so awkward. It was nice to have people [our center] introduced us to." Another stated, "I'm not confident approaching strangers, even in the U.S., so having activities helped to break the ice and get to know at least a few Japanese."

Students preparing to go on SA in the future might benefit from becoming aware of and understanding the importance of using a variety of strategies for networking. As a result, when they are in the host country they can take full advantage of opportunities to both build social networks and strengthen connections with individuals within these networks. Not all students will benefit equally from activities and arrangements initiated by their SA programs. As one student noted, "I didn't feel click with anyone associated with the program, so I just ventured out and found people on my own. Turns out I met people with the same interest like Masa, who shared more common interests and was not a student at [the university we were associated with]." Given that students have a variety of goals and interests, they may each have to take initiative to use whatever strategies they can to build their social networks. Being aware of what past students have done can be helpful in providing ideas for new strategies, such as volunteering at local schools, engaging in community service projects, visiting sites where local traditional crafts are produced, etc. One student interested in auto mechanics met a friend by stopping at an auto repair shop to admire a Mercedes Benz.

Also, since time was an important factor in developing friendships, students preparing to study abroad might focus their pre-program preparations on increasing their linguistic understanding so that time in country can be spent more exclusively on building relationships and opportunities to develop their linguistic knowledge. It is valuable to note here that language barriers were blamed as an inhibiting factor in 10% of the cases where participants had difficulty strengthening a relationship (see Table 6). These barriers may be overcome by additional focus on developing linguistic competence before leaving on SA. Some (e.g., Davidson, 2010; Dekeyser, 2007, 2010) have suggested that learners need to have a degree of linguistic competence prior to SA in order to be capable of taking advantage of the linguistic environment of SA.

Table 6. Choose three people …[who were] lowest in terms of friendship level. Describe anything that may have inhibited friendships with these people.

percentage per number of "lowest friends"	category	example
34%	Lack of time spent together/infrequent meetings	Was a friend of a friend that I saw only occasionally at parties or events
13%	Personality issues	She was nice, but kind of shallow

12%	Contact or SA was busy	Some of the Kyoto University students were very busy with theses and part-time work. People who I couldn't spend a lot of time getting to know didn't become my good friends.
12%	Lack of similar interests; different academic disciplines	They were very friendly, so we made small talk, but didn't have many common interests to deepen the friendship with.
10%	Language barrier	Clearly the language barrier was the largest opposition to our becoming better friends.
9%	Age difference	I'm an old man, age 25, and most of the people I dealt with at school were 19 or 20.
7%	Lack of interest in developing a friendship	They weren't very nice to me or didn't indicate much desire to talk with me a lot.
7%	Social status was an inhibiting factor	I think just them being more of a parental figure kept me from seeing them as a close friend.
7%	Contact was a teacher (similar to social status, but more specific)	We only knew each other as student-teacher and never talked outside of the classroom.
4%	Did not share mutual friends or did not want to branch out from established group of friends	I was never really invited to hang out all that much because she had another circle of friends.

Implications of the study

In short, the primary implication of this study is that students can benefit in terms of social networking from being placed in situations where they are bound to interact with native speaker peers. In addition to locating students on or near a university campus, where they can interact with native Japanese peers, programs might facilitate social network formation by bringing students together through a variety of experiences. Native Japanese students are more likely to have similar interests, have more time, and be more apt to interact with SA participants than many Japanese. Students highly valued opportunities to interact with native Japanese study buddies, tutors, classmates, etc. They appreciated social events organized by programs that connected them with Japanese university students.

While interactions with non-student Japanese natives were also available to and valued by SA participants, these interactions were not typically as available or productive. It appears that there are a variety of strategies that can be helpful for forming social networks, including attempting to be introduced to new friends through existing friends. Training in some of these strategies might be fruitful, but students' comments suggest that, more important than training, providing a range of formal and informal opportunities for social interactions (organizing social events, providing study partners, introducing to clubs and extracurricular opportunities, allowing direct enrollment in classes with native speakers, etc.) could be fruitful.

Limitations of the study

One of the major limitations of this study was that the data were all self-reported data from a single source (student questionnaires). To achieve a more comprehensive and objective understanding of students' social networking, additional data sources would be helpful. As Kinginger (2009) notes, "qualitative researchers should broaden their perspectives beyond the students, to include other people who shape the nature of study abroad" (p. 217). In particular, researchers could poll students' native speaker friends regarding how their friendships were formed, facilitating factors, inhibiting factors, etc. Furthermore, participant observation and journal writing would also provide richer detail. Having students record their experiences through journals would help overcome another limitation of this study. Students were reporting on their social network formation well after it occurred (in some cases several years after). Giving the SASIQ immediately after the SA experience, collecting journal entries, and interviewing students during and immediately after their experiences would provide a more immediate image of students' social network formation.

Recommendations for future research

In terms of other possible future research, programs could measure the results of specific types of interventions by collecting a variety of data after these interventions occur. For instance, if programs were to increase the number of integrated/direct enrollment courses (i.e., increase courses where SA participants study content alongside NS), then they might also measure the impact on social networks by having both SA students and NS students report on friendships that developed and/or time spent with their counterparts.

One additional possible line of research would be to conduct conversation analysis (see Liddicoat, 2007 for examples) to determine the specific nature of the conversations learners have within their social networks and then subsequently tie these conversations with language acquisition. Kinginger (2009) and [need Cohen's first name here – it is nowhere else in this document] Cohen (personal communication, March 23, 2011) have suggested that such detailed documentation of the nature of these interactions is an important next step if we are to understand the processes of second language acquisition experienced during SA.

Finally, we acknowledge that although the sample was rather diverse in nature, including students from a variety of home institutions and SA programs in Japan, it may not be representative of all students, in particular since our students were perceived by the Bridging Scholarship Awards Committee to be worthy of scholarships. Research involving students with a greater range of capabilities would allow for greater generalization of findings. Furthermore, research in other languages might also be informative. Our own research in Arabic (Dewey, Belnap, Kurzer & Palmer, 2011) has already shown that there can be differences across countries and/or programs in the ways that learners build social networks. One key variable that contributed to differences in the strategies students used to build social networks and even the types of interactions they had was location: in one case students studied on a Jordanian campus and therefore interacted often with young Jordanian students and in another case students were in a language center well away from any university campus and ended up interacting often with local service personnel and individuals who were often older or of vastly different social status. The value of English in these two settings also made a difference. For example, one setting where English was important to many locals contributed to the initiation of contact with the SA participants by these locals. In another setting, locals surrounding the students tended not to speak English and were therefore not inclined to initiate contact with the SA students. More detailed cross-program and cross-location analyses in Japan might yield similar results.

Conclusion

In this study, we presented data regarding how students build social networks during SA. We found that SA program interventions and location can play a large role in facilitating the formation of these networks through providing social activities with native speakers, placing learners in proximity to native speakers via housing, classes, and class location, introducing students to and encouraging participation in campus clubs, etc. We also found that students have their own means of building friendships as well. By being aware of these ways of building and strengthening relationships with native speakers, programs and faculty can better strategize ways of increasing learners' engagement in social networks in Japan.

Acknowledgments

We are grateful to Susan Schmidt, Executive Director of the Bridging Project Clearinghouse, for facilitating collection of the data used in this study. Data collection for this study was partially funded by a grant from the U.S., Department of Education (International Research and Studies Program, P017A080087).

References

Alred, G., & Byram, M. (2002). Becoming an intercultural mediator: A longitudinal study of residence abroad. *Journal of Multilingual and Multicultural Development, 23,* 339–352.

Badstübner, T., & Ecke, P. (2009). Student expectations, motivations, target language use, and perceived learning progress in a summer study abroad program in Germany. *Die Unterrichtspraxis/Teaching German, 42*(1), 41–49.

Brecht, R. D., & Robinson, J. L. (1995). On the value of formal instruction in study abroad: Student reactions in context. In B. F. Freed (Ed.), *Second language acquisition in a study abroad context* (pp. 317–334). Amsterdam, The Netherlands: Benjamins.

Brecht, R. D., Davidson, D. E., & Ginsberg, R. B. (1995). Predictors of foreign language gain during study abroad. In B. F. Freed (Ed.), *Second language acquisition in a study abroad context* (pp. 37–66). Amsterdam, The Netherlands: Benjamins.

Burns, P. D. (1996). *Foreign students in Japan: A qualitative study of interpersonal relations between North American university exchange students and their Japanese hosts* (Unpublished doctoral dissertation). University of Massachusetts Amherst, Amherst.

Campbell, C. (1996). Socializing with the teachers and prior language learning experience: A diary study. In K. M. Bailey & D. Nunan (Eds.), *Voices from the classroom* (pp. 201–223). New York, NY: Cambridge University Press.

Davidson, D. F. (2010). Study abroad: When, how long, and with what results? New data from the Russian front. *Foreign Language Annals, 43*(1), 6–26.

Dekeyser, R. (2010). Monitoring processes in Spanish as a second language during a study abroad program. *Foreign Language Annals, 43*(1), 80–92.

DeKeyser, R. M. (2007). Study abroad as foreign language practice. In R. M. DeKeyser (Ed.), *Practice in a second language: Perspectives from applied linguistics and cognitive psychology* (pp. 208–226). Cambridge, United Kingdom: Cambridge University Press.

Dewey, D. P. (2004). A comparison of reading development by learners of Japanese in intensive domestic immersion and study abroad contexts. *Studies in Second Language Acquisition, 26,* 303–327.

Dewey, D. P. (2008). Japanese vocabulary acquisition by learners in three contexts. *Frontiers: The Interdisciplinary Journal of Study Abroad, 15*(Winter), 127–148.

Dewey, D. P., Belnap, R. K., & Hillstrom, R. (in press). Social network development, language use, and language acquisition during study abroad: Arabic language learners' perspectives. *Frontiers: The Interdisciplinary Journal of Study Abroad, 22*(2013, Spring).

Dewey, D. P., Bown, J., & Eggett, D. L. (2012). Japanese language proficiency, social networking, and language use during study abroad: Learners' perspectives. *Canadian Modern Language Review, (68)*2, 111–137. doi:10.3138/cmlr.68.2.111

Díaz-Campos, M. (2004). Context of learning in the acquisition of Spanish second language phonology. *Studies in Second Language Acquisition, 26,* 249–273.

Fraser, C. C. (2002). Study abroad: An attempt to measure the gains. *German as a Foreign Language Journal, 1,* 45–65.

Freed, B. F. (1990). Language learning in a study abroad context: The effects of interactive and non-interactive out-of-class contact on grammatical achievement and oral proficiency. In J. E. Atlatis (Ed.), *Georgetown University Round Table on Languages and Linguistics 1990: Linguistics, language teaching and language acquisition: The interdependence of theory, practice and research* (pp. 459–477). Washington DC: Georgetown University Press.

Freed, B. F. (1995). What makes us think that students who study abroad become fluent? In B. F. Freed (Ed.), *Second language acquisition in a study abroad context* (pp. 123–148). Amsterdam, The Netherlands: Benjamins.

Freed, B. F., Segalowitz, N., & Dewey, D. P. (2004). Context of learning and second language fluency in French: Comparing regular classroom, study abroad, and intensive domestic immersion programs. *Studies in Second Language Acquisition, 26,* 275–301.

Ginsberg, R. B., & Miller, L. (2000). What do they do? Activities of students during study abroad. In R. D. Lambert & E. Shohamy (Eds.), *Language policy and pedagogy: Essays in honor of A. Ronald Walton* (pp. 237–260). Philadelphia, PA: Benjamins.

Glaser, B., & Strauss, A. (1967). *The discovery of grounded theory: Strategies for qualitative research.* New York, NY: Aldin.

Hashimoto, H. (1994). Language acquisition of an exchange student within the homestay environment. *Journal of Asian Pacific Communication, 4*(4), 209–224.

Hernández, T. A. (2010). The relationship among motivation, interaction, and the development of second language oral proficiency in a study-abroad context. *The Modern Language Journal, 94*(4), 600–617.

Hillstrom, R. (2011). *Social networks, language acquisition, and time on task while studying abroad in Jordan.* (Unpublished master's thesis). Brigham Young University, Provo, UT.

Huebner, T. (1995). The effects of overseas language programs: Report on a case study of an intensive Japanese course. In B. F. Freed (Ed.), *Second language acquisition in a study abroad context* (pp. 171–193). Amsterdam, The Netherlands: Benjamins.

Institute of International Education. (2010). *Open Doors 2010 fast facts.* Retrieved from http://www.iie.org/en/Research-and-Publications/~/media/Files/Corporate/Open-Doors/Fast-Facts/Fast%20Facts%202010.ashx

Isabelli, C. L. (2001). Motivation and extended interaction in the study abroad context: Factors in the development of Spanish language accuracy and communication skills. *Dissertation Abstracts International– Section A, 62*(8), 2703–A–2704.

Isabelli-García, C. (2006). Study abroad social networks, motivation, and attitudes: Implications for second language acquisition. In M. A. Dufon & E. Churchill

(Eds.), *Language learners in study abroad contexts* (pp. 231–258). Cleveland, OH: Multilingual Matters.

Iwasaki, N. (2007). Assessing progress towards advanced level Japanese after a year abroad. *Japanese Language and Literature, 41,* 271–296.

Iwasaki, N. (2008). L2 Japanese acquisition of the pragmatics of requests during short-term study abroad. *Japanese Language Education in Europe, 12,* 51–58.

Iwasaki, N. (2011). Learning L2 Japanese "politeness" and "impoliteness": Young American men's dilemmas during study abroad. *Japanese Language and Literature, 45,* 67–106.

Kinginger, C. (2009). *Language learning and study abroad: A critical reading of research.* London, United Kingdom: Palgrave Macmillan.

Kinginger, C., & Farrell-Whitworth, K. F. (2005). Gender and emotional investment in language learning during study abroad (CALPER Working Paper Series 2). Retrieved from http://calper.la.psu.edu/publications.php

Kline, R. R. (1993). The social practice of literacy in a program of study abroad. *Dissertation Abstracts International–Section A, Humanities and Social Sciences, 54*(5), 1785-A.

Kurata, N. (2004). Communication networks of Japanese language learners in their home country. *Journal of Asian Pacific Communication, 14*(1), 153–179.

Kurata, N. (2007). Language choice and second language learning opporunities in learners' social networks: A case study of an Australian learner of Japanese. *Australian Review of Applied Linguistics, 30*(1), 1–18.

Levin, D. M. (2001). *Language learners' sociocultural interaction in a study abroad context.* Indiana University, Bloomington.

Liddicoat, A. J. (2007). *An introduction to conversation analysis.* London, United Kingdom: Continuum.

Magnan, S. S., & Back, M. (2007). Social interaction and linguistic gain during study abroad. *Foreign Language Annals, 40*(1), 43–61.

Makino, S. (1996). *Hoomu sutee ni okeru nihongo gakushuu kooka* [The effect on Japanese learning of homestay]. In In O. Kamada & H. Yamauchi (Eds.), *Nihongo kyooiku/ibunka komyunikeeshon—kyooshitsu, hoomu sutee, chiiki o musubu mono* [Japanese pedagogy: Cross-cultural communication to bridge the classroom, the homestay, and the community] (pp. 41–59). Tokyo, Japan: Bojinsha.

Marcus, G. (Ed.). (2007). Study abroad for advanced skills [Special issue]. *Japanese Language and Literature, 41*(2).

Marriott, H. (1995). The acquisition of politeness patterns by exchange students in Japan. In B. F. Freed (Ed.), *Second language acquisition in a study abroad context* (pp. 197–224). Amsterdam, The Netherlands: Benjamins.

Marriott, H., & Enomoto, S. (1995). Secondary exchanges with Japan: Exploring students' experiences and gains. *Australian Review of Applied Linguistics Series S, 12,* 64–82.

Mathews, S. A. (2000). *Russian second language acquisition during study abroad: Gender differences in student behavior* (Unpublished doctoral dissertation). Bryn Mawr College, Bryn Mawr, PA.

Mendelson, V. G. (2004). *Spain or bust? Assessment and student perceptions of out-of-class contact and oral proficiency in a study abroad context* (Unpublished doctoral dissertation). University of Massachusetts, Amherst.

Miller, L., & Ginsberg, R. B. (1995). Folklinguistic theories of language learning. In B. F. Freed (Ed.), *Second language acquisition in a study abroad context* (pp. 293–315). Amsterdam, The Netherlands: Benjamins.

Milroy, L. (1987). *Language and social networks*. Oxford, United Kingdom: Basil Blackwell.

Noda, M. (2005, March). *Constructing study abroad experiences*. Paper presented at the University of Pittsburgh Japanese Pedagogy Workshop, Pittsburgh, PA.

Noda, M., Yuasa, E., & Quinn, C. J. (Eds.). (2005). Study abroad: Rethinking our whys and hows. *Occasional Papers of the Association of Teachers of Japanese, 5*.

Papatsiba, L. (2006). Study abroad and experiences of cultural distance and proximity: French Erasmus students. In M. Byram & A. Feng (Eds.), *Living and studying abroad: Research and practice* (pp. 108–133). Clevedon, United Kingdom: Multilingual Matters.

Pellegrino-Aveni, V. A. (2005). *Study abroad and second language use: Constructing the self*. Cambridge, United Kingdom: Cambridge University Press.

Polanyi, L. (1995). Language learning and living abroad: Stories from the field. In B. F. Freed (Ed.), *Second language acquisition in a study abroad context* (pp. 271–291). Amsterdam, The Netherlands: Benjamins.

Scott, J. (2000). *Social network analysis: A handbook*. Thousand Oaks, CA: Sage.

Segalowitz, N., & Freed, B. F. (2004). Context, contact and cognition in oral fluency acquisition: Learning Spanish in at home and study abroad contexts. *Studies in Second Language Acquisition, 26*, 173–199.

Segalowitz, N., & Ryder, A. (2006). *Montreal Index of Linguistic Integration (MILI)*. Unpublished questionnaire, Concordia University, Montreal, Quebec, Canada.

Shelley, H. (2011). *The female experience: Study abroad in Cairo, Egypt* (Unpublished master's thesis). Brigham Young University, Provo UT.

Siegal, M. (1995). Individual differences and study abroad: Women learning Japanese in Japan. In B. F. Freed (Ed.), *Second language acquisition in a study abroad context* (pp. 225–244). Amsterdam, The Netherlands: Benjamins.

Strauss, A., & Corbin, J. (1998). *Basics of qualitative research: Techniques and procedures for developing grounded theory* (2nd ed.). Thousand Oaks, CA: Sage.

Taguchi, N. (2008). Cognition, language contact, and the development of pragmatic comprehension in a study-abroad context. *Language Learning, 58*(1), 33–71.

Talburt, S., & Stewart, M. A. (1999). What's the subject of study abroad?: Race, gender, and "living culture." *Modern Language Journal, 83*(2), 163–175.

Tanaka, T., Takai, J., Kohyama, T., Fujihara, T., & Minami, H. (1997). Effects of social networks on cross-cultural adjustment. *Japanese Psychological Research, 39*(1), 12–24.

Twombly, S. B. (1995). Piropos and friendships: Gender and culture clash in study abroad. *Frontiers: The Interdisciplinary Journal of Study Abroad, 1*(Fall), 1–21.

Wang, C. (2010). Toward a second language socialization perspective: Issues in study abroad research. *Foreign Language Annals, 43*(1), 50–63.

Whitworth, K. F. (2006). *Access to learning during study abroad: The roles of identity and subject positioning* (Unpublished doctoral dissertation). The Pennsylvania State University, University Park.

Wilkinson, S. (1998a). Study abroad from the participants' perspective: A challenge to common beliefs. *Foreign Language Annals, 31*(1), 23–39.

Wilkinson, S. (1998b). On the nature of immersion during study abroad: Some participant perspectives. *Frontiers: The Interdisciplinary Journal of Study Abroad, IV*(Fall), 121–138.

Wilkinson, S. (2002). The omnipresent classroom during summer study abroad: American students in conversation with their French hosts. *Modern Language Journal, 86*(2), 157–173.

Xu, D., Wang, X., & Li, W. (2008). Social network analysis. In Li Wei & M. G. Moyer (Eds.), *The Blackwell guide to research methods in bilingualism and multilingualism* (pp. 263–274). Malden, MA: Blackwell Publishing.

Yager, K. (1998). Learning Spanish in Mexico: The effect of informal contact and student attitudes on language gain. *Hispania, 81*(4), 898–913.

Young, D. J., (1992). Language anxiety from the foreign language specialist's perspective: Interviews with Krashen, Omaggio Hadley, Terrell, and Rardin. *Foreign Language Annals, 25*(2), 157–172.

Appendix 1: Study Abroad Social Interaction Questionnaire (SASIQ), June, 2009 version

Study Abroad Social Interaction Questionnaire (SASIQ)

Thank you for agreeing to participate in this survey, conducted by the Bridging Program of the Association of Teachers of Japanese and by Dr. Dan Dewey of Brigham Young University. As a former Bridging participant, you have been selected to be part of an evaluation that will help us understand better how people form friendships with native Japanese while in Japan and how language is used outside of the classroom during study abroad.

This survey consists of four series of questions and should take you approximately twenty to thirty minutes to complete. There are minimal risks to participating in this study. The benefits are that we will be more able to provide assistance making friends and to help learners use the language more during their time in Japan.

Involvement in this study is voluntary. You may withdraw at any time without penalty or refuse to participate entirely. Your identity will be kept confidential as we report results from this survey. By participating in this questionnaire you agree to allow us to use your responses in our program evaluation and in presentations and written reports. Your responses will all be kept confidential and your name will never be associated with your answers as we present our research findings to others.

You will receive a gift certificate for completing this questionnaire, so please be sure that your name and email address are accurate and that you complete all of the items carefully.

If you have questions about this program evaluation, you may contact Dr. Dan Dewey, director of this survey project (ddewey@byu.edu, phone: 801-422-6005) or Susan Schmidt, Executive Director, Bridging Project, Association of Teachers of Japanese (susan.schmidt@colorado.edu, phone: 303-492-5487).

If you have questions about your rights as participants in this evaluation or have concerns about participating, you may also contact Dr. Christopher Dromey, Chair of the Institutional Review Board, 422 SWKT, Brigham Young University, Provo, Utah, 84602; phone, 801-422-3873, email christopher_dromey@byu.edu.

Your Name (First and Last):

Email address

What is your gender?
- ○ Male
- ○ Female

Where in Japan did you study as a Bridging scholarship recipient?

What year were you born?

Year

How long did you live in Japan during your Bridging study abroad experience?

Number of Months

Which situation best describes your living arrangements in Japan during your Bridging experience?
- ○ I lived in the home of a Japanese family.
- ○ I lived in the student dormitory.
- ○ I lived alone in a room or an apartment.
- ○ I lived in a room or an apartment with native or fluent Japanese speaker(s)
- ○ I lived in a room or an apartment with others who are NOT native or fluent Japanese speakers
- ○ Other (please specify)

Approximately how long had you studied Japanese prior to going abroad for your Bridging experience? Approximations are fine. Please start with the largest (academic years) and then add semesters or quarters if needed.

Academic Years
Semesters
Quarters

In this questionnaire you will be asked about people you spoke with in Japanese and in English while participating in study abroad as a Bridging scholarship recipient. Please respond carefully to each of the items based on your recollections of your Bridging experience in Japan. Your best recollections are acceptable.

In the boxes below, please write, from memory, the names of friends or acquaintances who you spoke Japanese with or native speakers of Japanese with whom you regularly spoke in English who fit the following description in all respects:

- You *at least occasionally* spoke Japanese to them or they *at least occasionally* spoke Japanese to you.
- You know them well enough to have spent at least some time socializing with them.

If you had more than twenty friends with whom you at least occasionally spoke Japanese, please simply list the twenty with whom you spoke Japanese most regularly.

To help you think about people you could name, think about people you met at school, in the community, through internships, or people you lived with, as well as people you were introduced to through friends or others.

Person 1
Person 2
Person 3
Person 4
Person 5
Person 6
Person 7
Person 8
Person 9
Person 10
Person 11
Person 12
Person 13
Person 14
Person 15
Person 16
Person 17
Person 18
Person 19
Person 20

Using the drop-down menu on the left, indicate the category that best describes how you met each person. In the text box on the right please elaborate on the details of your meeting. The boxes will fit more than it might appear. Please feel free to write as much as you need to.

	How you met this person	Please Elaborate How You Met
» Person 1		
» Person 2		
» Person 3		
» Person 4		
» Person 5		
» Person 6		
» Person 7		
» Person 8		
» Person 9		
» Person 10		
» Person 11		
» Person 12		
» Person 13		
» Person 14		
» Person 15		
» Person 16		
» Person 17		
» Person 18		
» Person 19		
» Person 20		

For each of the people in your list, please indicate the level of your friendship, ranging from mere acquaintance to very close friend/confidant.

Note that in terms of communication, level of friendship ranges from engaging in occasional friendly exchanges (low on the scale) to sharing one's deepest feelings or asking for advice regarding personal challenges (high on the scale). Refer to the diagram below to help interpret the range.

Acquaintance			Friend			Very Close Friend/Confidant	
1	2	3	4	5	6	7	8

	1	2	3	4	5	6	7	8
» Person 1	○	○	○	○	○	○	○	○
» Person 2	○	○	○	○	○	○	○	○
» Person 3	○	○	○	○	○	○	○	○
» Person 4	○	○	○	○	○	○	○	○
» Person 5	○	○	○	○	○	○	○	○
» Person 6	○	○	○	○	○	○	○	○
» Person 7	○	○	○	○	○	○	○	○
» Person 8	○	○	○	○	○	○	○	○

» Person 9	○	○	○	○	○	○	○	○
» Person 10	○	○	○	○	○	○	○	○
» Person 11	○	○	○	○	○	○	○	○
» Person 12	○	○	○	○	○	○	○	○
» Person 13	○	○	○	○	○	○	○	○
» Person 14	○	○	○	○	○	○	○	○
» Person 15	○	○	○	○	○	○	○	○
» Person 16	○	○	○	○	○	○	○	○
» Person 17	○	○	○	○	○	○	○	○
» Person 18	○	○	○	○	○	○	○	○
» Person 19	○	○	○	○	○	○	○	○
» Person 20	○	○	○	○	○	○	○	○

Choose three people from your list above that you marked as being the closest of friends (highest score). Pease tell why you think you were able to develop good friendships with these people? What allowed you to move up the scale from acquaintance to friend, etc.

Choose three people from your list above that you marked as being lowest in terms of friendship level. Please tell why you think you were not able to develop stronger friendships with these people? Describe anything that may have inhibited friendships with these people.

What topics did you talk most about with the people you listed? The text boxes are small, but will take as many topics as you wish to write for each person, so please list all common topics you can think of.

» Person 1
» Person 2
» Person 3

» Person 4
» Person 5
» Person 6
» Person 7
» Person 8
» Person 9
» Person 10
» Person 11
» Person 12
» Person 13
» Person 14
» Person 15
» Person 16
» Person 17
» Person 18

» Person 19

» Person 20

What were some obstacles that kept you from speaking Japanese with these people?

What did your study abroad program do to help you make native speaking friends or acquaintances while in Japan?

What more could your study abroad program have done to help you make native speaking friends or acquaintances while in Japan?

What sorts of things did *you* do to make friends with native Japanese speakers?

9. Please rate yourself on the following statements according to the scale given. Please think about your overall tendencies, **NOT** your time in Japan specifically. We are interested in your general tendencies.

	Strongly Agree	Agree	Neither Agree nor Disagree	Disagree	Strongly Disagree
I am a social person.	○	○	○	○	○
I have lots of friends.	○	○	○	○	○
I spend lots of time with other people.	○	○	○	○	○

SOCIAL GROUPS

There are four parts to this question (A-D).

Part A.

For this item you will help us identify which people know each other and how they know each other by grouping together the people you listed according to where they should know each other from (and possibly where you got to know them). For example, if three of the people are host family members, you would group them together by dragging their names to the "Host Family" box. If four of the people worked at your internship site and knew each other as a result, you would group them together by dragging their names to the "Group 1" box and then giving the box "Group 1" the label "Internship Site" in the blank below.

If people belong to more than one group, place them in their primary group (the group they are most tightly linked to).

After dragging people to their groups, please be sure to define each group in the text fields that follow (Part B) so we can understand how the people know each other. If you have more groups than there are boxes, please use the next question (Part C) to describe who these groups are and how they are made up (the people and the group names).

Items	Host Family (Homestay)	Group 1
» Person 1		
» Person 2		
» Person 3		
» Person 4		
» Person 5		
» Person 6		
» Person 7		
» Person 8	Group 2	Group 3
» Person 9		

- » Person 10
- » Person 11
- » Person 12
- » Person 13
- » Person 14
- » Person 15
- » Person 16
- » Person 17
- » Person 18
- » Person 19
- » Person 20

Group 4   Group 5

Part B

Label for Group 1
Label for Group 2
Label for Group 3
Label for Group 4
Label for Group 5

Part C
If there were more groups than six (Homestay plus five others), please list the groups and their members here.

Part D
If people belonged to more than one group, please list these people and their additional groups here. (Give each name with that person's additional group or groups.)

6

Grammar and Interactional Discourse: Marking Non-topical Subject in Japanese Conversation

インターアクションと文法:日本語の会話における「が」の非トピック明示機能

Michiko Kaneyasu
University of Colorado, Boulder

Abstract

This chapter aims to demonstrate the role of the postpositional particle ga in the collaborative organization of discourse topic in Japanese conversation. Discourse topic is not static; it is a dynamic notion that is interactionally achieved in dialogic communication under a "triadic interactional framework." The interactional triangle involves three nodes representing the speaker, the interlocutor, and the object or event on which the conversational participants place attention. The jointly attended object or event serves as a local discourse topic and a common reference point for achieving alignment and intersubjectivity (e.g., sense of shared understanding, awareness, feeling, or perspective), which is one major goal of conversational interaction. In this study, I examine face-to-face and telephone conversations involving two human referents, and analyze the role of ga in guiding and maintaining the co-participants' orientation to the common topic. I show that ga has the function of explicitly indicating the non-topicality of a ga-marked subject which participates in a sequence of actions expressed by upcoming predicate(s), and thereby contributes to the collaborative achievement of discourse topic. These findings shed light on the interplay between grammar and interaction.

要旨

本章では,日本語の会話の中でのトピックの協同的確立において後置詞「が」がどのような役割を果たしているのかを考察することを目的とする。トピックは静的な

Kaneyasu, M. (2013). Grammar and interactional discourse: Marking non-topical subject in Japanese conversation. In K. Kondo-Brown, Y. Saito-Abbott, S. Satsutani, M. Tsutsui, & A. Wehmeyer (Eds.), *New perspectives on Japanese language learning, linguistics, and culture* (pp. 123–144). Honolulu: University of Hawai'i, National Foreign Language Resource Center.

ものではなく「三項関係的な相互行為の枠組み」に基づいた対話において相互的に築きあげられる動的な概念である。相互行為の三項関係は話者, 対話者, そして二者が共同注意を向ける対象の三点で結ばれている。共同注意の対象は会話のトピックとしてだけでなく相互主観性(理解・認識・感情・観点などの共有感)を達成する為の指示対象としての役割も果たす。本研究では, 一つ以上の指示物が存在する対面会話と電話会話を分析し, 「が」には主語の非トピック性, そしてその主語がこれから述べられる述語の表す行為や事態と結びつくことを明示する働きがあり, トピックの相互的達成に重要に関わっていることを明らかにする。本研究結果は文法とインターアクションの密接な相互関係性を示唆している。

Introduction

The postpositional particle *ga* is one of the most discussed topics in the field of Japanese linguistics (e.g., Kuno, 1972, 1973; Tsutsui, 1983; Masunaga, 1988; Shibatani, 1990; Noda, 1996; Ono, Thompson, & Suzuki, 2000). The particle is most widely accepted as a grammatical subject marker, indicating the subject of a transitive or intransitive predicate. At the same time, the function of *ga* as a marker of new information is also recognized and discussed by a number of linguists (e.g., Kuno, 1972, 1973; Hinds & Hinds, 1979; Hinds, 1983; Iwasaki, 1985; Shibatani, 1990; Lambrecht, 1994).

Kuno (1972) first identified the correlation between *ga*-marking and new information, claiming that "[*ga*] as subject marker in [a] matrix sentence always signals that the subject conveys new, unpredictable information" (p. 273).[1] The following example illustrates the unpredictability requirement for *ga*-marking (Kuno, 1972, p. 277):

(1) *gootoo ga boku no ie ni haitta.*

'A robber broke into my house.'

sono gootoo *ga/wa boku ni pisutoru o tsukitsukete kane o dase to itta.

'The robber pointed a gun at me, and said, "Give me money."'

In (1), there is only one robber under discussion and the referent has been introduced into the discourse in the first sentence, hence the subject of the predicates 'pointed a gun and said...' in the second sentence is given. This is why the use of *ga* after *sono gootoo* 'the robber' results in ungrammaticality. However, as Maynard (1981, p. 115–116) shows in the modified example below, given the appropriate context, the use of *ga* following given information is grammatically acceptable.

(2) *gootoo ga boku no ie ni haitta.*

'A robber broke into my house.'

sono gootoo ga boku ni pisutoru o tsukitsukete kane o dase to itta.

'The robber pointed a gun at me, and said, "Give me money."'

sono toki tomodachi no Yamanaka-san ga heya ni haitte kita.

'Then my friensd Yamanaka came into the room.'

Yamanaka-san wa doa no soba ni atta raihuru o tsukamu to atarikamawazu uchidasita.

'As soon as (he) grabbed the rifle by the door, Yamanaka began to shoot wildly.'

Example (2) differs from (1) in that the writer introduces a third participant *Yamanaka-san* into the discourse and subsequently marks it with *wa*. Maynard (1981, 1987) argues that

---

[1] According to Kuno (1972), *ga*-marked NP in subordinate clauses can represent either new or old information.

the function of *wa* is to mark thematic information, while the function of *ga* is to mark non-thematic, subordinate information in narrative discourse (see also Noda, 1996). The acceptability of *sono gootoo ga* in the second sentence in Example (2) is counter-evidence against Kuno's claim that *ga* always marks new or unpredictable information.

My conversational data basically supports Maynard's claim that *ga* marks a non-topical subject in discourse involving two or more persistent referents.[2] However, the notion of topic that is relevant to written narratives seems to diverge from one that is relevant to conversational discourse. Maynard defines topic (or what she terms 'theme') as "the conceptual framework within which the story is told, presented and performed" (Maynard, 1981, p. 124). In written narratives, the topic is the central character from whose point of view the entire story is told. As I will discuss in the section on local discourse topic below, the notion of global discourse topic is suitable to the organization of written narratives whereas unplanned spontaneous spoken discourse, such as that found in conversation, requires a more open and labile notion of topic. Real-time production and comprehension of utterances in conversational discourse place a higher cognitive load on the participants in terms of how much information they can process at a time. Another important characteristic of conversation is its interactional nature. That is, the conversational participants do not just exchange information about a certain topic but they share their feelings, opinions, evaluations, and so on, with their co-participants concerning a given topic.

The primary finding in this study is that speakers use *ga*-marking to locally indicate the non-topicality of the *ga*-marked referent, and by doing so, they make sure that the co-participants' attentions are directed to the discourse topic. Securing joint attention is a prerequisite for collaborative sharing of the conversational participants' points of view in ongoing discourse. *Ga*-marking thus contributes to achieving successful dialogic interaction.

Let us look at an initial example to explore this function of *ga* in conversation. In the following excerpt (3), Hiro is telling his friend Jun about a Japanese fast food restaurant, Yoshinoya, and its first franchise restaurants in the U.S., In line 5, a former employee is introduced into the discourse with *ga*. Despite its given information status, the employee is marked by *ga* again in line 7.

(3) *ga*-marking in conversation (ja_4573)[3, 4]

1. Hiro: *de denbaa kara hajimete:, jukken gurai tsukuttan da kedo, kekkyoku nanka*

    'So (Yoshinoya) began (its overseas expansion) in Denver, and built about ten

    anmari umaku ikanakute:,

    restaurants, but it didn't go very well in the end,'

---

[2] The referent persistence is often equated with the notion of topicality (Givón, 1983; Clancy & Downing, 1987). See the section on referent persistence vs. topicality for further discussion on the correlations between the two concepts.

[3] The data source for each excerpt is indicated in the parentheses. See the section on data for more information about the data used in the present study.

[4] The segments from conversations provided in this study are transcribed based on the transcription system of Du Bois, Schuetze-Coburn, Cumming, and Paolino (1993), and the intonation unit (IU) is the basic unit of transcription and of analysis. The following intonation contours mark the end of each IU: [.] falling intonation; [,] continuing intonation; [?] rising intonation. Due to space limitations, in some cases, multiple IUs are presented on single lines. Other transcription conventions used in this study are listed in the Appendix.

2. Jun: *un.*
'Yeah.'

3. Hiro: *de hikiharaoo to shita toki ni:,*
'and when they were about to move out,'

4. Jun: *un.*
'Uh huh.'

5.→Hiro: *ano:: soko de hataraiteta hitori no hito ga, zenbu yoshinoya kara jukken*
'Ummm one of the employees who worked there bought all the ten restaurants
kaitottan desu yo.
from Yoshinoya.'

6. Jun: *a honto:.*
'Oh, really.'

7.→Hiro: *hai. de sono hito ga ima moritatete:, kaisha no namae kaete,*
'Yes. And that person has now revived (the company), and changed the company's name,'

The *ga*-marking in line 7 neither functions to introduce a new referent, nor is it employed just to indicate the grammatical subject of the predicate. As will be shown in the rest of this chapter, *ga*-attached given referents (i.e., those that are previously introduced) recurrently appear in the discourse environment in which there are two persistent referents. In the excerpt (3) above, for example, the second mention of the former employee in line 7 could have indicated a topic shift from Yoshinoya's franchise restaurants in the U.S., to the former employee. However, Hiro marks the given referent with *ga* in line 7 to explicitly indicate its non-topical status so as to maintain Yoshinoya as the ongoing topic of conversation. As seen in this example, the non-topic marking function of *ga* is observed in conversational data involving more than one referent potentially competing for topical status. The conversational data in the present study will explicate how conversational participants use *ga* as a local non-topic marking device so as to orient and maintain the co-participants' attention to the ongoing topic of the conversation.

Previous studies on *ga*

Kuno (1972, p. 273) distinguishes two kinds of *ga* functioning as a subject marker: neutral description and exhaustive listing. Exhaustive listing refers to a sentence that singles out the subject X, as in 'X (and only X)...' or 'it is X that...,' while neutral description refers to an objective observation of an event, an action, or a state of affairs. Although there are some instances of the exhaustive listing *ga* in my data,[5] most instances of *ga* found in the

---

[5] The following is an example of the exhaustive listing from my data (*Nihongo*). Prior to the following segment, Nao tells Yuko about some restaurants in the neighborhood she does not know. After Yuko displays her admiration of Nao's knowledge (line 1), Nao humbly says that everyone knows the restaurants (line 2).

1 Yuko: *ho:, yoku shitteru yone:?, ... ironna [resutoran].*
'Wow, you know various restaurants (in the area) so well.'

2 Nao: *[tabun minna shi]tte @masu @yo?*
'Probably everyone knows (them).'

present data are of the neutral description type. Observe the following example of neutral descriptive *ga* (Kuno, 1972, p. 272, with minor changes in the styles and glosses):

(4) Neutral description

oya, John ga kita.

'Oh, look. John has come.'

In (4), the speaker has just seen John coming. The utterance in (4) represents the event as a whole. Iwasaki (forthcoming) further notes that "when the speaker utters these [neutral descriptive] sentences, …no part of these sentences has been activated in the mind of the speaker, both [the entity and its temporary situation] are simultaneously activated on the spot" (p. 18). We can imagine a situation in which a speaker observes a state or event and immediately expresses his or her observation using *ga*. Although such use of *ga* is not common in dialogic interaction, the function of *ga* to mark a non-topical subject is closely related to the neutral descriptive *ga*. That is, *ga* presents the referent as being part of a state or event expressed by the predicate as if the scene is being observed in its entirety with no focus on individual components (see also Sunakawa, 2005, p. 178–182). The strategic use of *ga* functions to indicate the non-topic status of the referent, thereby preventing a false topic-shift.

In the study of turn-taking organization in conversation, Tanaka (1999) demonstrates how *ga* can be employed by conversational participants as an important grammatical resource for projecting further components of an unfolding utterance by creating a grammatical link between the preceding element and the following component yet to be produced. That is, when *ga* is uttered, it marks the preceding NP as a syntactic subject and at the same time projects that a predicate will follow at some point in the ongoing utterance. Figure 1, adapted and modified from Hayashi (2004, p. 350), is a schematic representation of this process:

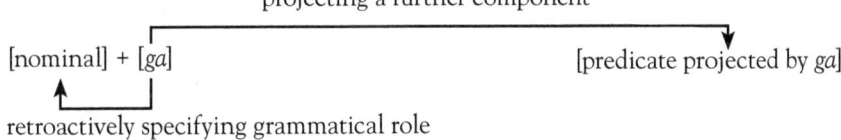

Figure 1. Grammatical link created by *ga*

While Tanaka (1999) and Hayashi (2004) emphasize the grammatical function of *ga* in conversation, Ono et al. (2000) focus on the pragmatic aspect of the particle. According to their research, the use of *ga* as a subject marker is highly infrequent in unplanned spontaneous conversation, and the particle only appears in pragmatically salient environments where the relationship between the *ga*-marked NP and the predicate is difficult to grasp. For example, *ga*-marking is observed under situations where an NP (1) is singled out, (2) introduces a concept, (3) is phonologically 'unusual,' i.e., a complex NP, a one-mora NP (see also Tsutsui, 1984) or a foreign NP (see also Yamaji, 1998), or (4) names a

---

3 Yuko: *e::? shi- sonna koto nain ja nai?*
          'What? kno- (I) don't think that's the case.'
4 →   *Nao chan ga, yoku shitten ja nai?*
          'It is Nao (you) who knows (the restaurants in the area) well, don't you think?'

In response to Nao's remark, Yuko says (line 4), *Nao chan ga yoku shitten ja nai?*, singling out Nao as the only person who knows these restaurants.

concept which is under negotiation.[6] Based on these findings, the authors conclude that *ga* is a pragmatic marker indicating that the *ga*-marked NP is a participant of the state or event represented by the predicate in pragmatically salient situations.

Iwasaki (1985) investigates the possible correlation between *ga*-marking and new information in spoken "pear story" narratives[7] with a particular focus on initial mentions of referents in terms of their grammatical roles, i.e., the subject of a transitive predicate (A), the subject of an intransitive predicate (S), or the direct object of a transitive predicate (O) (following the style of Comrie, 1978 and Dixon, 1979), and postpositional particle markings. He found that human participants were introduced most frequently in the S role (55.3%) and then by the A role (17.6%). The result of his study suggests that Du Bois' (1985) "given A constraint," i.e., avoiding introducing a new referent in the A role, is not fully operative in Japanese narrative discourse. In order to account for the disconformities, Iwasaki discusses, among other factors,[8] the use of *ga* to introduce a new referent into discourse. Out of 62 human referents who were introduced in either the S role or the A role, more than 90 percent (56 referents) were introduced with *ga*-marking.

The use of *ga* is often compared with that of *wa* in terms of given/new and topic/non-topic distinctions (e.g., Kuno, 1972; Hinds and Hinds, 1979; Maynard, 1981; Shibatani, 1990; Noda, 1996). Noda (1996), for example, states that when an NP has previously been introduced into the discourse, the NP can be topicalized by means of *wa*-marking. Thus, if the given NP is marked by *ga*, it means that *ga*-marking is chosen by the speaker over *wa*-marking to indicate the NP's non-topical status (Noda, 1996). Maynard (1981, 1987) also argues that the functions of *wa* and *ga* are in complementary distribution, with *wa* marking topical and *ga* non-topical information. However, this *ga-wa* dichotomy does not provide an account that reflects the use of these particles in actual spoken discourse. As Clancy and Downing (1987) show, many instances of *wa*-marking in spoken discourse do not mark the topical status of the NPs but instead mark a local contrast between *wa*-marked NPs and some other explicit or implicit elements. In addition, *wa*-marking is not the only means to indicate the topical status of an NP; zero-marking, *tte*-marking, the conditional *to ieba*, and zero anaphor are all possible means of encoding topic in Japanese (Suzuki, 1995).

---

[6] The following are some examples presented in Ono et al. (2000):

(1) NP is singled out: (p. 70)

   uchi tte hora onna ga minna dekai ja nai?

   'My family, see women are all big, aren't they?'

(2) NP introduces a concept: (p. 71)

   Harajuku ni Janiizu Shoppu ga dekita no.

   'Johnny's Shop has opened in Harajuku.'

(3) NP is phonologically 'unusual' (complex NP): (p. 68)

   nanka nikkori to suggoi kawaiku waratten no ga atta n da yo ne.

   'There was uh (this) very cute smiling one (i.e., photo).'

(4) NP names a concept which is under negotiation: (p. 72)

   A: *dono ko?* 'Which child?'

   B: *a, ue, oniichan ga.* 'Uh, older, the older brother.'

[7] Native speakers were asked to watch a silent film and describe what happened in the film. For a full description of "the pear stories" film, see Chafe (1980).

[8] Two other factors he presents are the constraint against animate objects and the lack of grammatical devices to place the agent in a non-subject position (Iwasaki, 1985).

This suggests that, in order to uncover its function, we must examine the use of *ga* in actual discourse, going beyond a mere comparison of *ga* and *wa*.

The present study investigates the use of *ga* in conversational discourse and illustrates its role in the discourse topic organization in ongoing interaction. It will demonstrate that conversational participants more often refer to topical NPs using zero anaphora to maintain discourse continuity unless there are some discourse boundaries, in which case *wa*- or zero-markings are employed (see footnote 21 for more details). In contrast, *ga*-marking is employed whenever the conversational participants see the need to explicitly indicate the non-topical status of an NP in order to maintain the topical status of another referent.

Triadic interactional framework

The triadic interactional framework represents the most fundamental structure of human interaction. In their earliest years, infants begin to learn how to establish joint-attentional focus with their caregivers on an object by constantly monitoring the caregivers' attention on both the object and themselves. These behaviors are "triadic in the sense that they involve infants coordinating their interactions with both objects and people, resulting in a referential triangle of child, adult, and the object or event to which they share attention" (Tomasello, 2003, p. 21).

This joint-attention frame (Carpenter, Nagell, & Tomasello, 1998; Tomasello, 2003), or what Du Bois (2007) terms a "stance triangle," is at work in adult-adult communication as well. For instance, when we share our opinion about something with someone, we must first make sure that our partner's attention is focused on the object of evaluation. In infant-adult interactions where interactional participants are face-to-face and the object of attention is physically present, non-linguistic resources such as gaze-following can be used to secure joint attention. On the other hand, in adult-adult conversational interactions, the object of attention is more likely not to be physically present and there may be more than one referent which could be a potential focus of attention. Conversational participants therefore need additional resources to gain and maintain their partners' attention to the object of focus (i.e., a discourse topic). The present study investigates discourse environments where more than one referent is involved in an attempt to demonstrate how the use of *ga*-marking contributes to locally securing and maintaining co-participants' attention to a discourse topic.

Local discourse topic

The notion of topic adopted in this study is a cognitive-pragmatic notion and is defined in terms of "aboutness," that is, what is being talked about (van Dijk, 1977a, 1977b; van Oosten, 1986). There are three dimensions of topic discussed in previous literature: sentential topic, local discourse topic, and global discourse topic. In what follows, the three types of topic are examined in light of the present conversational data (see the section on data for a description of the data). As will be seen later, the analysis of the conversational data suggests that it is the notion of a local discourse topic that is most relevant to the topic organization in Japanese conversational discourse. A local discourse topic is not only the entity about which the information is given at a local level of discourse, but also the focal referential point for various socio-interactional activities by the conversational participants.

Sentential topic

The concept of sentential topic has been effectively utilized in analyzing sentence structures (e.g., Kuno, 1972; Lambrecht, 1994). However, in the analysis of spontaneous conversation, the concept of sentential topic, together with the very concept of a sentence, may not be adequately applied. From the perspective of topicality, it is extremely difficult to identify a sentential topic in conversational data. For example, in excerpt (5) below, the sentences in lines 6, 11, and 12 each have two sentential topic candidates, but neither of them is expressed because of their given information status.

(5) Sentential topic (ja_0862)

1. Mom: *a, moshimoshi?*
   'Uh, hello?'
2. Aya: *un.*
   'Yeah.'
3. Mom: *nanka ne:,*
   'Well,'
4. Aya: *un.*
   'Mhm.'
5. Mom: *ima sono:* [*rokuon no:*],
   'Just now, uh:m, the recording's,'
6. → Aya: (zeroNP) (zeroNP) [*kiita desho*]?
   '(You) heard (it), right?'
7. Mom: [[*un*]].
   'Uh huh.'
8. Aya: [[*un*]].
   'Yeah.'
9. Mom: (zeroNP) *yu*[*tta kara*]?,
   'Because (on the recording, it) said,'
10. Aya: [*soo soo*].
    'Right right.'
11. → (zeroNP) (zeroNP) *ii?*
    '(Are you) fine (with it)?'
12. →Mom: (zeroNP) (zeroNP) *ii yo.*
    '(I'm) fine (with it).'
13. Aya: *hai hai.*
    'Okay.'

We could say that these sentences are about 'the speaker' (line 12) or 'the listener' (lines 6 and 11). At the same time, we could also say that the sentences are about 'the recording' (line 6) or 'being recorded' (lines 11 and 12). The fact that the interlocutors have no trouble understanding each other's utterances indicates that the identification of "sentential" topic is irrelevant or unnecessary in successfully carrying out conversation.

Global discourse topic vs. local discourse topic

In the previous section, we saw that the sentential topic was not a relevant notion to be employed in analyzing conversational discourse. In this section, the concepts of global and local discourse topics are compared in an attempt to understand how "aboutness" (van Dijk, 1977a, 1977b; van Oosten, 1986) is understood by conversational participants.

When we examine the subsequent development of the conversation between Aya and her mother in excerpt (6), we notice that none of the zero NPs in (5) are made into a topic of any larger segment. Instead, the speakers initiate new discourse topics, explicitly marking them with *wa* in lines 17 and 25.

(6) Self-initiated discourse topic (ja_0862)

14. Mom: [*hai*].
    'Yes.'

15. Aya: [*sor*]*ede ne?*
    'And,'

16. Mom: *un.*
    'Yeah.'

17.→Aya: *untenmenkyo wa:,*
    'The driver's license,'

18. *saisho ni jitchi shike- a: gakka shiken to:, me no shiken de ne?*
    'First, (there is a) driving te- u:m a paper test and, an eye exam, and,'

19. Mom: *un.*
    'Uh huh.'

20.→Aya: *tsugini are ga aru no, ano:, ano: ji- jitchi unten?*
    ' Next, there's that, uh:m, uh: a driving test?'

21. Mom: *un.*
    'Yeah.'

22. Aya: *sorede mada ukete nakute:,*
    'And, (I) haven't taken (it),'

23. Mom: *un.*
    'Mhm.'

24. Aya: *un.*
    'Yeah.'

25.→Mom: *jitchi wa sono:,*
    'The driving test uh:m,'

26. *anta, (H) ano: doraibingu suku:ru, iku tte itteta desho:.*
    'You, uh, a driving school, (you) said (you) were going to.'

In line 15, Aya marks the discourse boundary between the previous talk and what is to follow with the coordination marker *sorede*, which can be used to signal a return from a digression to a previously discussed idea (Ito, 1995; Sadler, 2006). In line 17, Aya reintroduces the idea of *untenmenkyo* 'the driver's license (application)' as the topic of discourse with *wa*-marking. Although this idea is not mentioned prior to line 17 in the ongoing telephone conversation, it is evident from her mom's remark in lines 25–26 that the concept is shared and has previously been discussed between the two speakers. The 'driver's license' continues to be treated as the topic until line 25 when Mom narrows the topic down to *jitchi* 'the driving test' with *wa*-marking. The notion of a driving test was initially introduced by Aya as a non-topic with *ga*-marking in line 20. The question is whether to categorize the two discourse topics as local or global. The second topic, 'driving test,' represents a narrower concept than the first topic, 'driver's license,' since the driving test constitutes part of driver's license application process. However, the broader-narrower distinction is not equivalent to the global-local topic distinction.

According to Moya Guijarro (2003), the global discourse topic "represents what a whole text or discourse is about," and "unifies all the local topics of the discourse under the same topical frame" (p. 136). This concept is most compatible with a planned, static, monologic discourse such as a newspaper article or written narrative. These written discourses are explicit with respect to the main topics conveyed in the form of headlines and titles.

Unlike planned written discourse, conversational discourse is generally spontaneous, dynamic, context-dependent, and interactive (Linell, 1982; Ong, 1982; Clancy, 1982). Because there is no top-down topic organizational framework in unplanned conversation, the concept of a global discourse topic is of little relevance. Since conversation does not have a self-contained beginning and end, although it is situated in a larger socio-interactional context, it is unfeasible for a researcher to judge the global-ness of a discourse topic. For these reasons, I regard explicitly marked discourse topics such as 'the driver's license' and 'the driving test' in the previous excerpt as "local" rather than "global" discourse topics.

In written narratives, having explicit global discourse topics in the form of titles affords more flexibility in shifting local topics in the course of the story itself. In my informal analysis of the folk tale *Momotaroo* 'Peach Boy' (Nishiyama, 1966), for instance, the protagonist *Momotaroo* is marked by *ga* in main clauses three times after its initial introduction while the supporting character *inu* 'dog' is marked by *wa* four times after its initial mention. Because the writers can assume that the readers understand *Momotaroo* as the main character and global topic of the story, they can freely shift local topics by means of *wa* and *ga* markings in a sentence-by-sentence fashion.

In contrast to written narratives, topic-maintenance or topic-shifting in everyday conversation must be accomplished dialogically since there is no top-down global discourse topic governing the entire conversation, as shown in (5)–(6). Collaborative establishment and maintenance of a local topic is important in conversational interaction as the local topic serves as the common target of expressing and sharing of perspectives and attitudes by the conversational participants within a triadic interactional framework. Securing joint attention to a common local topic becomes especially challenging when there is more than one potentially topical referent involved. The section on function of *ga* will illustrate the role of *ga* in marking a non-topical participant, thereby contributing to establishing and maintaining a joint attention to a local discourse topic.

Data

Data for this study comes from 10 face-to-face conversations[9] and 11 telephone conversations,[10] totaling over three hours of talk in length. All the conversational

---

[9] I would like to thank Tsuyoshi Ono for allowing me to use his data for this project.
[10] The data comes from Canavan and Zipperlen (1996) and Wheatley, Kaneko, and Kobayashi (1996).

participants are adult native speakers of Tokyo Japanese, and each conversation consists of either family members, close friends, or couples.

In the present study, I will limit the discussion to *ga*-attached human referents. This decision is based on the findings from past studies and my preliminary observation that *ga*-marked non-human referents appear in environments that are different from those in which *ga*-marked human referents appear.[11]

Function of *ga* as non-topical subject marker

New and given information status

Contrary to the claim that *ga* marks new information (e.g., Kuno, 1972), in the conversational data examined for this study, more than half of the *ga*-marked human referents (hereafter HR) represent given information,[12] as shown in Table 1.

Table 1. Information status of ga-marked HRs (in 21 conversational data)

	new	given	total
ga-marked HR	70 (45.8%)	83 (54.2%)	153 (100%)

One notable difference in the distribution of new and given *ga*-marked HRs is the type of predicates that follow them. As we can see in Table 2, the majority of the HR occurrences with existential predicates, i.e., *iru* 'exist' are new (79.3%).[13] This tendency is in accordance with the universal trend of introducing a new referent in conversation by referring to its existence (Givón, 2001). It also parallels the previous finding that *ga*-marking and existential verbs are strongly connected with the practice of new referent introductions in Japanese conversation (Kuno, 1972; Ono et al., 2000).

Table 2. *Ga*-marked new/given HRs and types of predicates

	new HR	given HR	total
existential predicate (*iru*)	23 (79.3%)	6 (20.7%)	29 (100%)
non-existential predicate	47 (37.9%)	77 (62.1%)	124 (100%)

A new referent introduced with *ga*-marking and the existential predicate *iru* may be subsequently topicalized as in (7), but the majority are only mentioned once in the ongoing discourse, as in (8).

(7) Subsequently topicalized new referent (*Ryuugaku*)

1. Chie: ... *nanka, uchi no kurasu ni [sa:, .. sono,]*

   'well, in my class, ... uh,'

---

[11] *Ga*-marked non-human NPs appear in the grammatical object position (e.g., Sugamoto, 1982; Ono et al., 2000) and some of the *ga*-marked non-human NPs appear to be lexicalized (Ono et al., 2000). *Ga*-marked human NPs may also appear in the syntactic object position, but the number of such NPs is extremely low compared to non-human NPs. In my data, I did not find any *ga*-marked human NPs in the object position.

[12] 'Given information' here refers to information that has been mentioned in the preceding discourse context, and thus likely to be active in the mind of the addressee (Chafe, 1994).

[13] The verb *iru* 'exist' is used with animate subjects. The inanimate counterpart of *iru* is *aru*. Since the present study only deals with *ga*-marked human referents, only *iru* is relevant here.

2. Fumi: [*kanbase*]*eshon*, ... *paato*[[*naa*]].
'conversation partner.'

3. Chie: [[*un*]].
'Yeah.'

4.→ ... *nihonjin no*, ... *otoko no*, ... *nijuusan gurai no hito ga*, *hitori iru-n* [*da kedo*],
'there is one Japanese, male, a person about 23 years old,'

5. Fumi: [*un un*].
'Mhm.'

6.→Chie: ... *sono hito wa nanka*, .. *isha ni narita-* ... *naritakute:*, *Amerika ni kitan da tte*.
'that person said (he) came to America to become a doctor.'

(8) Single-mentioned new referent (*Bukatsu*)

1. Ken: ... *yakyuu wa mada*, *dekiru kedo*,

2. ... *regyuraa wa*, .. *kore mo*, *dame jan*.
'(I) can play baseball fairly well, but (as far as) becoming a regular member, this is also impossible.'

3. Emi: ... [*un*].
'Yeah.'

4.→Ken: [*chuu*]*gakkoo kara yatteru yatsu ga*, *iru kara*.
'because there are those who have played it since middle school.'

In (7), a new referent is introduced with *ga*-marking in line 4, and in line 6, the same referent, now referred to as *sono hito* 'that person,' is explicitly marked by *wa*. The referent remains the topic for the next 70 IUs. (8) represents an instance of single-mentioned *ga*-marked new HRs introduced with the predicate *iru* 'exist.' These HRs are either non-referential (i.e., there is no specific referent for the NP) or unimportant referential nouns which are mentioned only once in the ongoing discourse. In (8), Ken explains why he would not become a regular member if he joined the baseball club at his high school. The *ga*-marked HR in line 4, *chuugakoo kara yatteru yatsu* 'those who have played (baseball) since middle school,' is non-referential and is mentioned only once in the entire conversation.

However, not all newly introduced HRs are subsequently topicalized or disappear after initial mention. Some *ga*-marked new HRs continue to be marked by *ga* in the subsequent mentions. These are *ga*-marked given HRs,[14] which is the focus of the next section.

Ga-marked given referents

In this section, I will present actual instances of *ga*-marked given HRs from the conversational data to demonstrate the function of *ga* in marking a non-topical subject. The first example comes from a story-telling sequence in which one of the speakers, Ken, recalls his after-school sports club experience in high school. The story features himself and a martial arts teacher (*kakugi no sensee*), who also turns out to be the judo club coach

---

[14] Not all *ga*-marked given HRs are initially introduced into the discourse with *ga*-marking. For example, if they are introduced in an object position, they may be marked by *o*, and if they are introduced in a dative position, they may be marked by *ni*.

(*juudoobu no komon*). Both participants have been introduced into the discourse prior to the following segment.

(9) *Ga*-marked given referent (*Bukatsu*)

1.→Ken: *tsugi no hi, ore, kaettetan da* [*yo*].

'The next day, I was going home.'

2. Emi: [*u*]*n*.

'Yeah.'

(several IUs omitted)

3. Ken: *kaetteta ra, ... tochuu de sa, ...*

4.→ *sono komon ga sa, ..*

'And as (I) was going home, that coach,'

5. Emi: *un. ..*

'Uh huh.'

6. Ken: *mukoo kara, aruite kite sa. ...*

'came walking towards (me),'

7. Emi: *n. ...*

'Mm.'

8. Ken: *mada, .. gakkoo, deru mae ni* [*ne*].

'Before (I) left school.'

9. Emi: [*un*].

'Yeah.'

10. Ken: *de sa, kyoo, renshuu wa dooshita, toka* @*itte.*

'And then, (he) said something like "what happened to the practice today?" '

(several IUs omitted)

11.→Emi: @*demo,* @*soshitara, ... nani:,*

12.→ *shizen ni haitchatta,* @*mitai* @*na kanji na no?*

'Then, is it like (you) joined (the judo club) unintentionally?'

At the beginning of the segment, Ken explicitly establishes himself as the primary participant of the subsequent discourse through zero-marked *ore* 'I'. First person pronouns are employed recurrently in conversational discourse to mark their discourse topic status (cf. Ono & Thompson, 2004). After providing short supplementary information in the first omitted IUs (that he went to the practice that day but did not stay), Ken makes an explicit reference to the judo club coach in line 4 with *ga*-marking. The given information status of the coach is evident from the use of the demonstrative pronoun *sono* 'that' as a discourse deictic. Then, in the immediately following context, Ken reports what the coach told him. Emi's utterance in lines 11–12 is a question about how Ken ended up joining the judo club (rather than, say, how the coach persuaded Ken to join the club). Despite the fact that the coach is crucially involved in the action sequence, Emi's utterance, which includes the predicate *haitchatta* 'entered,' clearly demonstrates that she understands the narrative segment as being about Ken instead of the coach. The use of the first pronoun *ore* 'I' in line 1 and the *ga*-marking in line 4 both contribute to jointly establish and maintain the local discourse topic, i.e., Ken. That is, *ga*-marking explicitly tells the addressee (Emi) that the coach is a non-topical referent and thus not the main target of comment.

The next example also involves the speaker and third person HRs as participants in a sequence of actions.

(10)   *Ga*-marked given referent (*Nihongo*)

1. Yuko: *de watashi wa tomodachi to shabettete:,*

    'and I was talking with a friend,'

2.   *de sono hito ni tsuite, komento o shiteta no yo.*

    'and commenting on that person.'

    (several IUs omitted)

3.→   *shitara sono futari ga:,*

    'then those two,'

4.   *totsuzen, eego de shabetteta noni:,*

    'though they were talking in English, suddenly,'

5.   [@*koro* @*tto* @*nihongo* @*de*] @*hanashi* @*dashite*,

    '(they) began speaking in Japanese,'

6. Nao: [*nihongo ni suicchi shita no*]?,

    '(they) switched to Japanese?'

7. Yuko: @*watashitachi no hoo o mita* @*no.*

    '(they) looked at us.'

8.   ... <VOX> *u* </VOX> @*to* @*omotte*,

    '(I) thought "ugh,"'

9.   *cho- chotto atozusari shitari shite,*

    'and (I) stepped back a bit,'

In (10), Yuko shares her embarrassing experience which resulted from her assuming that two strangers standing in front of her and her Japanese friend did not understand Japanese.[15] In line 3, the two strangers, who represent given information as evident from the use of *sono* 'those,' are marked by *ga*. The explicit encoding of the two strangers as non-topical entities helps maintain *watashi* (Yuko) as the local discourse topic. Notice that the second occurrence of the topic *watashi* (Yuko) in line 8 is zero anaphor. In the immediately subsequent discourse, Yuko clarifies what she said about one of the strangers upon Nao's request and gives the moral of the story by saying *ki o tsukenai to* '(I/we) have to be careful (not to assume a person does not understand Japanese just by his/her looks)'. Her remark confirms that her talk was about her and not the two strangers.

---

[15] Yuko's story is a response, or a "second" story, to Nao's preceding story about an American musician at a concert and how he unexpectedly and surprisingly spoke fluent Japanese. In general, a "second" story is related to the first one and displays how the teller of the second story understands the first story (e.g., Ryave, 1978; Sacks, 1992).

The previous two examples involved the speakers as the topical referents. The next excerpts, (11) and (12), each involve two third person participants, with one of them marked by *ga*. In (11), a married couple Mika (wife) and Ryo (husband) are talking about Mika's friend's plan to travel to Australia.

(11) *Ga*-marked given referent (*Ryokoo*)

1. Mika: ... *soshitara, kekkyoku nanka,*
   'and then, in the end,'
2. → *kareshi ga:,*
   'her boyfriend,'
3. Ryo: *un.*
   'Yeah.'
4. Mika: .. *shigoto ga ne, ... nanka, taihen de:, ... isogashikute:,*
   '(his) work was, like, troublesome, and busy,'
5. ... *de, yasumi ga, torenai toka i- tsutte,*
   'and, (he) said (he) can't take time off work,'
6. Ryo: .. *arara.*
   'Oh no.'
7. Mika: ... *nde:, ... iku?*[16]
   'and, the day of leaving?'
8. Ryo: ... *un.*
   'Yeah.'
9. Mika: .. *isshuukan mae, toka itta ka na?*
   'a week before that, or something like that?'
10. Ryo: .. *kyanseru?*
    'Cancel?'
11. Mika: ... *un.*
    'Right.'

The boyfriend (i.e., Mika's friend's boyfriend) has been introduced into the discourse prior to the segment. Nevertheless, the boyfriend is marked by *ga* in line 2. This segment consists entirely of the boyfriend's actions with no mention of Mika's friend, yet both Ryo and Mika understand that the discourse is about Mika's friend, not her boyfriend. This is clearly shown in the subsequent discourse when Ryo asks Mika *okotteta?* 'was (X) mad?' with subject ellipsis. Because the boyfriend was excluded from the possibility of being the local discourse topic through *ga*-marking, Ryo sees no need to explicitly state the topic of his question. Mika immediately understands the question with an unexpressed topic to be about her friend as she answers *moo atama ni kichau toka tte, ... atashi yori shigoto o totta tte koto da yo ne toka* "(My friend said) '(I'm) so upset,' (she said) 'it means that (he) chose his work over me, right?'" The conversation continues as Mika tells Ryo that the boyfriend actually did not tell his boss about the vacation plan at all because the company was too busy at that time.

---

[16] According to my transcription conventions, [?] simply indicates rising intonation, not a question.

Here too, when the boyfriend is overtly referred to in the subject position, he is marked by *ga* (*jibun ga* 'he himself').[17] In this way, *ga* explicitly marks the persistent HR as non-topical, which contributes to maintaining the conversational participants' attention to the local discourse topic, in this case, Mika's friend.

In the next excerpt (12), Tae is telling her sister Iyo about Tae's friend and how the friend had an arranged marriage with a politician. The politician was introduced into the discourse prior to the segment.

(12)   *Ga*-marked given referent (*Ojoosama*)

1.→Tae: ... *de soko ni, seijika no hito ga ittete,*

'and the politician was there,'

2.   .. *motte* .. *n mo nai hanashi,*[18] *mitai na toko atte:,*

'it was sort of like a windfall (for her parents),'

3.   ... *demo,* ... *kan-* .. *genjitsu ni:,*

'but, in reality,'

4.→   *kare ga,* .. *ofisu ni dehairi shite,*

'he was in and out of the office,'

5.   *kanojo no koto o, ki ni itchatta kara:.*[19]

'and because he took a fancy to her.'

6. Iyo: .. *un.*

'Yeah.'

Despite its given information status, the politician is marked by *ga* twice in lines 1 (*seijika no hito ga*) and 4 (*kare ga*). Unlike the previous excerpt, in (12), both the politician and Tae's friend (*kanojo*) are mentioned. However, as we can see in lines 4–5, the politician appears as the subject/agent while Tae's friend is the object/patient. As the subject/agent is much more likely to be treated as the discourse topic than the object/patient (Givón, 1983; Noda, 1996),

---

[17] The following is Mika's subsequent utterance following the excerpt (11):

1. *kaisha ga, dame da, tte itteru wake ja, nai rashii no yo.*

   '(It) seems that it is not the company that is saying that he cannot go on a vacation (lit. it is not okay).'

2. *jibun ga,* (several IUs omitted), *fudoosangyoo nan da kedo, ima chotto sugoi, isogashikute,*

   'He himself, (several IUs omitted), (the company) is a real-estate business, and (it) is very busy right now,'

3. (several IUs omitted) *soo iu toki ni, jibun dake nanka, yasumi toru no mo, ya da shi,*

   'In such a (busy) time, just he himself, um, did not want to take time off work.'

[18] It is difficult to tell whether the speaker is saying *omottemo nai hanashi* 'windfall' or *mottainai hanashi* 'more than one deserves.' The former interpretation is chosen here because it seems more appropriate in this particular context. In either case, the interpretation of this phrase does not affect the analysis of *ga*.

[19] *Kara* 'because' is a conjunctive particle. It generally marks an adverbial subordinate clause indicating the cause of an effect, but utterance final *kara* is also commonly observed in conversation (Iguchi, 1998; Haugh, 2008). *Kara* in line 5 is of the latter kind.

explicit marking of the politician as a non-topical entity is crucial to achieve or maintain the joint attention to the intended discourse topic, i.e., Tae's friend. In the subsequent discourse, Tae's friend remains as the focal point of their conversation as they talk about how Tae's friend ended up marrying the politician instead of her boyfriend.

In this section, it has been argued that the function of *ga* is to explicitly indicate non-topicality of the NP through the analysis of four conversational excerpts involving two persistent human referents (HR). Table 3 summarizes the topical referents and the *ga*-marked non-topical referents in the four conversations. In the next section, these topical NPs and *ga*-marked NPs will be further scrutinized using two quantitative measurements of topicality.

Table 3.   Topical and *ga*-marked referents

excerpt	topic	*ga*-marked
Bukatsu	1st (speaker)	3rd (club coach)
Nihongo	1st (speaker)	3rd (two strangers)
Ryokoo	3rd (speaker's friend)	3rd (friend's boyfriend)
Ojoosama	3rd (speaker's friend)	3rd (politician)

Referent persistence vs. topicality

According to the hierarchy of topicality (Givón, 1976, p. 152), a definite human referent who is more involved in the event or state under discussion is more likely to be a topic or what is being talked about. Givón (1983, p. 22) further notes that grammatical subjects and semantic agents are higher in the topicality hierarchy and thus more likely to be topics than other grammatical or semantic roles. From this perspective, two or more of the human referents that appeared in the previous four conversational segments all rank high in the topicality hierarchy.

As a more concrete measurement of topicality, Givón (1983) proposes two cross-linguistic quantitative measurements: (a) referential distance and (b) decay. These measurements are based on the assumption that topical referents figure more frequently in the discourse. Such measurements have been employed for Japanese data in previous research (e.g., Hinds, 1983; Clancy & Downing, 1987). Here are short descriptions of the two measurements (Hinds, 1983).

> (a) Distance—the distance from the present mention of a noun phrase by a particular device [(e.g., ellipsis, independent NP or pronoun, NP or pronoun marked by a particle)] to the last clause where the same referent was a semantic argument of that clause, in numbers of clauses. In a values of 1 to 20, 1 represents maximum continuity while 20 represents minimum continuity.
>
> (b) Decay—the number of clauses to the right from [the mention of a noun phrase in which] ... the same referent remains a semantic argument of the clause. The minimal value is zero, signifying an argument that decays immediately and hence minimum continuity. There is no maximal value (the higher the number, the greater the persistence). (p. 58)

In short, the distance looks back at the preceding context and measures the number of clauses between the current mention of the NP and the previous mention of the same NP, with a smaller number representing a higher continuity. The decay looks forward at the subsequent context and counts the number of clauses in which the NP continues to appear as a semantic argument (a higher number represents a higher persistence). I will refer to the two measurements as "persistence" for convenience. In order to compare the persistence of *ga*-marked and topical referents, I measured referential distance and decay. Table 4 presents the results of referential distance and decay measurements.

Table 4. Referential persistence measurements

excerpts	distance		decay	
	topic	*ga*-marked	topic	*ga*-marked
Bukatsu	1	1	11	8
Nihongo	1	1	4	3
Ryokoo	1	1	9	9
Ojoosama	1	1	4	3
average	1	1	7	5.75

The referential distance values in Table 4 indicate that both topical and *ga*-marked referents are maximally continuous. The difference in decay values between topical referents and *ga*-marked referents is found to be statistically non-significant, $t(3)=1.99$, $p=0.14$.[20] As mentioned before, the basic rationale for Givón's two referent persistence measurements is the assumption that the more important a referent is, the more frequently it appears in the current discourse. Based on this principle, both topical and *ga*-marked given referents are important as they both show high persistence values. In other words, the results show that both referents have high topicality. The quantitative findings substantiate the motivation for non-topical referent marking. The speakers exploit *ga*-marking to avoid the potential interference between the two persistent referents. Although *ga*-marked referents are crucial participants in the unfolding action sequence, they are explicitly marked as the non-focal reference point for socio-interactional exchanges between the conversational participants.

The question remains as to why the conversational participants explicitly mark the non-topical referent by *ga* instead of marking the topical referent by *wa* or other linguistic means. As we saw above, in informal conversation, zero anaphora is the unmarked form representing referent continuity (cf. Clancy, 1980; Hinds, 1983; Suzuki, 1995). Both *wa*-marked and zero-marked phrases indicate the topicality of referents, and as Suzuki (1995) and Iwasaki (1997) have found, they also express discourse boundaries.[21] When there is more than one persistent referent in the ongoing discourse, there are competing motivations between maintaining referent continuity and indicating the topicality or non-topicality of the referents. The findings in the present study suggest that the conversational participants prefer to refer to topical referents by zero anaphora to maintain discourse continuity unless there are some discourse boundaries to be marked, in which case *wa*- or zero-markings are employed.[22] In contrast, non-topical

---

[20] A paired t-test was used to compare decay values between topical referents and *ga*-marked referents.

[21] In the present conversational data, *wa*-marked *watashi* 'I' in (10) and zero-marked *ore* 'I' in (9) express discourse boundaries. According to Suzuki's (1995) findings, *wa*-marked phrases express major discourse boundaries while zero-marked phrases express minor discourse boundaries. Iwasaki (1997) calls these discourse boundaries "(unit-)floor transition."

[22] *Wa*-markings are also employed to mark contrastiveness (Clancy & Downing, 1987).

referents are marked by *ga* whenever the conversational participants see the need to explicitly indicate the non-topicality of the referent so as to keep the other referent's topical status.

Conclusion

This study examined one discourse-pragmatic function of the so-called subject marker *ga* in conversational discourse in the light of the triadic interactional framework. Conversational participants constantly monitor each other's attention and alignment not only to themselves but also to the local discourse topic on which they share their comments and perspectives. Achieving and maintaining joint attention to a common topic is especially challenging when there is more than one potentially topical referent continuously involved in the ongoing discourse. We have seen that *ga*-marking is an important grammatical device that conversational participants draw on to explicitly indicate the non-topical status of the referent, thereby contributing to successful socio-interactional communication.

Acknowledgments

The author would like to thank the audience at the 2011 ATJ Annual Conference for their helpful feedback. The author is also indebted to Maggie Camp, Shoichi Iwasaki, Michio Tsutsui, and two anonymous reviewers for their invaluable comments and suggestions. Of course, the author alone is responsible for any remaining shortcomings.

References

Canavan, A., & Zipperlen, G. (1996). *CALLHOME Japanese Speech*. Philadelphia, PA: Linguistic Data Consortium.

Carpenter, M., Nagell, K., & Tomasello, M. (1998). Social cognition, joint attention, and communicative competence from 9 to 15 months of age. *Monographs of the Society for Research in Child Development, 63*(4), 1–143.

Chafe, W. (1994). *Discourse, consciousness, and time: The flow and displacement of conscious experience in speaking and writing*. Chicago, IL: The University of Chicago Press.

Chafe, W. (Ed.). (1980). *The pear stories: Cognitive, cultural, and linguistic aspects of narrative production*. Norwood, NJ: Ablex.

Clancy, P. (1980). Referential choice in English and Japanese narrative discourse. In W. Chafe (Ed.), *The pear stories: Cognitive, cultural, and linguistic aspects of narrative production*. (pp. 127–201). Norwood, NJ: Ablex.

Clancy, P. (1982). Written and spoken style in Japanese narratives. In D. Tannen (Ed.), *Spoken and written language: Exploring orality and literacy* (pp. 55–76). Norwood, NJ: Ablex.

Clancy, P. & Downing, P. (1987). The use of *wa* as a cohesion marker in Japanese oral narratives. In J. Hinds, S. K. Maynard, & S. Iwasaki (Eds.), *Perspectives on topicalization: The case of Japanese wa* (pp. 3–56). Amsterdam, The Netherlands: Benjamins.

Comrie, B. (1978). Ergativity. In W. P. Lehmann (Ed.), *Syntactic typology* (pp. 329–94). Austin: University of Texas Press.

Dixon, R. M. W. (1979). Ergativity. *Language, 55*, 59–138.

Du Bois, J. W. (1985). Competing motivations. In J. Haiman (Ed.), *Iconicity and syntax* (pp. 343–365). Amsterdam, The Netherlands: Benjamins.

Du Bois, J. W., (2007). The stance triangle. In R. Englebretson (Ed.), *Stancetaking in discourse* (pp. 139–182). Amsterdam, The Netherlands: Benjamins.

Du Bois, J., Schuetze-Coburn, S., Cumming, S., & Paolino, D. (1993). Outline of discourse transcription. In J. Edwards & M. Lampert (Eds.), *Talking data: Transcription and coding in discourse research* (pp. 45–89). Hillsdale, NJ: Erlbaum.

Givón, T. (1976). Topic, pronoun and grammatical agreement. In C. Li (Ed.). *Subject and topic* (pp. 149–187). New York, NY: Academic Press.

Givón, T. (1983). Topic continuity in discourse: An introduction. In T. Givón (Ed.), *Topic continuity in discourse* (pp. 1–41). Amsterdam, The Netherlands: Benjamins.

Givón, T. (2001). *Syntax: An introduction* (Vol. 2). Amsterdam, The Netherlands: Benjamins.

Haugh, M. (2008). Utterance-final conjunctive particles and implicature in Japanese conversation. *Pragmatics, 18*(3), 425–451.

Hayashi, M. (2004). Discourse within a sentence: An exploration of postpositions in Japanese as an interactional resource. *Language in Society, 33*, 343–376.

Hinds, J. (1983). Topic continuity in Japanese. In T. Givón (Ed.), *Topic continuity in discourse* (pp. 43–93). Amsterdam, The Netherlands: Benjamins.

Hinds, J., & Hinds, W. (1979). Participant identification in Japanese narrative discourse. In G. Bedell, E. Kobayashi, & M. Muraki (Eds.), *Explorations in linguistics: Papers in honor of Kazuko Inoue* (pp. 201–212). Tokyo, Japan: Kenkyusha.

Iguchi, Y. (1998). Functional variety in the Japanese conjunctive particle *kara* 'because.' In T. Ohori (Ed.), *Studies in Japanese grammaticalization. Cognitive and discourse perspectives*. (pp. 99–128). Tokyo, Japan: Kuroshio.

Ito, R. (1995). *The function of the Japanese conjunction (sore)de as a discourse marker* (Unpublished master's thesis). Michigan State University, East Lansing.

Iwasaki, S. (1985). The "given A constraint" and the Japanese particle *ga*. In S. De Lancey & R. S. Tomlin (Eds.), *Proceedings of the First Annual Meeting of the Pacific Linguistic Conference* (pp. 152–67). Eugene: University of Oregon Press.

Iwasaki, S. (1997). The Northridge earthquake conversations: The floor structure and the 'loop' sequence in Japanese conversation. *Journal of Pragmatics, 28*, 661–693.

Iwasaki, S. (forthcoming). Grammar of the internal expressive sentences in Japanese: Observations and explorations. In K. Kabata & T. Ono (Eds.), *Functional approaches to Japanese grammar: Toward the understanding of human language*. Stanford, CA: CSLI Publications.

Kuno, S. (1972). Functional sentence perspective: A case study from Japanese and English. *Linguistic Inquiry, 3*, 269–320.

Kuno, S. (1973). *The structure of the Japanese language*. Cambridge, MA: MIT Press.

Lambrecht, K. (1994). *Information structure and sentence form: A theory of topic, focus, and the mental representations of discourse referents*. Cambridge, United Kingdom: Cambridge University Press.

Linell, P. (1982). *The written language bias in linguistics (Studies in Communication 2)* Linköping, Sweden: Linköping University.

Masunaga, K. (1988). Case deletion and discourse context. In W. J. Poser (Ed.), *Papers from the second international workshop on Japanese syntax* (pp. 145–56). Stanford, CA: CSLI.

Maynard, S. (1981). The given/new distinction and the analysis of the Japanese particles *-wa* and *-ga*. *Papers in Linguistics, 14*, 109–30.

Maynard, S. (1987). Thematization as a staging device in the Japanese narrative. In J. Hinds, S. Maynard, & S. Iwasaki (Eds.), *Perspectives on topicalization: The case of Japanese 'wa'* (pp. 57–82). Amsterdam, The Netherlands: Benjamins.

Moya Guijarro, A. J. (2003). Thematic and topical structuring in three subgenres: A contrastive study. *Miscelánea, 27,* 131–53.

Nishiyama, T. (1966). *Momotaroo [Peach boy].* Tokyo, Japan: Shogakukan.

Noda, H. (1996). *Wa to Ga* [Wa and Ga]. Tokyo, Japan: Kuroshio.

Ong, W. J. (1982). *Orality and literacy: The technologizing of the word.* London, United Kingdom: Routledge.

Ono, T., & Thompson, S. (2004). Japanese (w)atashi/ore/boku 'I': They're not just pronouns. *Cognitive Linguistics, 14*(4), 321–347.

Ono, T., Thompson, S., & Suzuki, R. (2000). The pragmatic nature of the so-called subject marker "*ga*" in Japanese: Evidence from conversation. *Discourse studies, 2*(1), 55–84.

Ryave, A. (1978). On the achievement of a series of stories. In J. Schenkein (Ed.), *Studies in the organization of conversational interaction* (pp. 113–132). New York, NY: Academic Press.

Sacks, H. (1992). *Lectures on conversation* (Vol. 1). Oxford, United Kingdom: Blackwell.

Sadler, M. (2006). A blurring of categorization: The Japanese connective *de* in spontaneous conversation. *Discourse Studies, 8,* 303–323.

Shibatani, M. (1990). *The Languages of Japan.* Cambridge, United Kingdom: Cambridge University Press.

Sugamoto, N. (1982). Transitivity and objecthood in Japanese. In P. Hopper and S. Thompson (Eds.), *Syntax and semantics, 15: Studies in transitivity* (pp. 423–447). New York, NY: Academic Press.

Sunakawa, Y. (2005). *Bunpoo to Danwa no Setten* [The Interface between Grammar and Discourse]. Tokyo, Japan: Kuroshio.

SuzUki, S. (1995). The functions of topic-encoding zero-marked phrases: A study of the interaction among topic-encoding expressions in Japanese. *Journal of Pragmatics, 23,* 607–626.

Tanaka, H. (1999). *Turn-taking in Japanese conversation: A study in grammar in interaction.* Amsterdam, The Netherlands: Benjamins.

Tomasello, M. (2003). *Constructing a language: A usage-based theory of language acquisition.* Cambridge, MA: Harvard University Press.

Tsutsui, M. (1983). Ellipsis of Ga. *Papers in Japanese Linguistics, 9,* 199–244.

Tsutsui, M. (1984). *Particle Ellipses in Japanese* (Unpublished doctoral dissertation). University of Illinois at Urbana-Champaign, Urbana-Champaign.

van Dijk, T. (1977a). Sentence topic and discourse topic. *Papers in Slavic Philosophy, 1,* 49–61.

van Dijk, T. (1977b). *Text and Context: Explorations in the Semantics and pragmatics of discourse.* New York, NY: Longman.

van Oosten, J. (1986). *The nature of subjects, topics, and agents: A cognitive explanation.* Bloomington: Indiana University Linguistics Club.

Wheatley, B., Kaneko, M., & Kobayashi, M. (1996). *CALLHOME Japanese Speech.* Philadelphia, PA: Linguistic Data Consortium.

Yamaji, H. (1998). *Ga-ellipsis in Japanese.* (Unpublished manuscript). Department of East Asian Studies, University of Arizona, Tucson.

Appendix: Transcription conventions

..	pause, short (<150 milliseconds)
...	pause, untimed (>150 milliseconds)
:	prosodic lengthening
[ ]	overlap (single)
[[ ]]	overlap (second instance)
(H)	inhalation
@word	laughter during the production of the word
wor-	word truncation
–	truncated intonation unit
<VOX> </VOX>	voice of another

「の」名詞化構文についての一考察：主要部内在型関係節とその周辺

A Study of the *No*-clause Construction in Japanese: Internally Headed Relative Clauses and Beyond

苗曉曼 (Xiaoman Miao)
スタンフォード大学 *(Stanford University)*

要旨

本章は「リンゴが机の上にあるのをとって食べた」のような, 主要部名詞が関係節の中に位置する, いわゆる「主要部内在型関係節」について論じる。従来の研究では重視されなかった主文動詞の項と主要部名詞との対応関係を考察した結果をもとに, 主要部内在型関係節は関係節とは言えず,「の」名詞化構文であることを主張する。そして, Croft (2001)のRadical Construction Grammar のアプローチを用いて,「の」名詞化構文全般の意味論的・語用論的特徴を考察することにより, 異なるカテゴリとされてきた関係節, 副詞節, 動詞補文および重文が, 実は「の」名詞化構文をを介して繋がり合った連続体をなすことを示す。さらに, これは日本語特有の言語現象ではなく, 他言語にも多く見られる現象で, 日本語の「の」名詞化構文 についても, 意味論的な観点を取り入れることにより「の」名詞化構文全体の妥当な分析が可能になることを主張する。

Abstract

This chapter discusses so-called "internally headed relative clauses" (IHRCs) in modern Japanese in which the head noun is placed inside the relative clause, as in the sentence *ringo-ga tukue-no ue-ni aru no-o totte tabeta* 'I picked up an apple which was (lit. is) on the desk and ate it.' The relationship between the nominalized argument of the main clause verb and the so-called head noun inside the IHRC has been neglected in previous studies. By examining this relationship,

---

Miao, X. (2013). 「の」名詞化構文についての一考察：主要部内在型関係節とその周辺 [A study of the no-clause construction in Japanese: Internally headed relative clauses and beyond]. In K. Kondo-Brown, Y. Saito-Abbott, S. Satsutani, M. Tsutsui, & A. Wehmeyer (Eds.), *New perspectives on Japanese language learning, linguistics, and culture* (pp. 145–161). Honolulu: University of Hawai'i, National Foreign Language Resource Center.

I argue that this construction in fact does not fit the definition of a relative clause, but rather should be seen as a construction marked by the bound nominalizer *no*. Furthermore, by adopting the approach of the Radical Construction Grammar developed by Croft (2001), I examine various semantic and pragmatic functions of this construction, and propose that the *no*-clause construction can span across the four prototypes of complex sentences, namely, relative clauses, adverbials clauses, complements, and coordination, and makes those Japanese complex sentences a unified continuum. This versatility of nominalization is not limited to Japanese and is observed in other languages as well.

はじめに

「主要部内在型関係節」の議論に入る前に，まず「関係節」一般について述べる。現代日本語においては，下記のような二種類の関係節がある。

(1) a. 太郎は [皿の上にあった] リンゴをとって，ポケットにいれた。

b. 太郎は [リンゴが皿の上にあったの] をとって，ポケットにいれた。

(1a)は通常の関係節で，ここでは [ ] 内の「皿の上にあった」が「リンゴ」を修飾し，普通，この部分が関係節と呼ばれる。そして，修飾される名詞や名詞句は「主要部名詞」[1]と呼ばれる。(1a)の関係節は，修飾される主要部「リンゴ」が関係節「皿の上にあった」の外に位置するため，「主要部外在型関係節」とも呼ばれる。これに対し，(1b)では，主要部名詞「リンゴ」が関係節の内部に位置し，主要部の位置に「リンゴ」の代わりに名詞化標識の「の」が置かれている。このように，「の」を含めて，主要部が節内に位置する関係節([ ]で表記)は「主要部内在型関係節」と呼ばれる。この場合は，節内の「リンゴ」が主要部名詞となる。

現代日本語における主要部内在型関係節は，Kuroda (1976)により，修飾や限定をされる主要部名詞が関係節の中に位置し，主要部名詞のかわりに名詞化標識の「の」が後続するものと定義された。その文法的役割については様々な議論がなされてきたが，名詞節説の代表であるKuroda(1976, 1992)，および黒田(1998, 1999, 2005)は，主要部内在型関係節は全体として名詞節として機能し，後続する主節動詞の格助詞の要求にかなう「格の一致現象」が見られると主張している。これに対して，三原(1994)は黒田の「格の一致現象」には問題があり，主要部内在型関係節は副詞節の性質を持つと主張した。さらに，坪本 (1997)は名詞節と副詞節の両方の性質を持つという二重性を提案した(詳しくは「内在型関係節の文法的機能」の節参照)。本章は主要部内在型関係節に関し，以下の三つの問題について論じる。

- 主要部内在型関係節と呼ばれる構造の定義は妥当か。
- 主要部内在型関係節のカテゴリは名詞節なのか副詞節なのか，あるいはそれ以外なのか(例えば，動詞補文)。
- このような構文は日本語だけの現象なのか。

本章はこれらの問題について考察し，以下の三点を主張する。

- Croft (2001) のRadical Construction Grammar (RCG)のアプローチを用いた，「の」名詞化構文で示される内容と主要部名詞との対応関係の考察結果から，主文の動詞にかかるものは主要部名詞ではなく，「の」名詞化構文全体の内容であり，

1　英語のように関係節が主要部名詞の後に位置する場合は先行名詞ともいう。

主要部内在型関係節は厳密には関係節ではなく,「の」名詞化構文(以下「の構文」)である。
- 「の構文」は関係節, 副詞節, 動詞補文, 重文と連続的に繋がり合う。
- このように名詞化構文が関係節, 副詞節, 動詞補文, さらに重文などと連続体をなす現象は他言語にも多く見られ, 普遍性がある。

以下では, 先ずこの内在型関係節の先行研究を紹介し, その性質を分析して行く。

先行研究

内在型関係節の文法的機能

主要部内在型関係節の性質については, 上記のように, 名詞節, 副詞節, それに名詞節と副詞節の両方の性質を持つという三つの説がある。以下に各説の代表的な議論を紹介する。

名詞節としての内在型関係節

名詞節説の代表としては, Kuroda (1976, 1992), および黒田(1998, 1999, 2005)が挙げられる。主要部内在型関係節の存在はKuroda (1976)によって指摘され, 最初pivot-independent relative clauseと呼ばれた。Kurodaは主要部が関係節の内部に移動し, その代わりに「の」がその主要部の指示物を指示し, 主文の述部と繋がっていると主張する。例えば, (1b)では主要部「リンゴ」が「の」の位置から関係節の内部に移動するが, 主文の述語「とる」の項[2]として, 関係節の外部と繋がっている。つまり, 内在型関係節は, 主要部が内部に移動するだけで, 全体が一つの名詞節として機能し, 後続する主文動詞の項になる。このため, 内在型関係節の後につく格助詞は必ず主文の動詞が要求する格助詞と一致すると黒田は主張している。これは,「格の一致現象」と呼ばれる。例えば, (2)では, 内在型関係節「学生たちが歩いてくるの」は「歩いてくる学生たち」のことを指し, 全体で一つの名詞句として機能する。そして, その後に付く格助詞「に」は, 主節の「出会う」が目的語を受ける時に要求する「に」格と一致している。

    (2) 田中が [学生たちが歩いてくるの] に出会った。(黒田2005:169)

このような「格の一致現象」から, 内在型関係節は全体として名詞節の機能を担うというのが黒田の主張である。

副詞節としての内在型関係節

三原(1994)は黒田の主張に対し, 主節動詞とかかわるのは内部に移動する主要部名詞ではなく, すべてゼロ代名詞であると主張し, 内在型関係節は副詞節の性質を持つとする。(3)は三原の提出する「格の一致現象」の反例である。

    (3) [村井にメモを残しておこうと思っていたの] が, あれやこれやですっかり忘れてしまった。(三原 1994:87)

三原によると, (3)において「忘れてしまった」のは「メモを」あるいは「メモを残しておくことを」である。つまり, この例では, 主文動詞は「を」格を要求するが, 実際には「を」

2　項(argument)とは, 統語論では, 語彙範疇(名詞, 形容詞, 動詞などの独立の意味を持つ語)によって選択される要素を指す。これに対して, 語彙範疇によって選択されない要素で文に現れるものを付加詞(adjunct)という。例えば,「花子が昨日ピザを公園で太郎と箸で食べた。」では, 動作主の「花子」と目的語の「ピザ」は動詞の「食べた」の項で,「昨日」「公園で」「太郎と」「箸で」は動詞の付加詞である(Tsujimura, 2007:162-163)。

格ではなく,「が」格が使われているので,「格の一致現象」は起こっていないと考えられる。このような例から,「格の一致現象」を名詞節説の根拠とするには無理がある, そして内在型関係節は主節の副詞節として機能し, 主節動詞の項はゼロ代名詞であるというのが三原の主張である。さらに, 三原は(4)のような両義性を持つ例を挙げ, 内在型関係節で示される内容は, 単に主語だけとは限らないとして, 内在型関係節は副詞節として機能することと, 主節動詞の主語はゼロ代名詞であることを主張する。

(4) ［警官が強盗を川のほうへ追い詰めていたの］が, 勢い余って, 川の中へ飛び込んだ。(三原 1994:88-89)

三原によれば, もし内在型関係節が名詞節として機能するのであれば,「川の中へ飛び込んだ」のは「警官」,「強盗」, あるいは「警官＋強盗」の三つの可能な解釈があるので, 曖昧文となるはずだが, 実際にはこの文に曖昧性はない。しかし, 内在型関係節が副詞節として機能し, 文全体の状況を描写しつつ後の主節に繋がっていくと考えれば, (4)に曖昧性がないことが説明できる。この場合, 主文動詞の主語は, ゼロ代名詞であり, 文全体の文脈から指示対象を選択することになる。

名詞節と副詞節との二重性

前述の二つの議論に加え, 名詞節と副詞節の両方の性質を持つとする説もある。例えば, 坪本(1997)は, 内在型関係節と「それを」との共起性を検討することによって, 副詞節と目的語としての名詞節との区別ができると指摘する。下の(5a)では内在型関係節は「それを」と共起できるが, (5b)ではできない。

(5) a. 警察は［ドロボーが逃げようとしたの］を([?]それを)捕まえた。
    b. 警察は［ドロボーが逃げるの］を(*それを)捕まえた。 (坪本 1997:161)

坪本は「二重対格目的語制約」[3]を議論の根拠とし,「それを」と共起できるのは副詞節であり, 共起できないのは名詞節であるという仮説を立てる。(5)において, (5a)は「それを」との許容度がより高いため, 副詞節として機能しているとみられる。それに対して, (5b)は「それを」を挿入できないことから, 名詞節と看做されるとする。つまり, 内在型関係節は一つのカテゴリに収まるのではなく,「それを」との許容度についての考察から分かるように, 名詞節の性質を持つ場合と副詞節の性質を持つ場合があるというのが坪本の主張である。

内在型関係節の成立条件の妥当性の検討

先行研究においては, 内在型関係節の性質と機能についての議論だけではなく, その成立条件についても, 様々な仮説が立てられている。本節では, 先行研究で指摘されている主要な条件を検討し, これらがいずれもすべての内在型関係節に共通する条件とは言えないことを示す。

意味論的・語用論的関連性

内在型関係節の意味論的・語用論的関連性に関しては, Kuroda (1992)のRelevancy Conditionという意味論的・語用論的条件が多くの言語学者に認められる条件の一つと

---

[3] 項(argument)とは, 統語論では, 語彙範疇(名詞, 形容詞, 動詞などの独立の意味を持つ語)によって選択される要素を指す。これに対して, 語彙範疇によって選択されない要素で文に現れるものを付加詞(adjunct)という。例えば,「花子が昨日ピザを公園で太郎と箸で食べた。」では, 動作主の「花子」と目的語の「ピザ」は動詞の「食べた」の項で,「昨日」「公園で」「太郎と」「箸で」は動詞の付加詞である(Tsujimura, 2007:162-163)。

考えられており、三原(1994)も同様の主張をしている。この条件は、外在型関係節で表される内容は主文の内容との関係が必須ではないのに対して、内在型関係節では、その構文の内容は主節の内容と何らかの関連性がなければならないとする。例えば、(6a)では、「ねじ伏せた」の目的語が「強盗」の場合、その内在型関係節の内容と主節の内容には自然な関連が感じられるが、(6b)でそれが成立するためには自然さを保障する文脈が必要である(三原 1994: 81–82)。

(6) a. 桜田は［強盗が襲いかかってきたの］をねじ伏せた。

b. ＊桜田は［娘がはるばる訪ねてきたの］をねじ伏せた。(三原 1994:82)

即ち、普通、「ねじ伏せた」の目的語は、「強盗」のような人間と想像できるので、内在型関係節で表される事態「強盗が襲いかかってきたこと」と主文で表わされる事態「ねじ伏せたこと」とは、意味的な関連性を見出しやすい。しかし、「娘がはるばる訪ねてきた」事態と「ねじ伏せた」事態とは、通常一つの関連した出来事とは想像しにくい。この例から分かるように、内在型関係節の事態と主文の事態とはその意味論的・語用論的な関連を必要とするというのがRelevancy Conditionである。

さらに、Kuroda (1992)はこの意味論的・語用論的関連性に関連して、内在型関係節と主文が表わす出来事が同時に起こっていなければならないという、内在型関係節と主節の「出来事同時性」と、それらが同じ場所で起こっていなければならないという「場所同一性」が満たされていることも指摘している。例えば、(7a)は適格文であるが、(7b)のように、「昨日」を加えると、「置いた」と「取った」との二つの動作が一連の動作にならないため、非文となる。

(7) a. 太郎は［花子がりんごを皿の上に置いたの］を取って…

b. ＊太郎は［花子が昨日りんごを皿の上に置いたの］を取って…(Kuroda, 1992:147)

しかし、この同時性は認めるとしても、場所の同一性には議論の余地がある。例えば、(8)は適格文であるが、「芋がらを干した」場所と「干した芋がらをどこかに入れた」場所は異なる可能性がある。

(8) 大麥小麥、三角畑の蕎麥あたれとみんなで聲を揃へて叫ぶのであつた、卷藁のなかへ［芋がらの干したの］を入れると音がいいといつて拵へて貰つたことであつた。(長塚節『月見の夕』)

この例から分かるように、この意味論的・語用論的関連性は内在型関係節の条件としては検討の余地がある。

「それを」の挿入による内在型関係節の名詞節と副詞節の区別

「名詞節と副詞節との二重性」の節で紹介したように、坪本 (1997) は、「二重対格目的語制約」から、「それを」と共起できるのは副詞節であり、共起できないのは名詞節であると主張する。しかし、下の例のように、名詞節の機能を果たすと考えられる補文でも、「それを」と共起する実例がたくさんある。

(9) お前は、［人の慰み物になっているの］を、それを出世と心得てるんだ。
(中里介山 『大菩薩峠 お銀様の巻』)

(9)では、「心得る」のは、「人の慰み物になっている」ことである。「人の慰み物になっているの」は全体で一つの事柄として後続する動詞の目的語として機能し、「それを」とも共起することができる。この補文は「を」という格助詞で受けられていることからも

分かるように「の」によって名詞化された名詞節であり,副詞節ではない。これは,坪本の「『それを』と共起できるのは副詞節,共起できないのは名詞節」とする議論の反証となる。つまり,「それを」との共起の許容度は,副詞節か名詞節かを区別するための適切な手段とはなり得ず,したがって,「それを」を挿入できるかどうかは,内在型関係節の性質を判断する条件とは言い難い。

現象文としての機能

小原(2002)は,内在型関係節は断定の機能を持ち,出来事や場面を報じる現象文[4]に相当し,現象文としての機能があるため,その節内では,「論理学的意味での主辞に相当する統語論的主語名詞句には主格の『が』は付くが,係助詞『は』はつかない」と主張する。例えば,(10a), (10b)では「母」と「息子」がそれぞれの内在型関係節内での名詞句であるため,そのあとに「は」が付かない。

(10) a. ［母が/*はセーターを送ってくれたの］が今日届いた。
 b. ［息子が/*は魚を釣ってきたの］を夫が料理した。(小原 2002:287)

しかし,(11)のように,主語名詞節に「は」がつく内在型関係節がないわけではない。

(11) ［合計特殊出生率は昭和二十五年には3.65だったの］が,四十年2.14,五十年1.91と下がり続け,五十六年にはどん底の1.74に。(レー・バン・クー 1988:75)

ここでは,内在型関係節の主語名詞句「合計特殊出生率」が「は」で受けられている。また,この内在型関係節は出来事や場面を報じる現象文ではなく,むしろ判断文の性質を持つと思われる。したがって,内在型関係節は全て現象文の性質を持ち,格助詞の制約があるという主張の妥当性には疑問がある。

以上,先行研究における内在型関係節の成立条件について,異なる主張を検討して来たが,どれも内在型関係節全般に当てはまる条件とは言い難い。このことから,はたして内在型関係節に共通した成立条件があるのか,この構文にはどのような統語的,あるいは意味論的・語用論的特性があるのか,さらに,内在型関係節はそもそも関係節と言えるのかという疑問が生まれる。そこで,以下では新しいアプローチとして,Croft (2001)によって提出されたRadical Construction Grammarを用いて,こうした疑問に答えながら内在型関係節の特性を再考して行く。

Radical construction grammar

内在型関係節を再考する前に,構文文法(Construction Grammar)一般について簡単に述べる。構文文法は,構文(grammatical construction)という「形式と意味と機能の結びつき」(Fillmore et al., 1998; Lambrecht, 1994; Goldberg, 1995; Croft, 2001)を文法記述の基本単位とする文法理論である。語彙要素間の統語的関係や要素の移動などに関する抽象的な構造規則によって文が生成されるという生成文法の立場を取らず,二つの構文が統語的に異なれば,両者は意味的・語用的にも異なるとする文法理論である。例えば,内在型関係節は,統語論的に外在型関係節とは異なるため,必ず意味論的・語用論的にも異なるという立場を取る。

4 　小原(2002: 286–287)によれば,現象文というのは,「出来事や場面を報じる」文である。(英語では"neural description" (Kuno, 1972) "sentence-focus structures" (Lambrecht, 1987; 1994)などと呼ばれる。)これに対し,「主題をまず提示しそれに対する判断を述べる文」は判断文である。(英語では, "topic-comment sentences," "predicate-focus structures" (Lambrecht, 1994)。)日本語では,この二種類の文は主辞(主題)に係助詞「は」がつくかどうかによって区別される。現象文には「は」を用いることができないのに対し,判断文には「は」を用いるとができる。

Radical Construction Grammar(RCG)はこの構文理論を踏まえた上で, 一つの構文内の要素間の関係を, いわゆる「統語的関係」としてではなく, すべて「部分─全体の関係」として捉え, 構文と構文の間のダイナミックな相互関係を強調する。そして, 類型的文法現象についても, 構文のプロトタイプと, 構文間あるいは言語間のバリエーションを考察し, 人間が構造を認知するための普遍的な性質を持つ「概念空間」(conceptual space)を用いて分析する。また, この「概念空間」によれば, 様々な言語のにおける,「重文」(coordination),「副詞節」(adverbial clauses),「補文」(complements),「関係節」(relative clauses)など異なる構造として扱われてきた構文が, 一つの関連したネットワークとして捉え直されるとする(「複文の連続体」の節の図1参照)。Croft (2001)の分析では, 主要部内在型関係節(internally headed relative clauses)は, 動詞補文(complements)と関係節(relative clauses)との中間に生じるものとされ, それら両方の特性を兼ね備えるとされている。Croftの主張は, 多言語の分析に基づいたもので, すべてが日本語に当てはまるものではないかもしれないが, その複文間[5]の関連性についての分析は, 現代日本語における「の構文」の性質の解明に極めて有益であると考えられる。

以下, RCGのアプローチを取り入れて, その構文理論を説明しながら, 内在型関係節の定義付けや, 内在型関係節と副詞節や補文など他の複文との関係について, 考察を行っていく。

RCGの主要部内在型関係節への適用

部分(主要部名詞)と全体(「の構文」)の関係

RCGは「形式と意味と機能の結びつき」である構文を基本的な分析単位とし, 構文内部の要素間の関係は, 統語関係ではなく, 部分と全体の関係として扱う。この観点に立ち, まず主要部内在型関係節の定義の妥当性を再考してみたい。

まず, 問題となるのは, 果たして主文動詞の項は関係節内の主要部名詞と一致するかという点である。RCGでは, 構文は形式と意味を統一したものであり, 単に要素の移動などによって, 構造の全体を説明することには無理があるとしている。本章でも, 主要部名詞は節外から節内に移動するものではなく, しかも, 主文動詞の項として働くことができず, 意味上も構造上も単に構文の部分でしかないと主張する。この点を明らかにするために, 以下では, 従来重視されなかった主文動詞の項, 即ち,「の構文」の指示物と主要部名詞との対応関係を, 主要部名詞と「の構文」の指示物が一致しない場合をいくつか取り上げて考察する。

「の構文」の指示物が主要部名詞の指示物から変化する場合

従属節の動詞が変化をもたらす動詞の場合,「の」が指示するものは主要部名詞の指示物から変化したものであり, もとの主要部名詞の指示物とは一致しない。(12)はこの例である。

---

[5] Croft (2001:320–321)によると, 従来の複文(complex sentences)についての分類は, 重文(coordination)と従属文(subordination)との二つに分かれる。重文は等位接続詞によって結合された二つあるいはそれ以上の節によって並列的に構成される文である。従属文はさらに, 副詞節(adverbial clauses), 補文(complement clauses), 関係節(relative clauses)の三つに下位分類される。そして, 従属文は重文のように並列的に二つの節が結ばれるのではなく, 主節と従属節のような節同士に従属性をもつという。しかし, RCGでは, 従来の分類と違う視点をとり, それぞれの複文にははっきりした切れ目がなく, 中間的な構文を介して互いにネットワークのように関連していることを一つの「概念空間」の図で示した(「複文の連続体」の節の図1「概念空間における意味図式」を参照)。

(12) 私への土産は，［駝鳥の羽を赤と黒とに染めたの］を，幾本か細いブリキの筒へ入れたのです。(小金井喜美子　『兄の帰朝』)

(12)では，「の構文」で指示されるのは元の色の「駝鳥の羽」ではなく，「赤と黒とに染めた駝鳥の羽」のことである。この例から分かるように，その主要部名詞は関係節で修飾，あるいは限定されるという意味での主要部とは言えず，その名詞を主要部名詞と呼ぶこと自体が不適切であると言える[6]。

「の構文」の指示物と主要部名詞の指示物との量的不一致の場合

黒田(1999, 2005)は内在型関係節が副詞節の性質を持つことを認めず，名詞節であると主張し，副詞節説への反論として，内在型関係節の主要部名詞が遊離数量詞のホスト[7]となることを示した。(13)は黒田の例である。

(13) a.　田中が男の学生を三人と女の学生を二人，同時に見かけた。

b.　田中が［男の学生が坂を降りてきたの］を三人と［女の学生が坂を上がっていったの］を二人同時に見かけた。(黒田　2005:187)

黒田(2005:186-187)によると，数量詞が名詞の直後の位置を占めている場合は，数量詞とそれがかかる名詞とがいっしょになって一つの名詞句を構成するという。例えば，(13a)では「男の学生」と「女の学生」はそれぞれ数量詞「三人」と「二人」のホストになって，これらの数量詞といっしょに名詞句を構成する。そして(13b)において，(13a)の「男の学生」と「女の学生」が内在型関係節「男の学生が坂を降りてきたの」と「女の学生が坂を上がっていったの」でそれぞれ置き換えられることから分かるように，内在型関係節も通常の名詞の場合と同様に振る舞う。したがって，遊離数量詞は，内在型関係節が名詞節であることを支持する証拠となると主張する。そして(13b)では，内在型関係節の主要部名詞「男の学生」と「女の学生」がそれぞれ「三人」と「二人」のホストとなるという。本章は，この例文の内在型関係節が名詞節である点は認めるが，問題は，遊離数量詞のホストが内在型関係節の主要部名詞であるかどうかということである。例えば，下の例を見られたい。

(14) 田中が［十人の男の学生が坂を降りてきたの］を三人途中で見かけた。

(14)では，関係節中の主要部名詞は「十人の男の学生」であるのに対し，主文の動詞「見かけた」に関わるのは「十人の男の学生」ではなく，「三人の男の学生」である。つまり，主要部名詞と「の構文」の指示内容は量的に一致しない。したがって，黒田の主張には疑問が残る。

主要部名詞が現れない場合

次に，主要部名詞が関係節内に表われない場合を見てみよう。例えば，(15)では節内に現れる名詞は主要部名詞とは言えない。

(15) けさ，［顔をそったの］が，夕方にはまた伸びてきた。(Nomura, 2000: 119)

---

[6]　この点については柴谷(2011)も言及している。

[7]　遊離数量詞」(floating quantifier)とは，形容詞のように前から名詞を修飾するのではなく，前の位置から後方に遊離し，後位から名詞句を修飾する数量詞である(加藤1997)。例えば，「3本のビールを飲んだ。」での「3本」は「ビールを3本飲んだ。」のように名詞の前位から後位に遊離する。「遊離数量詞のホスト」とは遊数量詞が修飾する名詞句のことである。

(15)では，主節の動詞から「伸びてきた」のは「髭」だと判断できるが，前の「の構文」には節内の名詞として「顔」があるだけで，「髭」には言及すらされてない。「伸びてきた」にかかるものが「髭」であるとすれば，[ ]内の名詞「顔」は「主要部名詞」とは言えない。これから，「の構文」の指示物は必ずしも節内の名詞の指示物とは限らないことが分かる。

以上見て来たように，内在型関係節の主要部名詞は，一見「の」の位置から関係節内部に移動したかのように見えるが，実際に主文動詞の項，即ち「の構文」の指示物とは一致しない場合もある。主文動詞にかかる名詞句は，場合によって，節内の名詞の指示物から変化したり，節内の名詞とは数量的に違ったり，節内に現れなかったりする。したがって，主要部名詞の指示物を解明するには，「の構文」を一つの全体として捉え，その意味を考えなければならない。つまり，要素間の統御関係や要素移動に基づく枠組ではなく，構文を分析の単位とし，部分(主要部名詞)と全体(「の構文」)の関係を明確にするRCGの方が，この内在型関係節の分析に適していると考えられる。

構文と構文の間のダイナミックな相互関係

急進構文文法では，構文間の関係(例えば，「の構文」と主文の関係)は，構文内の要素の間の関係と同じく，ある決まった一つの統語関係ではなく，構文間のダイナミックな相互関係や文脈情報などを考え合わせて適切な解釈を得ることが重要になる。

「先行研究」において見たように，三原は「の構文」を副詞節として取り扱い，その理由の一つとして，「の構文」で指示される名詞は，多義性があることをあげている。例えば(16)([4]の再録)では，「川の中へ飛び込んだ」のは「警官」，「強盗」，もしくは「警官＋強盗」という三つの可能な解釈があり，「の構文」は文全体の状況を紹介し，副詞節として働くと述べている。

(16) ［警官が強盗を川のほうへ追い詰めていたの］が，勢い余って，川の中へ飛び込んだ。(三原 1994:88-89)

三原によると，主文の述語と呼応するのは，ゼロ代名詞であり，文全体の文脈からゼロ代名詞の指示対象を選択することになる。しかし，本章は文法的カテゴリとしてのゼロ代名詞の存在を前提とする必要はなく，文脈情報によって多義性をなくすことで，「の」によって名詞化される内容を確定するという立場をとる。つまり，ゼロ代名詞の指示対象を文脈によって選択することと同じように，単に「の構文」の指示対象を文脈から限定すれば，「ゼロ代名詞」という抽象的な概念を導入することなしに多義性の問題を解決することができると考える。

次に，従来「の構文」と知覚動詞の補文との区別については，金水(1995)は，下に例示するように，「の構文」は「もの」を指示するのに対し，知覚動詞補文は「出来事」全体として動詞の項となると述べている。

(17) a. ［犬が走ってきたの］を捕まえた。(の構文)

b. ［犬が走ってきたの］を見た。(知覚動詞補文)

しかし，RCGの理論では，構造的に同じように見える二つの構文は本質的に同じ構文と見なす。よって，本章では，「の構文」と知覚動詞補文とは，本質的には同じものとして取り扱う。即ち，両方とも「の」によって名詞化される構文であり，その名詞化された内容が主文の述語とある意味関係を有していると考える。具体的には，主文の動詞が知覚動詞である場合，「の構文」の指示物はその知覚動詞が意味する知覚に関わる事象全体 と見ることができる。これに対し，主文の動詞が知覚動詞ではない場合は，その動

詞の意味要求によって,「の構文」の指示物が決まる。この点を説明するために,長谷川(2002:7)から引用した黒田(1999)の例を見られたい。

(18) 京子が [道子がそのハエがまた飛んで来るかどうか怪しがっていたの] を見つけ出した。

黒田の統語理論に基づく議論では,普通,述語の項は,「リンゴを食べた」の「リンゴ」のように動詞と隣接するなど,構造的に限定された範囲内に位置しなければならない。しかし,(18)では,主要部内在関係節全体が主文の動詞「見つけだす」の項の位置を占めるが,実際に,節内主要部とされる「ハエ」は,いくつかの構造(つまり,関係節とその内部の節)に囲まれて,かなり離れた動詞「見つけだす」の統御範囲に含まれないにもかかわらず,その動詞の項とされるという[8]。

これに対し,本章は,RCGの枠組に基づいて統語関係は認めず,「の構文」の指示内容を決定するには,その構文だけではなく,それと主文の構文がどう関係しているかを考えることが不可欠であると主張する。例えば,(18)を「道子がそのハエがまた飛んで来るかどうか怪しがっていたの見る」という文にしたとすると,「の」の指示物は「ハエがまた飛んで来るかどうか怪しがっていた道子」,「道子が怪しがっていたハエ」,「道子がそのハエがまた飛んで来るかどうか怪しがっていたという場面」など,いずれの可能性もあり,一つに限定することができない。そして,この多義性の問題は統語関係だけを分析していては解決できない。つまり,「の構文」を分析する場合,単にこの構文だけでは意味が確定できず,主文の構文との意味的な関連を考えなければならない。(18)から分かるように,動詞が具体的な「もの」を対象物として要求する「見つけ出す」であれば,「の構文」の指示内容は「もの」になり,動詞がもし場面全体を指す「出来事」や具体的な「もの」(あるいは「者」)を対象物として要求する「見る」であれば,「の構文」の指示内容は多義性があり,文脈によって選択しなければならない。このように,「の構文」は主文の動詞構文とダイナミックな相互関係を持ち,その意味もこの二つの構文の相互の意味関係によって決まり,次いで文全体の意味が確定される。

プロトタイプ分析と構文の意味・形式の分化

プロトタイプというのは,カテゴリにおけるもっとも典型的な代表例のことを指す。たとえば,鳥というカテゴリなら,スズメ,カラスなどがまず典型的な代表例として考えられる。また,スズメやカラスなどより,典型的特徴が薄れる例としては,ペンギンやダチョウなどが考えられ,これらは,周辺的なタイプと言える。一般にこのプロトタイプと周辺的タイプが共に存在することから,構文の意味と形式においても,プロトタイプと分化によって生じる周辺的タイプの共存が予測される。以下では,「の構文」のプロトタイプと周辺的タイプの共存について説明する。

ここで先のKuroda (1976, 1992),および黒田(1998, 1999, 2005)と三原(1994)の論争を振り返ると,下の(19)([1b]の再録)に示すように,Kuroda (1976)が最初に提出した「の構文」は主文の述語の要求する項を満たす名詞節であり,しかも,ここでは修飾される主要部名詞が「の構文」の内部に現れるものであった。

(19) 太郎は [リンゴが皿の上にあったの] をとって,ポケットにいれた。

三原(1994)は(20)([3]の再録)のような「格一致現象」の反例を取り上げ,「の構文」は副詞節であると主張する。

---

[8] 黒田(1999: 51)によると,これは「主部内在関係節はθ統率される位置を占めるが,この位置に放下されるべき意味役割はSの境界を越えて主部内在関係節に含まれる名詞句に放下される」ためと考えられる。

(20) ［村井にメモを残しておこうと思っていたの］が, あれやこれやですっかり忘れてしまった。

黒田(1999)は三原の副詞節説に異論を唱え, (20)のような文の存在を認めたとしても, 三原の主張するような逆説の意味を持つ副詞節はいわゆる内在型関係節とは性質を異にするとする。そして, 遊離数量詞の例をもとに, (20)のような「の構文」は副詞節ではなく名詞節であると論じる。(詳しくは「『の構文』の指示物と主要部名詞の指示物との量的不一致の場合」の節を参考)

本章では, 名詞節であれ, 副詞節であれ, いずれも「の構文」としてその存在を認めるという立場を取る。そして, プロトタイプと周辺的タイプが共存するという視点から,「名詞節」が「プロトタイプ」であり,「副詞節」がやや周辺的なタイプであると考える。つまり, プロトタイプでは, 名詞節の後につく格助詞は常に主文の動詞が要求する格と一致する。しかし, 典型性が下がるにつれて, 形式上の要求も変化する。その結果, 格助詞への要求も変化し, 例えば, 明確に動詞の目的語を表示するものから, (20)のように名詞節の格の要求を満たさない副詞節に変化していく。

このプロトタイプから周辺的なタイプに変化する現象は, もともと「の＋格助詞が」と「の＋格助詞を」であったものが逆説の意味を表す接続助詞「のが」と「のを」に変化することにも見られる。Ohara (2005)によると,「のが」と「のを」はお互いに入れ替えできることから,「のに」「ので」のように, その性質が動詞とその項との間の格関係を表す機能から分離し, 逆説の意味を表す接続助詞の機能に変化し, その結果,「の構文」も名詞節から周辺的なタイプへ変化し副詞節になるという。例えば, (21)では,「のを」はすでに一つの逆説の接続助詞に近い働きを持つと考えられる。

(21) 彼は欠席したほうがいいのを, 無理をした。(レー・バン・クー 1988: 86)

このように, プロトタイプから周辺的なタイプへ分化し, 変化していくことによって, 新たな構文が誕生することになる。さらに, 分化というプロセスを経て周辺的タイプが生まれることから, こういうプロトタイプと周辺的なタイプの間にははっきりした切れ目がなく, 一つの全体として繋がっていることが分かる。以下では,「概念空間」における「意味図式」で「の構文」のプロトタイプと周辺的なタイプの関係を論じる。

複文の連続体

Croft (2001)は,「意味図式」において「重文」,「副詞節」,「補文」,「関係節」という従来提案される四つの構文を取り上げ, これらの構文と他の構文との関連について論じた。(22)はこの四つの複文の日本語の例である。

(22) a. 重文：太郎は歌を歌うのが上手だが, 踊るのが苦手だ。

b. 副詞節：太郎が歌っているとき, 花子は踊っている。

c. 補文：太郎は教室で花子が踊っているのを見た。

d. 関係節：太郎は教室で踊っている花子を見た。

Croft (2001)は様々な言語の複文を分析し, それらの間の関連を図1のようにまとめている。

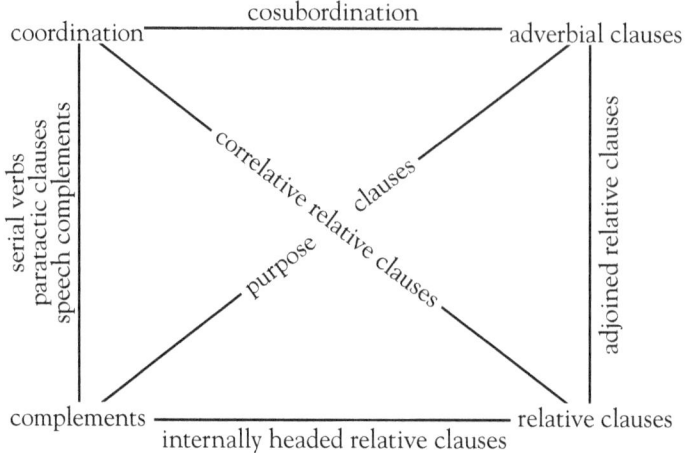

図1　概念空間における意味図式(Croft 2001: 322)

この図が表すように, Croftによると, 各複文は孤立した存在ではなく, ほかの複文と関連し合い, 一つのネットワークを形成する。この図のように, 本章の対象である「主要部内在型関係節(internally headed relative clauses)」は, 補文(complements)と関係節(relative clauses)との中間に位置し, それら両方の特性を兼ね備えるとされている[9]。この提案は, 言語類型論の立場から, 多言語を分析した結果としてなされたもので, 必ずしも日本語に当てはまるものではないかもしれないが, 複文間の繋がり, 各複文が一つのネットワークのように連続体をなすという視点は「の構文」の意味と形式のバリエーションを解釈するのに有用であると考えられる[10]。以下では, このCroftの理論に基づき, 「の構文」がいろいろな複文と関連し密接に繋がっており, 「関係節」の枠にとどまらず, 様々な複文構造の範疇にも関連していることを示す。

関係節との繋がり

「主要部内在型関係節」は, 主要部名詞を修飾, あるいは限定する節内にその主要部名詞が位置するという条件を満たす節と定義付けられる。その名称から分かるように, 「主要部外在型関係節」と共に, もともと「関係節」の一種として分類されてきた。(23)([1]の再録)に示すように, それと「主要部外在型関係節」, 即ち通常の「関係節」とは, 主要部の位置の違いと「の」の有無によって区別される。

(23) a. 太郎は [皿の上にあった] リンゴをとって, ポケットにいれた。

(主要部外在型関係節)

b. 太郎は [リンゴが皿の上にあったの] をとって, ポケットにいれた。

(主要部内在型関係節)

---

[9] Croft (2001:325)は, 「internally-headed relative clauses span the region between relative clauses and complements」としている。例えば, Imbabura Quechuaでは「the structure of internally-headed relative clauses is identical to that of complements, including the nominalizing suffixes used in both」という。

[10] この複文連続体の観点を取り入れた日本語の連体修飾構文の先行研究には, Wang, Horie & Pardeshi (2009)がある。

しかし,「部分(主要部名詞)と全体(『の構文』)の関係」の節で見た「主要部内在型関係節」の特徴から分かるように,その節内に現れる名詞は必ずしも主文動詞の項に対応する名詞とは限らないことから,主要部内在型関係節が完全に関係節だとするには無理がある。本章では,主要部内在型関係節は関係節の一種ではなく,「の」による名詞化構文(即ち「の構文」)であると主張する。ただし,これは「の構文」と「関係節」が全く別の構文で相互に関係がないという意味ではなく,この二つは,統語的,あるいは意味的に連続していると考える。

統語的,意味的に連続性が見られるのは主文動詞の項に対応する名詞が節内に現れない場合である。例えば,(24 a)において,主文動詞の項,即ち「の構文」の指示物は,節内に現れる名詞「玄米」ではなくて,「玄米」からできた「ご飯」のことを指している(この種の「の構文」の分析は「部分(主要部名詞)と全体(『の構文』)の関係」の節を参照)。

  (24) a. [新鮮な玄米を炊いたの]を食べた。(の構文)

    b. [新鮮な玄米を炊いた]ご飯を食べた。(関係節)

(24 a)と(24 b)の連続性は,間に(24 a')を挿入して見ると分かりやすい。

  (24) a. [新鮮な玄米を炊いたの]を食べた。

    a'. [新鮮な玄米を炊いた]もの　を食べた。

    b. [新鮮な玄米を炊いた]ご飯　を食べた。

即ち,(24 a')の主要部「もの」は,「形式名詞」あるいは「機能的な名詞」(奥津 1975)として「の」と共通している一方,実体を指示する点においては「ご飯」とも共通している。そして,これら異なる構文を持つ3つの文は意味的にもそれほど変わらない。

RCGにおいては,一つの構文がプロトタイプから徐々に周辺的なタイプへ変化していくこと,そして,プロトタイプと周辺的なタイプが共存していることを認める。さらに,構文間においては,それぞれが孤立した存在ではなく,お互いに中間的な構文を介し,ネットワークのように繋がっていることを主張している。この理論によると,(24)においては,主文動詞の項に対応する名詞が節内に現れないという特徴をもつ「の構文」(24 a')はプロトタイプ的な(1b)よりやや周辺的なタイプと言えよう。そして(24 a')は,関係節のカテゴリにおいては,主要部名詞が普通名詞ではなく形式名詞であることから,プロトタイプと言うより周辺的タイプと考えられる。つまり(1b)と(24)の3文は,「の構文」プロトタイプ—「の構文」周辺的タイプ—関係節周辺的タイプ—関係節プロトタイプという連続体を成していると見ることができる。

副詞節との繋がり

次に「の構文」と副詞節との関係を見てみよう。図1のCroft (2001)の図では副詞節と「の構文」とは繋がっていないが,これは多言語を分析した結果であって,必ずしも日本語に当てはまるものではない。例えば,下の(25)と(26)の「の構文」はいずれも副詞節のように文全体の状況を述べ,「の構文」全体が一つの意味単位となって主節と繋がる。したがって,このような「の構文」は,厳密には 関係節とは言いがたい。

  (25) だが,四目になると,[最初の一番は直木が有利な形勢であったの]を,最後まで打って見ると意外にも,僕が一目の勝であった。(菊地寛　『碁の手直り表』)

(26) ところが同じ船と海の事を書いたものでも，船長が［眼病で，船の操縦ができないの］を，眼の見えるふりでどこまでも押し通す様子などになると，筋は海を離れて，船長自身の個人の身の上話しに移ってしまう。(夏目漱石　『コンラッドの描きたる自然について』)

(25)と(26)の「のを」は，共に「のに」で置き換えてもそれほど意味が変わらない。このことから，ここの「の構文＋を」は，主節の背景情報を提供する逆接の副詞節であると言える。三原(1994)では，内在型関係節はすべて副詞節であるとしているが，本章は，内在型関係節の一部に副詞節の性質を持つものがあると主張したい。そして，副詞節の性質を持つ「の構文」は周辺的なタイプとして「の構文」と副詞節を繋がり，一つの連続体を形成していると言えよう。

知覚動詞補文との繋がり

「構文と構文の間のダイナミックな相互関係」の節で述べたように，本章は知覚動詞補文と主要部内在型関係節は，その性質に共通性がみられるという立場を取る。そして，それらを区別するには，「の構文」と主文間の意味関係という視点が不可欠だと考える。つまり，動詞補文と「の構文」はまったく別物で，それぞれが孤立した存在であるというのではなく，どちらの解釈が生まれるかは「の構文」と主文との意味関係によって決まると主張したい。例えば，(27)では，主節に「見つけて取ろう」という二つの連続した動作があり，前者は感覚動詞であるのに対し，後者は具体的な対象物を指す目的格名詞を要求する動詞である。

(27) ［池に美しい帯が浮いているの］を見つけて取ろうとすると，たちまち巻き取られて飲み込まれる。(岡本綺堂　『半七捕物帳』)

(27)では，「見つける」は感覚動詞なので動詞補文を取り，動作動詞「取る」が要求するのは「の構文」の指示物とするのが普通の解釈であるが，この二つの動詞にかかるのはただ一つの「の」節なので，この「の」節はどちらの性質を持つのかが問題になる。「池に美しい帯が浮いているのを見つける」とした場合には動詞補文と解釈でき，「池に美しい帯が浮いているのを取る」と見るなら，「の構文」になるため，いずれの解釈もできると考えられる。このように，一つの「の」節が動詞補文にも「の構文」にもなり得るという事実は，この構文が二つ特性を併せ持つことを示している。言い換えれば，動詞補文と「の構文」は別々の独立した存在なのではなく，一つの連続体であり，主動詞によって特定の特性が顕著に表われると考える方が事実をよく説明できると思われる。

重文との繋がり

ここで特に注目したいのは重文における対比関係の場合である。まず，(28a)と(28b)を比較してみよう。

(28) a. 全土の米の収穫は，［八三年に百六十万トンに達したの］が，自然災害で逆戻り。(朝日新聞『天声人語』レー・バン・クー　1988: 77)

b. 全土の米の収穫は，八三年に百六十万トンに達したが，自然災害で逆戻り。

(28a)は「の構文」であり，(28b)は接続詞「が」を用いた対比関係の重文である。しかし，(28a)と(28b)は意味上ほとんど差がないと考えられる。レー・バン・クー(1988: 84)によると，(28a)のような「の構文」の「主文へ展開する役割を果たす『の』」は，従属節を名

詞化するという機能を「喪失」しており,そのため「の」がなくなっても,意味上は大した違いがない。

さらに,Ohara (2005)も,「の構文」の「の」とそれと受ける格助詞は一つの文法単位となり,「のが」や「のを」が全体として,対比関係の重文に現れる接続助詞「が」と類似の機能を担って,主文と逆説的な意味を表現すると述べている。つまり,「のが」や「のを」は名詞化マーカー「の」と格助詞「が」・「を」の複合体ではなく,一つの独立した接続助詞に変化する傾向がみられる。ちなみに,この文法的な変化は二十世紀から変遷し始め,すでに接続詞として定着している「のに」[11]よりかなり遅れているという。このように,「の構文」の「の」はその名詞性を失い,後ろの格助詞と一緒になって接続助詞に変化することから,「の構文」は重文とも密接に繋がっていることが分かる。

以上見て来たように,RCGにおける「構文の連続体」という理論に基づいた分析では,現代日本語の「の構文」は,単一の性質を持つものではなく,そのプロトタイプと周辺的タイプが共存し,関係節,副詞節,動詞補文,重文などの構文と意味上で重なり合い,一つの連続体をなしていることが分かる。

結論

本章ではRCGの理論を基に,これまでの研究で論じられて来た内在型関係節の成立条件や特徴などが一つの理論で統一的に説明できない理由について考察を行った。これまでの研究はいずれも,「の構文」の全体像を把握せず,その性質の一部しか論じていなかったため,副詞節や動詞補文や重文などの性質を持つ側面が十分に扱われてこなかったように思われる。本章は,Croft (2001)の複文連続体の観点を取り入れ,「の構文」の働きが幅広い範囲で他の様々な構文と繋がっていることを明らかにし,その性質の多様性を示した。下に「の構文」と各種複文との繋がりを示す例文をまとめる。

(29) a. 関係節:［新鮮な玄米を炊いたの］・もの・ご飯を食べた。

b. 副詞節:だが,四目になると,［最初の一番は直木が有利な形勢であったの］を,最後まで打って見ると意外にも,僕が一目の勝であった。

c. 知覚動詞補文:［池に美しい帯が浮いているの］を見つけて取ろうとすると,たちまち巻き取られて飲み込まれる。

d. 重文(の先行節):全土の米の収穫は,［八三年に百六十万トンに達した(の)］が,自然災害で逆戻り。

このように,「の構文」を介して,日本語の関係節,副詞節,動詞補文,重文が一つの連続体として,お互いに繋がり合っていることが明らかになる。

ところで,「の構文」のような名詞化構文が関係節,副詞節,動詞補文,重文などと連続体を成し,多機能を担うという言語現象は,日本語の特有のものではなく,他言語にも見られる。例えば,Noonan(1997)は,チベット・ビルマ語のChantyalという言葉は,名詞化標識-waによって,動詞補文,名詞補文,目的節,関係節など10種類の構文を作ると報告している。また,Kimura(2003)やYap, Choi, & Cheung (2007)は,中国語の名詞化標識「的」によって成り立つ文型の多機能性を研究している。さらに,Epps (2009)は,アマゾン語のHupという言葉では主要部を欠く関係節が副詞節に変化したことを指摘している。このように,いろいろな複文が互いに連続体をなす現象は 他言語にも多く見られこと

---

[11] Ohara (2005)によると,「のに」は歴史的にも名詞化マーカー「の」と「に」から一つの複合接続詞へ変化したという(Ohara, 2005: 67)。また,「ところが」「ところを」「ものを」などにも類似の文法現象が見られる。

から,日本語の「の」名詞化構文 においても,構文間の意味的な関連性に注目するアプローチを取ることにより,妥当な分析が可能になると思われる。

謝辞

本章は2011年4月のハワイ大学でのATJ年次学会での発表内容に修正を加えてまとめたものである。本章の作成にあたり,終始丁寧かつ熱心に指導してくださった松本善子教授,本章の草稿を精査し,詳細で有益な助言を与えていただいた筒井通雄教授に深謝する。また,表現上の訂正に多くの援助をいただいた車田千種氏に感謝の意を表する。残された問題は著者の責任である。

引用文献

奥津敬一郎 (1975)「程度の形式副詞」『都大論究12』都立大学

小原京子 (2002)「構文理論から見た主要部内在型関係節の意味と機能」『シリーズ言語科学3認知言語学II:カテゴリー化』東京大学出版会, 277–295.

加藤重広(1997)「日本語の連体数量詞と遊離数量詞の分析」『富山大学人文学部紀要26』, 31–64.

金水敏 (1995)「日本語史から見た助詞」『言語』24 (11), 78–84.

黒田成幸 (1998)「主要部内在関係節」『言語の内在と外在』東北大学文学部, 1–7.

黒田成幸 (1999)「主要部内在型関係節」『ことばの核と周縁』くろしお出版, 17–103.

黒田成幸 (2005)「主辞内在関係節」『日本語からみた生成文法』岩波書店, 169–235.

柴谷方良 (1978)『日本語の分析−生成文法の方法』大修館書店

柴谷方良 (2011)「理論研究と習得研究をつなぐ−準体助詞『の』と誤用「赤いのくつ」をめぐって」Proceedings of seventh international conference on practical linguistics of Japanese, 22–29.

坪本篤郎 (1997)「状況の文連結」『モダリティと発話行為』研究社出版, 155–202.

長谷川信子 (2002)「主要部内在型関係節:DP 分析」Scientific approaches to language 1, 1–33.

三原健一 (1994)「いわゆる主要部内在型関係節について」『日本語学』13 (7), 80–92.

レー・バン・クー (1988)『「の」による文埋め込みの構造と表現の機能』くろしお出版

Croft, W. (2001). *Radical construction grammar*. New York, NY: Oxford, United Kingdom University Press.

Epps, P. (2009). Escape from the noun phrase: From relative clause to converb and beyond in an Amazonian language. *Diachronica, 26*(3), 287–318.

Fillmore, C., Kay, P., & O'Connor, C. (1988). Regularity and idiomaticity in grammatical constructions: The case of let alone. *Language, 64*, 501–538.

Goldberg, A. E. (1995). *Constructions: A construction grammar approach to argument structure*. Chicago, IL: The University of Chicago Press.

Kimura, H. (2003). 'De' zi ju de jushi yuyi ji 'de' zi de gongneng kuozhan [The semantics of the 'de' construction and the extended function of 'de']. *Zhongguo yuwen, 4*, 303–314.

Kuno, S. (1972). Functional sentence perspective: A case study from Japanese and English. *Linguistic Inquiry, 3*, 269–320.

Kuroda, S.-Y. (1976). Headless relative clauses in Modern Japanese and the relevancy condition. *Proceedings of the Annual Meeting of the Berkeley Linguistics Society, 2*, 269–279.

Kuroda, S.-Y. (1992). Pivot-independent relativization in Japanese. In S.-Y. Kuroda (Ed.), *Japanese syntax and semantics: Collected papers* (pp. 114–174). Dordrecht, The Netherlands: Kluwer Academic.

Lambrecht, K. (1987). Sentence focus, information structure, and the thetic-categorical distinction. *Proceedings of the Annual Meeting of the Berkeley Linguistic Society, 13*, 366–339.

Lambrecht, K. (1994). *Information structure and sentence form: Topic, focus, and the mental representation of discourse referents.* Cambridge, United Kingdom: Cambridge University Press.

Nomura, M. (2000). The internally-headed relative clause construction in Japanese: A cognitive grammar approach. (Unpublished doctoral dissertation). University of California, San Diego.

Noonan, M. (1997). Versatile nominalizations. In J. Bybee, J. Haiman, & S. A. Thompson (Eds.), *Essays on language function and language type. In Honor of T. Givón* (pp. 373–94). Amsterdam/Philadelphia, PA: Benjamins.

Ohara, K. H. (2005). From relativization to clause-linkage: Evidence from modern Japanese. In M. Fried & H.C. Boas (Eds.), *Grammatical constructions: Back to the roots* (pp. 57–70). Amsterdam, The Netherlands: Benjamins.

Tsujimura, N. (2007). *An introduction to Japanese linguistics.* Malden, MA: Blackwell.

Wang, L., Horie, K., & Pardeshi, P. (2009). Toward a functional typology of noun modifying construction in Japanese and Chinese: A corpus-based account. *Studies in Language Sciences, 8*, 213–228.

Yap, F., Choi, P., & Cheung, K. (2007). Delexicalizing di: How a Chinese noun evolves into a nominalizer, with attitude (Unpublished manuscript). Chinese University of Hong Kong.

Transmissive Feminism: The Evolutive Mind as Displayed in the Overseas Letters of Yamada Kakichi to Yamada Waka

伝達されるフェミニズム：山田嘉吉から山田わかへ，二人の往復書簡が明かす女性思想の新たなかたち

Rika Saito
Western Michigan University

Abstract

This chapter examines handwritten letters exchanged across the Pacific and Atlantic Oceans between a Japanese feminist critic, Yamada Waka (1879–1957) and her husband and mentor, Yamada Kakichi (1865–1934) in 1922. The letters between the couple are privately owned and were buried in the warehouse of their grandson, Mr. Yaheiji Yamada, for decades. The letters relate to the Yamadas' articles in Fujin to Shin-Shakai (FTS, Women and the New Society) and indicate how Waka developed her intellectual relationship with her husband, Kakichi, and how she learned to exercise her independence as a critic. Before and during the period when she established her career, Waka received constant intellectual and emotional support from Kakichi. Some researchers and critics directly acquainted with the couple called them "one in body and spirit" (isshin dōtai). Their collaboration has never been closely scrutinized perhaps because of the scant primary evidence available until now that showed the exact and precise degree of inspiration that Kakichi gave to Waka. These exchanged letters, however, shed new light on the collaborative, transmissive, and feministic views of this unique couple and show how their relationship advanced feministic thinking.

要旨

本章は，戦前から戦後にかけ女性問題評論家として活躍した山田わか(1879–1957)と夫・山田嘉吉(1865–1934)の間で，1922年に太平洋と大西洋を隔てて交換され

Saito, R. (2013). Transmissive feminism: The evolutive mind as displayed in the overseas letters of Yamada Kakichi to Yamada Waka. In K. Kondo-Brown, Y. Saito-Abbott, S. Satsutani, M. Tsutsui, & A. Wehmeyer (Eds.), *New perspectives on Japanese language learning, linguistics, and culture* (pp. 163–181). Honolulu: University of Hawai'i, National Foreign Language Resource Center.

た手紙について考察している。二人の孫に当たる山田弥平治氏が長年私蔵されてきたこの手紙を見ると, 夫婦による雑誌『婦人と新社会』にまつわる情報や, わかが嘉吉との協働によって, どのように知的発展を遂げ, 自立性を育んでいったのかを, うかがい知ることができる。わかは評論家として活動する以前も, その活動中も絶えず嘉吉から知的かつ精神的なサポートを受けてきた。二人を知る学者の中には, 彼らを「一心同体」と称する者がいるが, これまでその協働のあり様が詳しく考察されることはなかった。おそらくそれは嘉吉がわかにどのような感化を与えたのかを具体的に知る手立てがなかったためとも思われる。しかし, この往復書簡は, 二人の協働性に基づく女性支援というフェミニズムの実践, およびその夫婦間での伝達を詳らかにしている。

Introduction

Ninety years ago, a remarkable couple exchanged letters in English and Japanese across the Pacific and Atlantic Oceans, discussing their love and hope in the home and family as well as feminism and social criticism regarding developing further ideas for modernizing Japan. These two were the Japanese feminist critic, Yamada Waka (1879–1957), and her husband and mentor, Yamada Kakichi (1865–1934). Yamada Waka is primarily known as a contributor to the journal, *Seitō* (Bluestocking), published by Japan's first feminist literary group, the Seitō-sha, which was active in the early 1910s, and as a social critic and columnist on women's issues in Japan before and after World War II. Waka was also well recognized as a social worker and an advocate for motherhood and devoted herself to helping widows and their children. In 1934, she became the first President of the Alliance for the Mother and Child Protection Act (*Bosei hogo renmei*).[1] Yamada Kakichi, her husband, ran a private academy in Tokyo where he taught several foreign languages and sociology to *Seitō* members and other intellectuals. He supported his wife's learning and intellectual evolution, and her research and social activism before and during their marriage.

This study examines their letters and the journal that they jointly produced, *Fujin to Shin-Shakai* (*FTS*, *Women and the New Society*) to illustrate how Yamada Waka developed an apprenticeship for intellectual work with her husband, Kakichi, and how she learned to exercise her independence as a critic. Before and during the period when she was establishing these careers as a social activist and writer, Waka received constant intellectual and emotional support from Kakichi. Waka was a very productive writer, whose books and journal articles were compiled by a scholar on social work, Hayashi Chiyo (Yamada, 2007), in *Yamada Waka chosakushū* (*Collection of Works of Yamada Waka*). In contrast, Kakichi left only two publications, a sociology textbook titled *Shakaigaku gairon* (1924, *The Outline of Sociology*) and *Seiyō ryōrihō taizen* (1923, *Western Cuisine Cookbook*). However, certain researchers and critics who were directly acquainted with the couple often called them "one in body and spirit" (*isshin dōtai*). These comments imply that most of the work done under the name of Waka was actually the embodiment of Kakichi's thought and spirit as well.

In a sense, Waka may have been a living spiritual medium for Kakichi, a person of encyclopedic knowledge. Waka describes him as her greatest mentor and someone who extended to her much knowledge about different social theories, foreign language skills, and other historical cultural values that she grew to greatly appreciate.[2] The couple's likely intellectual collaboration, however, has not been closely scrutinized previously, as little

---

[1] The original name was the "Alliance for the Promotion of a Mother and Child Protection Act" (*Bosei hogo hō seitei sokushin fujin renmei*). This alliance led to establishing the Mother and Child Protection Act in 1937.

[2] See Gomi (1980) and Fukushima (1935). As for Waka's life and works, see Saji (1974), Gomi (1978, 1980, 1993), Yamazaki (1978, 1985), and Imai (2006).

evidence existed to indicate exactly what Kakichi contributed or how much inspiration Kakichi gave Waka for her own work. The letters exchanged between the two are new sources that can shed valuable light on the collaborative, transmissive, and feminist views of this couple. Examining their journal in detail also sheds new light on their collaboration in discussing and writing their thoughts down, and on implementation of Japan's social and feminist issues. Indeed, they may be evidence of still another type of gender relationship that occurred in early twentieth century Japan. The relationship was unique in that devotion of a husband/male spouse whose support for his wife's/partner's intellectual development and career achievement promoted feminism in an indirect manner.

Background of the couple

Yamada Waka is distinct among the famous Japanese feminists living at the beginning and the middle of the twentieth century in Japan because of her background and the life experiences she had prior to becoming a popular critic. She is probably best known as a contributing author to the journal *Seitō*, mentioned above. Her translations of the works of Western intellectuals and writers appeared in the 1914–1916 issues of the journal. Her translation skills were excellent. Among those whose works she selected for translation were the New Women who argued for expanded rights for women: Ellen Key (1849–1926), a Swedish scholar and eugenicist who advocated the protection of motherhood, and Olive Schreiner (1855–1920), a South African novelist and activist. While the majority of Waka's contributions to *Seitō* were translations of Western thought, one of her essays titled, "Watashi to sono shūi" ("Myself and My Surroundings)," which appeared in *Seitō* in 1916 and was translated for English readers by Jan Bardsley in 2007, "includes one of the most heated displays of anger" (p. 232) that she ever expressed toward the abuse and violence suffered by women.

This unusual public display of Waka's deep-seated fury was rooted in her own unbearable misfortune; she was deceived into thinking that she was travelling to North America to obtain a good job, but was forced into prostitution instead as soon as she arrived, as I describe in detail below. Surviving such brutality is a feat in itself. It is nothing short of amazing that Waka overcame this trauma and even more incredible that she went on to pursue a career as a critic and social advocate. By the end of the 1910s, she was known as a popular critic who worked on women's issues, in particular, those related to motherhood protection and women's roles based on family-oriented policy. Most famously, Waka was a contributor to the "Debates over the Protection of Motherhood" (Bosei hogo ronsō) during 1916–1919, which included several famous feminists, such as Hiratsuka Raichō (1886–1971), Yosano Akiko (1878–1942), and Yamakawa Kikue (1890–1980).[3] Waka declared that the government should financially support mothers who rear children, so they would not have to work outside the home to help with family finances. This opinion was extreme for that time, when compared to those conservative debaters who argued instead that the government should support mothers who were rearing children by providing childcare so that they could work outside the home.

Yamada Waka viewed the home as the center of life and society and saw the role of women as being almost exclusively inside the home. Because of that view, she is generally considered today to be a conservative maternalist in terms of motherhood and other women's issues, such as abortion. The most striking episode detailing her anti-abortion viewpoint appeared in the *Asahi Newspaper* column titled, "Advice for Women" on March 30, 1932. She advised

---

[3] For discussion of "Debates Over Protection of Motherhood" in English, see Rodd (1991), Tomida (2004), Mackie (2002), and Bardsley (2007a).

a woman pregnant by rape not to abort the pregnancy, but instead to devote all her energies to raising that child. Waka even traveled to the U.S., in late 1937 as a writer for the popular women's magazine *Shufu no tomo* (*Housewife's Companion*), meeting Eleanor Roosevelt at the White House. Unfortunately, however, Waka's maternalism was integrated into the Japanese government propaganda to advocate for producing a higher birth rate before and during World War II. By request, she often wrote opinion articles for the media to promote the militant government of the 1930s–1940s. During the war period, she was delegated to go to European countries, including Germany and Italy, Japan's fellow Axis powers, to give speeches on womanhood that were dedicated to supporting the home front.

Few who met Waka in the 1930s would have imagined that this transnational diplomat came from humble beginnings. Waka was born into a farmer's family in the rural area of Kanagawa Prefecture and as a girl, was enthusiastic about learning. However, she was not able to continue on to further schooling after four years of elementary education because her parents were not interested in giving more education to girls. Her family was large—the parents, three boys and five girls— so it became difficult to make ends meet. She had to give up her education to strive to earn money. Waka unwillingly married a local man who was expected to help the Yamada family financially. However, the marriage lasted for less than a year since the family did not get any money from him. At eighteen, Waka decided to go abroad to earn money to help the family finances.

In the 1890s, only a few governmental elites or wealthy higher class people went to Europe and the U.S., to learn about Western civilized culture. For the rest, including women from the lower classes, going abroad was to earn money, and it usually produced extreme hardships. The women often ended up becoming involved in prostitution. Waka was unaware of this pitfall when she sailed for Vancouver; however, she soon discovered her unfortunate destiny. Right after arriving at the port, she was sold into a brothel in Seattle, Washington in 1897. She stayed trapped in the web of prostitution for nearly seven years.

In 1903, Waka escaped the brothel, reached San Francisco, and was rescued through Cameron House, a settlement house for refugee girls established by the Presbyterian Church in 1874.[4] Most girls in the settlement house had been illegally sent from China and other Asian countries to the United States to be forced into prostitution. During her three-year stay there, Waka worked to help her fellow Japanese women who had experienced similar misfortune. She became a translator of English into Japanese. Although she had little formal education, she was talented and absorbed everything she heard. Her talent was clearly recognizable to Yamada Kakichi, who ran a private academy to teach foreign languages and sociology in San Francisco. Waka began to attend his academy soon after she arrived at Cameron House. Kakichi was an immigrant also. He had come to the U.S., twelve years prior to Waka's arrival. He had no formal education either, but he had taught himself all his acquired academic, social, and political knowledge.

Waka and Kakichi married and returned to Japan in 1907. Soon afterwards, they settled in Tokyo, where Kakichi opened the Yamada Language School to teach foreign languages and other academic subjects to Japanese intellectuals, college students, white collar workers, and educated wives and daughters from the middle and upper classes. Through this work, the Yamadas became acquainted with Hiratsuka Raichō, the founder of the journal, *Seitō*.

---

[4] According to Yamazaki (1985), Cameron House was founded for young girls sent to the West Coast from China for forced prostitution. The home was named for Donaldina Cameron (1869–1968), the director of the settlement house, who saved more than five hundred women while serving there for twenty-five years (p. 84-86). Also see Yasutake (2004).

As previously mentioned, Waka soon became a contributor to *Seitō*, creating a series of translations, social criticism, and personal essays. By the 1920s, she had achieved nationwide fame as a social critic on women's issues. She was always enthusiastic and grateful, crediting her success to Kakichi, who dreamed that he could "train" his wife to be a prominent feminist intellectual. He gave her as much support as he could. Their mentor-disciple relationship began shortly after their first meeting and continued until Kakichi's dream came true. Our discussion here, however, presents new examples of their collaboration by looking at their unpublished letters and their less often examined journal articles.

Letters overseas

The letters examined here are ones that Waka and Kakichi exchanged when he traveled to the United States, Cuba, Europe, and then through the Suez Canal to Southeast Asia from April to October of 1922. This was a business trip on which he worked as a translator and negotiator to help a Japanese businessman. Kakichi wrote his letters in English, while Waka responded in Japanese. As Kakichi had finished only a few years of elementary education in Japan and then went to the United States to work, he seemed to be more comfortable writing in English rather than in Japanese.

The first letter from Waka to Kakichi is dated April 19, 1922, the day the *Taiyō-maru*, the passenger boat that Kakichi was on, departed from the port in Yokohama. Waka wrote that she and her children as well as friends had decided to go to the Sankeien Park near the port, as the children were eager to go. Waka wanted to go home straight away rather than stopping on the way as she had a lot of editing to do for the journal. However, from the hill in the park, they luckily saw the boat sailing away and all of them became excited. She sent twenty-nine more letters following this one. Kakichi began writing letters on April 23, 1922, on his way to Honolulu, Hawai'i, from which the ship would then put off for San Francisco. There are sixty-two correspondences from Kakichi to his wife. The ninety-two handwritten letters of the couple that I studied are all privately owned and have been stored in the warehouse of their grandson, Mr. Yaheiji Yamada for several decades.[5] It was a rare opportunity to read these letters and I was honored to be able to examine so many personal letters that had never been scrutinized.

Kakichi always used letterheads with nice photographic drawings and the logo of the hotels or boats where he stayed. He had a dynamic and flowing penmanship, so much so "that even a short note might take a few pages of stationary" (Bardsley, 2007b, p. 1) as noted by Jan Bardsley, who was involved in typing up Kakichi's handwritten English. Kakichi also sent Waka many postcards from various places. The letters from Kakichi are largely private exchanges with his wife. He almost always begins with such greetings, as "My Dearest," or "My Dearest Waka," and ends with "Your loving husband," "Your love, Kakichi." These openings and endings make his letters sound very affectionate. With tenderness, he writes, "Do not forget that I am nearing you every day" in his first letter written and then again several times in his later correspondences to her. His strongly emotional remarks seem to suggest that he was unwilling to go abroad and leave his family behind. He had been strongly encouraged, however, to take the role of international business assistant because it might bring financial benefit to the Yamada family. The Yamada family almost always had difficulty making ends meet, as they had many to take care of in the family, not only their

---

[5] In 2009, I contacted Mr. Yamada and found that the unpublished letters are available for consultation through Dr. Jan Bardsley, Associate Professor of Japanese Studies at the University of North Carolina at Chapel Hill. See Saito (2010b, 2011) for previous analysis of a few examples from the letters and *FTS*. As of April 2012, the couple's letters are accessable in the Japan Center for Women and Governance (Ichikawa Fusae Kinenkai) in Tokyo.

adopted children, but also Waka's older and younger sisters, and several non-paying lodgers, including male students who were economically underprivileged and wives or daughters who were refugees from their families. At one time, the Yamadas were all told fourteen people (Yamazaki, 1978, p. 216–217).

There is one episode that tells about the Yamadas' financial situation written by Gomi Yuriko, the couple's acquaintance and social work scholar. She reflects that Waka often went to a fish store at closing time to get leftovers to sell as they were cheaper (Gomi, 1980, p. 2).

In describing those he meets on this trip, Kakichi often verbally sketches typical Japanese tourists who behave indecently in public and offers his sarcastic views of them. For example, he describes Japanese passengers on the *Taiyō-maru* as being of three types: one, "real business men," two, "young men who are going back," and three, "the luxurious fools who only go for fooling" (K. Yamada, personal communication, April 23, 1922). He grows impatient with Japanese businessmen because they are "narrow-minded men who know only how to make money and nothing else. I am not wealthy, but [have] human worth...." (K. Yamada, personal communication, May 26, 1922). This criticism of Japanese businessman can be read as a thinly veiled complaint of his travel companion and employer, a Japanese businessperson referred to "Mr. A.," whose profile in detail is not known. Apparently, Mr. A. hired Kakichi as a translator and negotiator for his business trip abroad.

Waka describes Mr. A. in her essay for the journal, *Fujin to Shin-Shakai* (FTS), as a person to whom the couple owed a lot (*Fujin to Shin-Shakai*, 1993, No.27 (May 1922), p. 60). Waka writes that Mr. A. influenced the two to become converts from radicalism to conservatism in terms of their ideology. She even refers to him as a person of virtuous character. However, during his travels with this individual, Kakichi came to dislike what he saw as Mr. A.'s ignorance of the world and his insensitivity toward other cultures as well as his mammonism or money-madness. He criticizes him at every turn in his letters to his wife. Kakichi writes,

> Mr. A. understands America so little that it is very difficult to guide him to understand. He thinks of nothing, but sugar. He is sugar crazy. He is so dull in other things. I am surprised that he could do business. Japanese businessmen are too far from the American. They must become much more intelligent (K. Yamada, personal communication, June 9, 1922).

It appears in Kakichi's eye that Mr. A. represented the typical sort of Japanese national whom Kakichi resented, but often happened to see outside Japan. Kakichi also expressed discomfort when he had to interact with such travelers from Japan and this experience too leads Kakichi to write unpleasant comments about Mr. A.. Yet, Kakichi does not just criticize the Japanese; he also finds fault with the attitude of the Western colonizers whom he sees as prejudiced toward local Southeast Asians. On his travel in Asia, he sees the local people more sympathetically. For example, he writes to Waka when he arrives in Surabaya:

> ...The Dutch have succeeded in colonizing Java and Sumatra and other Dutch colonies. They only cultivated the nature and got sugar and other things. But they never try to educate the people; perhaps they think it is wise not to touch the spiritual side of the natives. Of course, the Dutch like the natives in the sense that cattlemen like cattle and feed them well so that the cattle get fat and bring in larger income (K. Yamada, personal communication, September 13, 1922).

This remark on education makes one recall that Kakichi was likely one of the many worried Japanese nationals who knew they had to catch up with the civilized Western countries soon; otherwise, they were in danger of being colonized as well.

Another topic on which Kakichi often reports is women in the West. First Kakichi notices women's dress, and it seems to be too gaudy and superficial for him. He puts his observations of women in the letters to his wife. Below is one observation that appears in his second letter.

> …This evening there was a special dinner for those who got off the ship at Honolulu and there is fancy dancing; several American girls dressed fancy ways and came to table this evening. They made a round of the large dining room to show their fancy makeup. They are going to dance this way this night (K. Yamada, personal communication, April 25, 1922).

This comment is written in an objective way, but his remarks gradually get more subjective.

> …The latest style of women's dress is much longer, which means that they are getting saner than used to be, and I am glad for Americans are moving back to the better mode (K. Yamada, personal communication, May 16, 1922).

This comment is included in a letter written in Chicago where Kakichi might have seen a flux line of pedestrians on the main street. The next is also written in a big city—New York City.

> …I have seen many girls looking at themselves reflecting in the glass while walking through streets. They are so materialistic and sensualized that they are nothing, but sensuality itself, and trying to attract men's attention. This is, its seems to me, their only business (K. Yamada, personal communication, June 15, 1922).

Now Kakichi appears censorious when he sees American women in New York City right after his visit to Havana, Cuba. He observes Cuban women in a very different way.

> …Women are here very pretty, but they are not working. Most of them are eating, drinking, and dancing. That is what they are doing here, not like in America. They [American women] are working, but much too fat. Very few [Cuban women] take outside outdoor work; therefore, there is hardly a woman question here (K. Yamada, personal communication, June 15, 1922).

Kakichi seems to prefer a plain mode of women's fashion and lifestyle. The very last line of the above quote saying that there is not a woman's problem ("question" in this line means a "problem" or "issue") as Cuban women hardly work outside the home, reflects his basic ideas regarding women and their working style. It might be exaggerated of course to say that he believes women should eat, drink, and dance at home every day without any obligated work. Yet it seems he wishes women freedom from labor and wants to give them protection as a breadwinner for the home. He has conservative ideas on home, married couples, and women working outside the home. Perhaps those ideas are the source of what Waka proclaimed in the "Debates over the Protection of Motherhood"—a women's role should be exclusive to that inside the home.

Almost every topic in Kakichi's letters was later transformed into world reports like his "World Travel Journals" for the periodical *Fujin to Shin-Shakai* (*FTS*). In it, Waka introduced various details about Europe, the U.S., and other foreign countries where only a very small number of Japanese people went at that time. It is obvious that Waka utilized almost all the information from the newspapers, magazines, and books that Kakichi sent her. She quoted from them or translated portions of them into these articles.

The letters from Waka are written on her private letter paper where the characters "*Yamada yōsen*" (letter paper for the Yamadas' use) appear. Hiratsuka Raichō once described Waka's penmanship as "childish," (Hiratsuka, 1971/2006, p. 237) remembering the time when she saw Waka's translation of Schreiner's "Dreams," her first contribution to the journal, *Seitō*. After reading these letters to Kakichi, however, I did not find her handwriting particularly illegible. Of course, by the time she wrote these letters, six to seven years had passed after she showed her initial work to Raichō; therefore, her script very likely had improved considerably from practice. She writes both *kanji* and *kana* in the cursive style, and she seems to put pen to paper with relatively strong pressure because all the letters are placed very clearly and precisely. Mr. Yaheiji Yamada, a grandson of the couple, who typed up his grandmother's handwritten letters did note that:

> I am decoding my grandmother's writing which is idiosyncratic, so it is a little difficult to figure out. These are letters written by a forty-three year old wife to her fifty-eight year old husband. It's natural that my grandmother wrote about love and longing toward her husband in a straightforward way. The content was just miscellaneous news picked up in everyday life, but I found it remarkable how sincere and profound was her love and respect for my grandfather (Yamada, 2011, p. 3).

It is true that her letters are full of her affection for Kakichi, and at the same time, one can see that they are also logs of the work Yamada Waka had done. I introduce that work as she was editing articles for her own monthly periodical, *Fujin to Shin-Shakai* (*FTS*) and discuss it in detail in the following sections. When comparing the items and events described in the letters with those that appeared in the *FTS* articles, one can see that what Waka was working on for the journal at this time consisted of items that she produced on her own accord. We also observe how that work simultaneously indicated her independence and yet her still strong intellectual/emotional collaboration with her husband, Kakichi.

Independence and collaboration and the reverse

As mentioned above, contemporaries of Waka and Kakichi considered them to be "one in body and spirit" (*isshin dōtai*) and their works as very collaborative. Waka stands at the forefront to present thoughts that originally came from Kakichi. Because of their relationship, it is fair to say that her thinking was developed through having a loving companion, but also within a master-disciple relationship. That resulting collaboration is indicated clearly in Kakichi's answer to an interview undertaken by the women's journal, *Shufu no tomo* (*Housewife's Companion*) in 1933.

> Although Waka was uneducated, she was remarkably intelligent with a fine memory and an ability to grasp subtleties. She seemed anxious to learn, anxious to be given the opportunity. I, in turn, wanted to teach her everything she requested, certain that given the chance, her natural talents would help her overcome a late start in life (as cited in Yamazaki, 1985, p. 100).

In 1929, Kakichi also wrote about his "three hopes." One hope was for the career success of his wife. This passage appears on the back page of the front cover of *FTS*.

> My first hope was that I wanted to make my wife a pioneer of a feminism that is based on Japan and the Japanese people; this effort [has] now eighty percent succeeded... (*Fujin to Shin-Shakai*, 1993, No.114 [September 1929], the back page of the cover).

Kakichi did not try to make himself "somebody" in Japan since, as Gomi Yuriko points out, he was not comfortable writing in Japanese due to having been away from Japan for more than twenty years (Gomi, 1980, p. 71). That view is reinforced in Kakichi's comments, such as "I am not good at both speaking and writing in Japanese; therefore, I wish that you never expect me to give a great speech. It must be just a small talk." This comment appeared in the local newspaper that was reporting on his public talk at the Nihon Club in Singapore.[6]

On the other hand, Waka describes Kakichi when she met him for the first time in San Francisco around 1903 as follows:

> There was a huge distance between Kakichi and me at that time; he was familiar with almost any kind of things and thought in the world, while I was unable to even read Japanese very much. In terms of knowledge, he was an adult, whereas I was a baby (*Fujin to Shin-Shakai*, 1993, No.27 [May 1922], p. 59).

Waka was around 24 to 25 years of age when she met Kakichi and started her study with him. In her essay that appeared in 1934, Waka notes that meeting and its aftermath.

> When I met him, I felt I was the worst kind of human being, an illiterate, nothing but a poor farmer's daughter. But Kakichi did not look at me as a lesser being. He treated me like a lady, which made me reexamine myself. Eventually, I gained self-respect (Yamazaki, 1985, p. 100).

Hiratsuka Raichō also remembered Kakichi, when he visited her to introduce his wife for the first time, writing below in her 1971 autobiographical volume titled, *In the Beginning, Woman Was the Sun*.

> …He (Kakichi) spoke with great animation, occasional peculiarities of speech, and lapses in grammar (he had lived in the United States for many years) about how they had met in the United States and fallen in love, about their life since returning to Japan, and his future hopes for his wife. In effect, he was asking me to take his wife on as a writer for the journal (Hiratsuka, 1971/2006, p. 236).

It seems true that Waka was not able to think or write without Kakichi's help at the initial stage of her career even though she was the more fluent in Japanese. As previously mentioned, Waka played the role of a living medium who transformed deep, but raw, material of intellect received from her husband into readable Japanese sentences. As Kakichi did not write in Japanese, Waka wrote for him and the process of this transmission is somehow quite visible in a written form. The couple's jointly owned journal *Fujin to Shin-Shakai* (*FTS*) does indicate such collaborative traces in its articles.

Fujin to Shin-Shakai (FTS)

Seven years after Waka's debut in 1913 as a critic/writer for *Seitō*, the couple decided to start their own journal, *Fujin to Shin-Shakai* (*FTS, Women and the New Society*), so Waka could express her thoughts more freely. Gomi Yuriko assumes it was Kakichi who was eager to produce their journal as a showcase for his wife's talents. Her writing on women's issues and her translations gradually gained in popularity in the intellectual circles of that time. *FTS* was surely a collaborative product for the couple. However, unlike Gomi, I focus more on another aspect of this work, namely, that it was Waka who clearly took the initiative in organizing and managing the journal. I am limited here, however, to only a few examples of her enterprise as introduced from their letters and journal articles, but they are intriguing in their tone. Before discussing these examples, it is advantageous first to describe the couple's journal, *FTS*.

The first issue of *FTS* was published in March 1920 right after the year when the New Women's Association (NWA, Shin fujin kyōkai), Japan's first association demanding women's political rights, was launched and began to publish its own newsletter, *Josei*

---

[6] The name of the newspaper is unknown.

dōmei (*The Women's League*). While Waka was initially involved in organizing NWA with Hiratsuka Raichō, Ichikawa Fusae (1893–1981), and Oku Mumeo (1895–1997), she later declined to work for the association as an executive member. According to Fusae, who was also invited by Raichō to work with her, Kakichi told Fusae to be careful working with Raichō, who was not a good organizer. Although Fusae did not follow Kakichi's advice and did become a co-founder of NWA along with Raichō, Waka added her name to only the list of the journal associates. It seems Kakichi had persuaded Waka to give up any strong involvement in the NWA. Possibly Kakichi had observed Raichō's activities and leadership at *Seitō* and concluded that the leader of *Seitō* was not a good team player. Waka did not necessarily oppose the vision of NWA, however, and was willing to offer help to NWA, contributing a few articles to *Josei dōmei*. Yet it seems that the Yamadas did have good timing in creating their own journal, as the couple could present their own views and have them stand out as fresh and different from those of Raichō and other female critics.

Initially the publisher of *FTS* was Abe Sentarō, a philanthropist and supporter of the Yamadas. However, after Abe's business declined, Kakichi took over the position of publisher in July of 1920. Issues of the journal were 64 pages long, and publication was consistent until September 1923 when the Great Kanto Earthquake destroyed much of the city of Tokyo and its surroundings. In the wake of this disaster, the number of pages in the journal declined to only 16, and the journal then continued with even fewer pages until the No. 160 issue (July, 1933). It then ceased abruptly about a year before Kakichi passed away from a stroke in 1934.

In the first issue of *FTS*, Waka explains that the objective of the journal was to encourage women to understand and discuss their own issues. It also promoted her family-centered viewpoint. She says,

> …I believe that it is love that matters in discussing women's issues. In Europe and the U.S., it was women's rights that really mattered in order to have women equal to men. However, recently, people have realized that women and men should be differentiated. Claiming that difference is the right that women are supposed to hold and doing so is their responsibility as human beings…(*Fujin to Shin-Shakai*, 1993, No.1 [March 1920], p. 3).

It is clear that Waka has a maximalist and gender distinctive view of feminism; that is, she wants to emphasize the difference between women and men, but keep women from competing against men for equal rights. Waka further states that the socialist ideal regarding cooperative production and distribution of profits is only a fantasy. Instead, women should nurture altruistic morality in the home and bring that philosophy into the broader society. If a woman did go outside the home to work for financial independence, then how could she take care of the home and train herself and her family members to be altruists?

Waka's advocacy of maternalism also led her to oppose socialist feminists, in particular, Yamakawa Kikue, whom Waka had already confronted in the "Debates over Protection of Motherhood." In an article published in the No. 35 (January, 1923) issue of *FTS*, Waka criticized Kikue, who promoted a socialist ideology among women. According to Waka, women's demand for equal rights with men would never bring any good results to either these women or their families (*Fujin to Shin-Shakai*, 1993, No. 35 (January, 1923), p. 55–60). Thus, in general, *FTS* represented a conservative feminist view that advocated distinctly gendered and separate roles for men and women when managing the family.

On the other hand, *FTS* is full of altruism (*rita shugi*), the key concept to understand to see Waka's theoretical backbone and personal belief. Altruism made her an admirable figure in charitable activities after 1934—when Kakichi passed away and one year after *FTS* ceased. It seems Waka was influenced by selfless love, Christian love, as she was baptized while staying in Cameron House. At the same time, Waka was probably unselfish by nature, according to her biographical note in *FTS* (*Fujin to Shin-Shakai*, 1993, No. 7 [September, 1920], p. 52–63) Waka, the seventh child among nine, reflects on her childhood when she was never doted on and almost neglected by her parents. That treatment for children was not uncommon at the time in a farmer's household with many children. She was an easygoing, innocent, and sympathetic little girl. For example, Waka continuously gave food to a wandering beggar in her neighborhood village and was teased by her friends and siblings badly for that. This episode may make the reader of *FTS* feel closer to Waka who was indeed an honest and down-to-earth personality.

Transmissive feminism

Before doing any comparative analysis, we should discuss the key term of this study, transmissive feminism. Transmissive feminism is obviously a new gendered term that I define as a form of feminism that provides direct/indirect courage, motives, and collaborative efforts to women, the beneficiaries of feminism, from men and the supporters of feminism. Men's support for women is so great that the men nearly sacrifice themselves for the success of women. This term could be particularized from the other forms of feminism, such as liberal feminism, radical feminism, Marxist and socialist feminism, psychoanalytic feminism, and others despite the philosophical, ideological background each may have. All are based on women's initiated agency; that is, women themselves seek feminism, which is defined as "the advocacy of women's rights on the grounds of political, social, and economic equality to men" (Feminism, n.d.). While some men may also be concerned with such advocacy for women and help their counterparts promote equality in society, women are mostly the primary agents who demand reform of laws and the social structure, as well as reform of the woman-man relationship in the home. None or very few men, if any, would likely devote themselves sacrificially to women for their equality and independence.

In Japan, First-wave feminism can be traced back to the 1870s, just as its counterpart in Europe and North America, and it is found occasionally as being very transmissive. Considering women's status and the education system during this time period, any women who were aiming to become scholars, writers, and other intellectuals had to learn their basic knowledge and skills from their counterparts, men. For example, a male master and a female disciple combination is very common in modern Japanese literature. One such example is the pioneering professional woman writer Higuchi Ichiyō (1872–1896) who needed initiation help from her male mentor as well as her unrequited first love, Nakarai Tōsui (1860–1926).

In this case, Ichiyō learned from that individual male a gender specific normative rule of writing, which was nearly forcibly applied to all women writers. Namely, the male dominated modern literary circle expected women to write something in a graceful style, such as the pseudo-classical style. Some colloquial expressions that sounded particularly lowbrow were taboo for the women writers, most of whom came from the middle to upper-middle class. Ichiyō's learning of this style seems to have been a transmissive gendered lesson. However, she eventually transformed that gendered transmissiveness into her own writing style and her personal individuality of independence (Saito, 2010a). In this manner, it could be said that such transmissive teaching to women by men in this particular period was feministic in the sense that it helped women to promote their own intellectual endeavors enough to become independent of men and their rationale. Thus, transmissive feminism could balance the gendered power relationship that was likely overdetermined from the start as not an equal circumstance between women and men.

Another example of transmissive feminism is the collaboration of Takamure Itsue (1894–1964) and her husband Hashimoto Kenzō (1897–1976). Itsue was a pioneering feminist scholar who wrote an extended women's history that focused on the ancient matrilineal system in Japan. Itsue was a brilliant woman who was born and educated in Kumamoto and joined Japan's emerging feminist movement in the 1920s with other feminist peers, such as Hiratsuka Raichō. While participating in writing for the anarchist feminist journal *Fujin sensen* (*Women's Vanguard*) at the beginning of the 1930s, she decided to enter a life of seclusion to engage in her grand work on historical feminism. Concentrating on writing her life's work, six volumes of *Josei no rekishi* (1954–1958, *Women's History*), while also secluding herself from the outside world gave her the status of being the most mythical feminist figure of that period.

During this scholarly hard work, her husband Kenzō constantly took all everyday practical responsibilities, including contracts and negotiations with publishers as well as completing the household chores. Kenzō acted "both as intellectual companion and as project-maker and promotion manager" (Ryang, 2009, p. 4). Without his self-sacrificing support, Itsue might not have been able to complete her admirable scholarly venture. Itsue's work is credited as her own; yet, at the same time, a trophy could be awarded to Kenzō's indirect efforts on the homefront. This kind of contribution is typically observed in the role of wife for husband or woman for man and usually not recognized as particularly admirable since the wife's collaboration with the husband tends to be accepted as a matter of course. In contrast, any husband's constant dedication to his wife's lifetime career success is rare in this particular period and indeed in any other period. This is a transmissive act with feministic elements; in this case the husband's devotion to his wife helped her to deeply engage in feministic work.

Yamada Waka and Kakichi may also be a model of transmissive feminism. Certain thoughts shared between the two parties were creatively transmissive. Further, such transmissive thoughts and the transmissive acts themselves between this unique couple are purely feministic, especially in the sense of expanding women's agency and opportunities for intellectual expression. In exploring this feminist transmissiveness, we examine their letters and journal articles in a comparative manner. In particular, I focus on Waka's ability to develop her independence with Kakichi's input and further, I illuminate her creativity in writing and as a journal editor.

Comparative analysis of the letters and articles

Collaboration, influence, gratitude

When focusing on the *FTS* articles that come from issues No. 27 (May, 1922) to No. 38 (April, 1923), one can see Waka and Kakichi's collaboration implicitly, but also explicitly. A comparison of the articles in terms of their descriptions of events and thoughts is found in their letters. Basically, through a precise comparison of the two different texts (articles and logs) from two different viewpoints (those of Waka and then Kakichi), we can see the effects of an intellectual dynamism in the texts as well as in the persons.

In issue No. 27 (May, 1922), Waka writes "Seeing My Husband's Departure On An Around-the-World Trip" (*Sekai isshū ryokō no to ni otto o okutte*). This essay begins with an introduction of Kakichi's background, explaining that he lost his mother as a small boy, and then his family had the misfortune to be broken apart. He had to work to take care of himself when he was only eight years old. She talks about his unbelievable efforts to study on his own and expresses her deep gratitude to Kakichi for helping her to learn everything she now knows and helping her from the very beginning.

The tone of the essay is full of her emotion, though Waka does not write about her concerns and loneliness at missing her husband directly. Instead, she brings up a poem that symbolizes her feelings. That poem is *Evangeline, A Tale of Acadie*, an epic poem published in 1847 written by Henry W. Longfellow, an American poet. Waka describes herself in a crowd at Tokyo station, just like Evangeline, who although decrepit with age continued looking for her fiancé whom she had lost in the crowd when she was a maiden.

In the end of the essay, Waka writes that she feels she was obligated to report to the readers of *FTS* that Kakichi had gone abroad because he was the editor and publisher of the journal. In fact, it is the first time that she refers to Kakichi in the two years and two months since the journal started. The reader may know who the publisher is, as it is of course Kakichi, Waka's husband, although Waka holds the actual role of editor for the journal. It seems that Waka is still reminding the readers of her husband's role as publisher and a financial supporter to publish the periodical. She is saying that he was helping her all the time even though he was totally invisible on the actual pages of the journal. When comparing this *FTS* essay that refers to Kakichi in light of Waka's personal letters that she sent to Kakichi, I think the essay was more likely a declaration that Waka would be writing and editing the journal more independently during her partner's absence.

Her first letter written to Kakichi on April 19, 1922, corresponds to the essay described above. Waka writes in her first letter the following:

> Today, I have finished writing "Seeing My Husband's Departure On An Around-the-World Trip (*Sekai isshū ryokō no to ni otto o okutte*) instead of editorial notes.... Yesterday, Mr. Seto dropped by to tell me that he had finished copyediting the first 350 pages of the book (*Katei no shakaiteki igi*, The Social Importance of Family). It will have about 450–460 pages (W. Yamada, personal communication, April 19, 1922).

She is briefing her husband here about what is going on in terms of her work editing the journal and also the processing of their other publications.

In her second letter, dated April 24, 1922, she comments:

> ...We often have guests, such as Ichikawa and Yamazaki, but I usually ask my sister to attend to them to keep doing work upstairs. I have to do much better work while you are away.... The price of *The Social Importance of Family* will be 2 yen 80 sen. Several newspapers have advertised that the book will be published. The journal is supposed to be done tonight or tomorrow morning. I'll send it to you as soon as it comes out (W. Yamada, personal communication, April 24, 1922).

Also, in her third letter, dated April 29, 1922, she writes,

> ...Last night, Mr. Seto (the printer) came here to give me back the manuscripts before he put them into type. The book will be finished around May 10th. He also asked me for a seal for the last page of the book. He has not charged us yet.
>
> ...Please do not worry. I can somehow manage the work by myself (W. Yamada, personal communication, April 29, 1922).

While Waka talks about miscellaneous news about her, their family, and neighbors, she also always lets Kakichi know if the journal editing is going well. She does so probably because she believes that is what Kakichi is concerned about and wants to know. It is assumed that when Kakichi was home, Waka could always ask him when she had something problematic to review. Now she has to deal with every problem on her own.

In the next issue of *FTS*, No. 28 (June 1922), there is a small column published under the name of Yamada Kakichi titled, "On the way to the Pacific Ocean (*Taiheiyōjō yori*)." This column is an abridged version of Kakichi's letter from April 23, translated into Japanese. (The quotation below is from the original English letter).

> ...There are about one hundred and forty Japanese passengers total. The number of first-class passengers is 271; second, 103; and second "B," 93; with steerage, 534. That makes a grand total of 1,001 on board. The *Taiyo-maru* is a colony indeed. There is a post office, barbershop, photo developing, [winter] garden, all kinds of physical exercise all arranged. There is nothing left out to make a man happy, I mean externally.
>
> The kind of passengers, I mean Japanese passengers, are three: #1 is a real businessmen; #2 are young men who are going back; #3 are the luxurious fools who only go for fooling (K. Yamada, personal communication, April 23, 1922).

In her letters sent to Kakichi, Waka does not refer to the column she writes for the No. 28 issue, which is a Japanese translation of her husband's letter.

In her letters on June 22, 1922 and on July 18, 1922, she writes to him that she did translate his letters and published them as a kind of traveling abroad diary under the name of Yamada Kakichi. Here is her message to him.

> ...I wrote a four-page article titled, "North American Transcontinental Diaries (*Hokubei gasshūkoku*)" using your name. When there was nothing special in your letters I could use for the journal, I looked up information in an encyclopedia and added more details to the journal article (W. Yamada, personal communication, June 22, 1922).

The article titled "North American Transcontinental Diaries (*Hokubei gasshūkoku*)" in No. 29, the July 1922 issue of *FTS*, includes a diary log from Kakichi's letter dated April 26, 1922. It reports that Kakichi arrived in Hawai'i and had a quick sightseeing trip in town. The actual date of the letter in which this information is included is April 25, and Kakichi writes, "I am going to reach Honolulu tomorrow morning." Waka puts the date of April 26 on the diary log for the *FTS* article based on this information. Thus, it appears that she read his letters carefully and then organized them in a proper way. There are ten logs dated from April 26 to May 20. These letters were written in Honolulu, San Francisco, Yosemite, Los Angeles, Salt Lake City, Chicago, Detroit, Niagara Falls, and New York City. Most of the translated descriptions in the "North American Transcontinental Diaries" do reflect the original order of dates and descriptions. The only difference is that the journal diaries do not include any affectionate and romantic messages from a lonely husband to his beloved wife.

The brief Editor's note on the last page of the diaries includes the following message to the reader:

> ...Letters from Kakichi who forgot how to write Japanese are all written in English. I (Waka) wanted to put them in the article in the original language. But it might be inconvenient for those who do not read English, and using both languages takes so much space. Therefore, I decided to put them only in a Japanese translation (*Fujin to Shin-Shakai*, 1993, No. 29 [July, 1922], p. 62).

This note tells the reader that Kakichi does not write in Japanese, so all the Japanese articles appearing under the name Kakichi are actually written by Waka.

In addition, it seems that Waka's younger sister also translated some English into Japanese. In the passage below from Waka's letter dated July 18, 1922, one learns that Ohisa, who worked as a typist, helped Waka to do a translation of the materials sent by Kakichi.

For the August 1922 issue of *FTS*, I wrote "Cuba and the South of the United States Tour (*Kyūba oyobi gasshūkoku nanbu meguri*)." ...I asked Ohisa to help out for the August issue. We used the newspaper articles you sent me as a report titled, "New York News." (W. Yamada, personal communication, July 18, 1922).

"Cuba and the South of the United States Tour" in No. 30, which appeared in the August 1922 issue of *FTS* also has the same format as the travel log article in the previous issue. Waka writes a preface for the diaries article, revealing that she had received letters from Havana, Cuba, which she did not expect. The travel plan that Waka was aware of was that Kakichi would stay in New York and might be able to travel to Cuba, but only when he finished all his assigned work. She explains to the readers that Kakichi and his employer's party changed their original plans for some reason and extended their journey to go to Cuba.

However, Kakichi's letter dated May 20 and written in New York and letters dated May 25, 26, and 30 in Havana, include no explanation for the possible schedule change. It seems the schedule change was reported in the article as only a note in passing because of Waka's decision to do so, not because of Kakichi's suggestion. Thus, one can see that Waka was fully responsible for translating and editing Kakichi's letters. Her Japanese translation transfers the meaning of Kakichi's English passage quite well to present a good factual report, but she does not use his description verbatim because she sometimes makes changes to expressions, so the reader can more easily follow the article and find it interesting.

Similar tour reports authored by Yamada Kakichi, such as "Around Great Britain" (*Eikoku isshū*), "Observation Tour to Europe"(*ōshūshokoku junsatsu*), "From France to the South Seas" (*Furansu kara naiyō made*), and "Finished My Around-the-World Trip" (*Sekai isshū ryokō o owatte*), appeared in *FTS* from September to December of 1922. All are easy to read because of Waka's careful re-organization of them and her translations of them into Japanese. Kakichi's letters are not always chronological and sometimes include several different events, referring to one event as done "yesterday" and then another event to be done tomorrow. Waka arranges the order of these dates and their corresponding events, putting them in proper order for better reading. For example, the journal entries "Observation Tour to Europe" in the October 1922 issue of *FTS* have an entry for July 19, which states "Arrival in Berlin." "I left Amsterdam at 8:47 a.m., this morning, arriving in Berlin at 9:00 p.m., tonight" (*Fujin to Shin-Shakai*, 1993, No.32 (October 1922), p. 40). The actual letter reads "... We are going to Berlin tomorrow morning by 8:47, arriving in Berlin by 9 p.m" (K. Yamada, personal communication, July 18, 1922). She changes the date of the journal entry and arranges it as though Kakichi wrote it after he arrived in Berlin instead of predicting his arrival there. It is thus much easier for the readers to follow the log because it is clearer about precisely when Kakichi was where.

Learning, development, independence

Thus, I have found some indications that Waka was a capable editor for the journal and very independent, as opposed to a comment from Gomi Yuriko, mentioned above and a social work scholar, who had direct contact with Waka and Kakichi while they were alive and compiled the *Collection of Works of Yamada Waka*. Although Gomi admits *FTS* was primarily credited to Waka, she tends to overestimate Kakichi's role as supervisory over Waka, and considers him to be a political moderatist, as shown in the passage below.

> ...I'm sure the articles published in this journal (FTS) belong to Waka, but I also assume some of them are their collaborative works. I am wondering whether there are quite a few works reflecting a philosophy and ideology that were shared by the two. Because Kakichi did not write a book of his own on this,* we cannot get to know his thoughts

in a direct manner.... He might have learned about and had been attracted to the labor movement and socialism because he had a hard time when he was working as an unskilled worker in the U.S. for a long time. However, it is amazing that he did not hold any radical ideology at all (Gomi, 1993, p. 59)

note: Kakichi published at least one book on sociology, one on Western cuisine.

Part of the answer to Gomi's question—why Kakichi did not become a radical despite his past wage-worker background and his attraction to socialism—is explained by Waka in her essay in the May 1922 issue of *FTS*. Kakichi's travel companion, Mr. A.—who is previously referred to in this essay as being a negative stereotype of Japanese businesspersons—influenced him to become an anti-socialist. Interestingly, in his letters, Kakichi criticizes Mr. A.'s attitude, which he feels is totally lacking in cultural and artistic sensitivities. Waka does not refer to Kakichi's comments about Mr. A. in her letters, however. Accordingly, it could be said that Waka was not necessarily in complete agreement with Kakichi on how to view Mr. A. in terms of ideology. In this respect, Waka and Kakichi apparently had different views of the Japanese businessperson. Or Waka just wanted to be nice to the person who had hired her husband. Waka might tolerate a person's behavior more than Kakichi would. Yet, Gomi still calls Kakichi a "moderatist" who avoids conflicts between wage-labor and capital in order to pursue the goal of social improvement commonly expected by any party. She considers Waka as having a more conservative and nationalistic state of mind. Here are Gomi's comments from another article on a biographical exposition of Yamada Waka:

> ...I assume Waka always acted as a spokesperson for Kakichi's thought and philosophy and the couple worked on writing together all the time. Still, I believe, it is Waka who actually wrote them, though.

> ...Kakichi advocated gradualism, shunning anything too radical. He learned to be a cosmopolitan. How should such a man have reacted if he survived after the Pacific War? Waka was devoted to patriotism. In addition, around 1936 to 1937, she was influenced by the Nichiren sect of Buddhism. Since then, she spent most her time transcribing a sutra until she died in 1957 (Gomi, 1980, p. 43).

Gomi is likely to have formed these conclusions as a result of knowledge of Waka's family and Waka's maternal-oriented thoughts that had been easily integrated into the government's wartime home-front policy.

However, at this point there is no clear way to figure out which person, Waka or Kakichi, was the more radical or conservative and who influenced the other the most to change his/her state of mind. Nonetheless, Waka was definitely not a person who simply shadowed her husband's ideas, as the previous examples clearly show. At the beginning of her intellectual development, she learned the "alphabet" in Japanese from Kakichi and wanted to become absorbed in the latest theories and discussions. Later she stepped up further and behaved more independently to reorganize and restructure what Kakichi was thinking in language that her mentor and husband was likely less comfortable with.

Good examples of these elaborate efforts are the couple's two articles which do follow and support each other. Waka's piece on "Historical Contents of the Conservatism and the Progressivism (*Hoshu shugi to shimpo shugi no rekishiteki naiyō*)" appeared in the February 1923 issue of *FTS*. In this article, she explains that the aspiration for political revolution in France came from the view of conservatism (*hoshu shugi*), while gradualism in Great Britain derived from progressivism (*shimpo shugi*). That means, as she elucidates, that in France, the people encountered several political fluctuations in the many changes of regimes from the French Revolution to the French Third Republic, and precise intellectual deliberation among the people was totally missing. French "conservatism" seems to be interpreted by Waka as having the power of hampering the progression of the country by bringing about a surge of revolutionary fever. The people in France merely acted with great emotion in their series of French political revolutions. In contrast, in Great Britain, there was no major change in the political regime after the Glorious (Bloodless) Revolution of 1688–89 and British life remained relatively stable. In general, the British way was considered conservative, and in its own way, did enable the British to achieve successful industrialization. Thus it was called progressivism because of the progress that took place over time.

Waka's article is followed by an article written under the name of Kakichi, "France: Won't Change While Seeking Change (*Henka o motomete henka sezaru Furansu*)," published in the March 1923 issue of *FTS*. The main argument here seems to be that France had experienced many intellectual and artistic changes, and yet the strong interest of the French in these areas had not changed at all. In conclusion, France rarely changed because of its unique "French spirit" which values cultural tradition as well as cultural creation. Kakichi quotes some lines of French thinkers and artists, such as Bergson and Baudelaire, to illustrate how the French people have engaged in philosophical discussions and experienced violent oscillation because of their aesthetic values. This article was written to continue the discussion of Waka's article in the previous issue, in which France's conservatism was described as a negative consequence of the extreme level of emotion that always hinders the French from achieving a progressive mind. Kakichi's article may have supplemented the content of Waka's to show another aspect of French conservatism, namely, its enthusiastic inclination to arts and philosophy. Thus, the two articles are complementary and help the reader understand the topic more deeply. As written in Japanese, both articles are indeed under Waka's control. Waka wisely distinguishes one from the other by using different writing styles. Waka's article is written in a polite narrative style using the sentence endings "*-desu,- masu*" in Japanese. This style sounds more communicative in its written form than the formal written "*-da, -dearu*" style used in Kakichi's article. In this way, Waka, who learned much from Kakichi, now ironically bolsters her intellectual mentor in a reverse way—by writing her own articles in Japanese, she transmits a better way to him to articulate his thought and create a bridge between him and the *FTS* readers.

Conclusion

As Gomi Yuriko hypothesizes, *FTS* is in truth a collaborative work by both Waka and Kakichi. Gomi, however, assumes that Waka was shadowing what Kakichi originated, based on his encyclopedic knowledge of world events and social/political theories. A comparative analysis of the pair's personal letters and published journal articles show that Waka's efforts at composing and organizing relatively mixed information from the letters actually made the articles more readable and informative. In particular, Waka's ability in the translation of English texts to Japanese bridges the gap between the journal reader who may not be able to read text in English and her husband and author of the travel logs who does not have a good command of Japanese and thus writes in English.

This study has touched on the collaborative aspect of one remarkable intellectual couple by examining a few written examples of their written communication, namely, their handwritten letters and journal articles in a comparative manner. Although I do not elaborate on further examples of their collaborative works in this essay, it is apparent that the outcome of their relationship and collaboration is a clean example of transmissive feminism, wherein Kakichi passed on his intellect and passion to a younger willing wife instead of standing alone as a male front-liner for women's issues. The example also shows the transmissive nature of marriage and the relationship when both parties truly respect and trust the opinions and intellect of the other and the capability of growing and expanding thought. Waka eventually evolved into an intellectual, developing true, perhaps even greater maturity in her thinking and ideology, while still remaining loyal to Kakichi. The couple worked together to theorize and create a family unit that centered on mothering-centered feminism through both their publications and her speeches in the 1920s and 1930s until Kakichi died. After his death, Waka realized and expressed her own family-oriented thought through effective social work practices, supporting single mothers and their children. It would be still more intriguing to explore her later transmissive feministic acts and thoughts through a closer analysis of more of the writings that the couple produced in both the private and public spheres.

Acknowledgements

I am most grateful to Mr. Yaheiji Yamada, a grandson of Yamada Waka and Kakichi, for kindly showing me the letters used to write this article. I also thank Dr. Jan Bardsley for introducing me to Mr. Yamada and encouraging me to work on this project.

References

Bardsley, J. (2007a). *The bluestockings of Japan: New woman essays and fiction from Seitō, 1911–16*. Ann Arbor: Center for Japanese Studies, University of Michigan.

Bardsley, J. (2007b). *A Taishō romance: Travel letters from Yamada Kakichi (1865–1934) to Yamada Waka (1879–1957)*. Unpublished manuscript.

Feminism. (n.d.). In *Oxford dictionaries online*. Retrieved from http://oxforddictionaries.com/definition/feminism?region=us.

Fujin to Shin-Shakai [Women and the New Society]. (1993). Reprint of 160 issues originally published monthly, March 1920–July 1993, in 7 volumes, plus Supplement in separate volume, *Bessatsu sōmokji*, kaisetsu [Supplementary volume: Complete table of contents, Commentary]. Tokyo, Japan: Kuresu Shuppan. LCCN Permalink: http://lccn.loc.gov/2009211528

Gomi, Y. (1980). Yamada Waka: Hito to ayumi [Waka Yamada: Her personality and life history]. *Shakai jigyō kenkyū, 8*, 69–84.

Gomi, Y. (1993). Kaisetsu [Commentary]. In *Fujin to Shin-Shakai* [Women and the New Society] (1993), *Bessatsu sōmokji*, kaisetsu [Supplementary volume: Complete table of contents, Commentary]. Tokyo: Kuresu Shuppan.

Hiratsuka, R. (2006). *In the beginning, woman was the sun: The autobiography of a Japanese feminist*. (T. Craig, Trans.). New York, NY: Columbia University Press. (Original work published 1971).

Imai, K. (2006). Yamada Waka: Kunan no hansei kara bosei hogo undō no kishu e [Waka Yamada: Her suffering of life and working on the movement of protection for motherhood]. In Y. Murota (Ed.), *Jinbutsu de yomu kindai nihon shakaifukushi no ayumi* [Reading the history of social welfare in modern Japan through biographies] (pp. 163–169). Tokyo, Japan: Mineruba shobō.

Mackie, V. (2002 [1997]) *Creating socialist women in Japan: Gender, labour and activism 1900–1937*. New York, NY: Cambridge University Press.

Rodd, L. R. (1991). Yosano Akiko and the Taisho debate over the 'new woman.' In G. L. Bernstein (Ed.), *Recreating Japanese women, 1600–1945* (pp. 175–198). Berkeley: University of California Press.

Ryang, S. (1998). Love and colonialism in Takamure Itsue's feminism: A postcolonial critique. *Feminist Review, 60, Feminist Ethics and the Politics of Love*, 1–32.

Saji, E. (1974). Yamada Waka to boseishugi [Waka Yamada and motherhood ideology]. *Ochanomizu Shigaku, 18*, 15–30.

Saito, R. (2010a). Writing in female drag: Gendered literature and a woman's voice. *Japanese Language and Literature, 44*(2), 149–177.

Saito, R. (2010b). Taishō roman no unda feminisuto: Yamada Waka & Kakichi no kyōdō to shisō, sono 1 [Feminists born in the Taisho romanticism: Waka & Kakichi Yamada's collaboration and thought, part 1]. *Kotoba, 31*, 113–126.

Saito, R. (2011). Taishō roman no unda feminisuto: Yamada Waka & Kakichi no kyōdō to shisō, sono 2 [Feminists born in the Taisho romanticism: Waka & Kakichi Yamada's collaboration and thought, part 2]. *Kotoba, 32*, 151–165.

Tomida, H. (2004). *Hiratsuka Raichō and Early Japanese Feminism*. Boston, MA: Brill.

Yamada, K. (1922). Taiheiyōjō yori [On the way to the Pacific Ocean]. In *Fujin to Shin-Shakai*, 3(28), 60.

Yamada, W. (1922). Sekai isshū ryokō no to ni otto o okutte [seeing my husband's departure on an around-the-world trip] In *Fujin to Shin-Shakai*, 3(27), 59–61.

Yamada, K. (1922). Kyūba oyobi gasshūkoku nanbu meguri [Cuba and the south of the United States tour]. In *Fujin to Shin-Shakai*, 3(30), 34–39.

Yamada, K. (1922). Eikoku isshū [Around Great Britain]. In *Fujin to Shin-Shakai*, 3(31), 43–47.

Yamada, K. (1922 October). Ōshūshokoku junsatsu [Observation tour to Europe]. In *Fujin to Shin-Shakai*, 3(32), 39–44, 58.

Yamada, K. (1922). Sekai isshū ryokō o owatte [Finished my around-the-world trip]. In *Fujin to Shin-Shakai*, 3(34), 41–47.

Yamada, K. (1923). Henka o motomete henka sezaru Furansu [France: Won't change while seeking change]. In *Fujin to Shin-Shakai*, 4(37), 35–45.

Yamada, W. (1923). Puroretaria o katsugu Yamakawa Kikue shi e [To Ms. Kikue Yamakawa who willingly acts as a cat's-paw of proletarians]. In *Fujin to Shin-Shakai*, 4(35), 55–60.

Yamada, W. (1923). Hoshu shugi to shimpo shugi no rekishiteki naiyō [Historical contents of conservatism and progressivism]. In *Fujin to Shin-Shakai*, 4(36), 52–56.

Yamada, W. (2007). *Yamada Waka Chosakushū* [Collected works of Waka Yamada]. Hayashi Chiyo (Ed.). Tokyo, Japan: Gakujutsu shuppan.

Yamada, Y. (2011). Kakichi to Waka no tegami 1922 nen [The letters written by Kakichi and Waka in 1922]. Unpublished manuscript.

Yamazaki, T. (1978). Ameyuki san no uta: Yamada Waka no sūkinaru shōgai [The song of a woman bound for America: Ups and downs in the Life of Waka Yamada]. Tokyo, Japan: Bungei shunjū.

Yamazaki, T. (1985). *The story of Yamada Waka: From prostitute to feminist pioneer*. New York, NY: Kodansha International.

Yasutake, R. (2004). *Transitional women's activism: The United States, Japan, and Japanese immigrants in California, 1859–1920*. New York, NY: New York University Press.

About the Contributors

Editors

Kimi Kondo-Brown is a professor in the Department of East Asian Languages and Literature at the University of Hawai'i at Mānoa. She is also presently serving as the associate dean of the College of Languages, Linguistics, and Literature at the University. She has published books and articles in the fields of Japanese pedagogy, assessment, and heritage language education. Her newest book entitled *Assessment for Japanese language teachers* (2012, with Kuroshio in Tokyo) examines theoretical issues and practical ideas for conducting assessments for formative and summative purposes at course and program levels.

Yoshiko Saito-Abbott is a professor of Japanese, the chair of the School of World Languages and Cultures, and the director of the Monterey Bay Foreign Language Project at California State University, Monterey Bay. She is an editorial member of the *Foreign Language Annals* and has served on the board of directors for professional organizations such as the National Council of Japanese Language Teachers and the Association of Teachers of Japanese (AATJ). Her research interests include the acquisition of Japanese as a foreign language, technology in language instruction, business Japanese, and teacher education. She publishes in journals such as *Modern Language Journal* and *Foreign Language Annals*.

Shingo Satsutani is a professor of Asian Languages at College of DuPage in Illinois. He received an MA in Asian Studies from Seton Hall University in New Jersey. He continued his studies in the doctoral program at Fordham University in New York. In 2008, he won the Japanese Teacher of the Year from the National Council of Japanese Language Teachers. His current, keen interests are Japanese education for heritage speakers and the seamless articulation of K–16 Japanese education. He is currently serving on the board of directors of AATJ and is in charge of the Japanese National Honor Society and other student activities at his college.

Michio Tsutsui is the director of the Technical Japanese Program at the University of Washington. He is a Donald E. Petersen Professor and a professor in the Department of Human Centered Design and Engineering. His research areas include Japanese linguistics, technology for language learning, and Japanese for special purposes. His publications include *A dictionary of basic Japanese grammar*, *A dictionary of intermediate Japanese grammar*, and *A dictionary for advanced Japanese grammar* (The Japan Times; with Seiichi Makino). He coauthored *Tobira: Gateway to advanced Japanese* (Kuroshio) and has codeveloped several software applications, including *Language partner online*.

Ann Wehmeyer is an associate professor of Japanese and Linguistics at the University of Florida. She received a PhD in Linguistics from the University of Michigan. Her research interests include the history of linguistic thought in Japan, contemporary language use in Japan, and folklore. Her translation of Motoori Norinaga's commentary, the *Kojiki-den, Book 1*, appeared in the Cornell East Asia Series. She has also published on nonstandard speech in the media, the history of Japanese grammatical studies, and early perspectives on the Japanese sound system.

Authors

Yuka Akiyama is a Japanese lecturer at the Massachusetts Institute of Technology. In the past, she has also taught Japanese at Boston University and Middlebury College in Japan. Her research interests include written/oral corrective feedback, eTandem language learning (reciprocal teaching and learning of L1 and TL using CMC tools), task-based language teaching (TBLT), and language assessment. She holds a Master of Education in TESOL from Boston University and has been coordinating task-based eTandem language exchange projects between schools in Japan and the United States. In Fall 2013, she will enter the doctoral program in Linguistics at Georgetown University.

Kiyomi Chinen is an assistant professor of Japanese in the Department of Asian and Asian American Studies at California State University, Long Beach. Her research interests include Japanese heritage language learning, language learning and identity, and ethnolinguistic vitality. With Masako Douglas and Hiroko Kataoka, she coauthored "The role of familial factors in Japanese heritage language development" in *Proceedings of the 2nd International Conference on Intangible Heritage* (2011), and authored "Ni-gengo de sodatsu kodomo no aidentiti" in *Amerika de sodatsu Nihon no kodomo tachi: Bairingaru no hikari to kage* (2008).

Dan Dewey is an associate professor of Linguistics at Brigham Young University in Utah. He received his PhD from Carnegie Mellon University in Second Language Acquisition (specializing in Japanese). His research interests include language acquisition through informal out-of-class language exposure (in particular during study abroad), second language testing, and individual differences in second language acquisition. He has published in *Studies in Second Language Acquisition*, *Foreign Language Annals*, *Japanese Language and Literature*, and *The Canadian Modern Language Review*.

Masako O. Douglas is a professor of Japanese at California State University, Long Beach. Her research interests include Japanese Heritage Language (JHL) development, the pedagogy of young and adult learners, and curriculum design with a special focus on content-based instruction. She created a textbook for young JHL learners, *Ken Ken Pa* (2010). Her papers include "Analysis of *kanji* ability of heritage learners of Japanese" in *Heritage Language Journal* (2010), and "Scaffolding in content-based instruction of Japanese" (with Hiroko Kataoka) in *Japanese Language and Literature* (2008). She is the chair of JHL special interest group of American Association of Teachers of Japanese, and an editorial board member of the *Heritage Language Journal*.

Mayumi Fleshler is a statistical consultant with experience in fields ranging from education to biomedical applications. She has been involved in research at Harvard Medical School, Boston University, and Osaka University in Japan. Her research interests include boundary-crossing problems in sequential analysis applied to mathematical finance and experimental design in medical and social sciences. She holds a PhD in Mathematics (Probability/Statistics) and has taught a wide variety of statistics courses at Harvard University (Department of Statistics, where she currently holds a preceptor position), Harvard Extension School, and Boston University (Department of Mathematics and Statistics).

Daniel Gardner received a bachelor's degree in Linguistics with a minor in Scandinavian Studies from Brigham Young University in 2011. He completed his senior thesis on language use and intercultural sensitivity. He has coauthored presentations and publications regarding social network development in Japanese and Arabic. Currently, he is working for Ancestry.com.

Atsushi Hasegawa received his PhD in Second Language Acquisition (SLA) (with a minor in Japanese) from University of Wisconsin-Madison. His research encompasses various aspects of classroom SLA. In particular, he is specialized in conversation analysis (CA) and its application for SLA research. He has written on such topics as "Toward 'contents' in the beginning language class" (with Noriko Hanabusa, Mano Yasuda, and Kazumi Matsumoto) and "Doing being a foreign language learner in a classroom: Embodiment of cognitive states as social events" (with Junko Mori). He is currently a language lecturer at New York University.

Tomoko Iwai teaches Japanese in the Department of East Asian Languages and Literatures at the University of Hawai'i at Mānoa, where she also earned her PhD in Japanese Linguistics. Her research interests are language pedagogy and pragmatics. She is a cocreator of a pragmatics-focused oral communication curriculum at the University of Hawai'i at Mānoa, and a coauthor of *Japanese for oral communication: A new approach to Japanese language and culture* (2001). She was a 2011 recipient of the Frances Davis Award for Excellence in Undergraduate Teaching at the University of Hawai'i at Mānoa.

Uichi Kamiyoshi is the senior chief Japanese language specialist and chief consultant of the Overseas Human Resources and Industry Development Association, HIDA Research Institute. He received his MA degree (Language and Culture) in 2001 from Osaka University Graduate School. His areas of research interest are language policy, business Japanese, and psychology of learning of language. He is the author of "A study of the second language acquisition process through language-mediated activity in the workplace: The limits and possibilities of language development from the perspective of primary and secondary speech" in *Journal of Japanese Language Teaching* (2010).

Michiko Kaneyasu received a PhD in Asian Languages and Cultures (Japanese Linguistics) from the University of California, Los Angeles in 2012. She is currently a full-time instructor of Japanese at the University of Colorado, Boulder. Her research interests center on understanding the interrelationships between linguistic forms, their functions, and contexts of use, including pragmatic and socio-cultural factors. In her dissertation, she explored the patterns and functions of recurrent multi-morphemic sequences in Japanese spoken discourse. Her current research projects include the use of copulas as stance markers, formulaic language in conversation, and the role of technology and media in language instruction.

Hiroko C. Kataoka is a professor of Japanese at California State University, Long Beach. Her current research focuses on young learners of Japanese, including heritage speakers of Japanese and Japanese immersion program students. Her most recent book is *Amerika de sodatsu Nihon no kodomo tachi: Bairingaru no hikari to kage*, coedited with Gun'ei Sato (2008). Her recent papers include "Japanese language proficiency and home language use among children of international marriages: Breaking free from common assumptions" in *JHL Journal: Japanese Heritage Language Education* (coauthored with Setsue Shibata, 2011).

Yuri Kumagai received her EdD in Language, Literacy, and Culture from the University of Massachusetts, Amherst. Her specializations are foreign language education and critical literacy. She has coedited books, *Assessment and Japanese language education* (2010), and *Japanese language education for global citizens* (2011). Her articles appear in journals such as *Critical Inquiry in Language Studies, Japanese Language and Literature, Japanese Language Education around the Globe, Critical Studies in Education,* and *Social Identities*. She has been teaching Japanese as a foreign language to college students in the US for more than 20 years. Currently, she is a senior lecturer at Smith College.

Xiaoman Miao is a PhD student in the Department of East Asian Languages and Cultures at Stanford University. Her research interests include Japanese semantics and pragmatics, Japanese and Chinese contrastive linguistics, and the acquisition of Japanese as a second language. She authored "Aspectual shifts of *moo* and *mada*" in *Foreign Language and Culture Studies* (volume 5, Shanghai Foreign Language Education Press, 2005), and with Fangqiong Zhan coauthored "A comparative study on Japanese and Chinese noun modifying constructions: A semantic and discourse approach" in *Rice Working Papers in Linguistics* (volume 3, 2012).

Spencer Ring is an undergraduate at Brigham Young University student majoring in Economics and minoring in Japanese. He has copresented on Japanese and Arabic language use and acquisition at the Annual Conference of the Association of Teachers of Japanese, the American Association for Applied Linguistics, and the Second Language Research Forum. Recently, he coauthored an article involving Japanese language learners with Dan Dewey and others entitled "Social capital and language acquisition during study abroad" in *Proceedings of the 33rd Annual Conference of the Cognitive Science Society*.

Rika Saito is an assistant professor of Japanese at Western Michigan University. She is interested in feminist issues in modern and pre-modern Japanese literary texts, language and gender, and language policy. Her publications include "Writing in female drag: Gendered literature and a woman's voice," in *Japanese Language and Literature (2)44* (Fall, 2010), "Constructing and gendering women's speech: Integrated policy of language through textbooks" in *U.S.–Japan Women's Journal(31)* (2006), and "Was women's speech included in the official language policy of Meiji Japan?: The case of *kōgo bunten*, guidebooks for grammar in spoken Japanese" in *Nihongo to Jendā [Japanese Language and Gender]*.

Shinji Sato received his PhD degree in Anthropology and Education from Teachers College, Columbia University. His specialization is educational anthropology, focusing on language education. He is the coauthor of several publications, including *Culture, language, and education: Beyond standards in Japanese education* (2008), *Assessment and Japanese language education*" (2010), *Japanese language education for global citizens* (2011), and "Communication as intersubjective activity" in *Native speakers effects: Standardization, hybridity, and power in language politics* (2009). He has taught Japanese at Columbia University and Harvard University. Currently Sato is a senior lecturer and the director of the Japanese Language Program at Princeton University.

NATIONAL FOREIGN LANGUAGE RESOURCE CENTER
University of Hawai'i at Mānoa

ordering information at nflrc.hawaii.edu

Pragmatics & Interaction
Gabriele Kasper, series editor

Pragmatics & Interaction ("P&I"), a refereed series sponsored by the University of Hawai'i National Foreign Language Resource Center, publishes research on topics in pragmatics and discourse as social interaction from a wide variety of theoretical and methodological perspectives. P&I welcomes particularly studies on languages spoken in the Asia-Pacific region.

PRAGMATICS OF VIETNAMESE AS NATIVE AND TARGET LANGUAGE
CARSTEN ROEVER & HANH THI NGUYEN (EDITORS), 2013

The volume offers a wealth of new information about the forms of several speech acts and their social distribution in Vietnamese as L1 and L2, complemented by a chapter on address forms and listener responses. As the first of its kind, the book makes a valuable contribution to the research literature on pragmatics, sociolinguistics, and language and social interaction in an under-researched and less commonly taught Asian language.

282pp., ISBN 978-0-9835816-2-8 $30.

L2 LEARNING AS SOCIAL PRACTICE: CONVERSATION-ANALYTIC PERSPECTIVES
GABRIELE PALLOTTI & JOHANNES WAGNER (EDITORS), 2011

This volume collects empirical studies applying Conversation Analysis to situations where second, third, and other additional languages are used. A number of different aspects are considered, including how linguistic systems develop over time through social interaction, how participants 'do' language learning and teaching in classroom and everyday settings, how they select languages and manage identities in multilingual contexts, and how the linguistic-interactional divide can be bridged with studies combining Conversation Analysis and Functional Linguistics. This variety of issues and approaches clearly shows the fruitfulness of a socio-interactional perspective on second language learning.

380pp., ISBN 978-0-9800459-7-0 $30.

TALK-IN-INTERACTION: MULTILINGUAL PERSPECTIVES
HANH THI NGUYEN & GABRIELE KASPER (EDITORS), 2009

This volume offers original studies of interaction in a range of languages and language varieties, including Chinese, English, Japanese, Korean, Spanish, Swahili, Thai, and Vietnamese; monolingual and bilingual interactions; and activities designed for second or foreign language learning. Conducted from the perspectives of conversation analysis and membership categorization analysis, the chapters examine ordinary conversation and institutional activities in face-to-face, telephone, and computer-mediated environments.

430pp., ISBN 978-0-8248-3137-0 $30.

Pragmatics & Language Learning
Gabriele Kasper, series editor

Pragmatics & Language Learning ("PLL"), a refereed series sponsored by the National Foreign Language Resource Center, publishes selected papers from the biannual International Pragmatics & Language Learning conference under the editorship of the conference hosts and the series editor. Check the NFLRC website for upcoming PLL conferences and PLL volumes.

PRAGMATICS AND LANGUAGE LEARNING VOLUME 13
TIM GREER, DONNA TATSUKI, & CARSTEN ROEVER (EDITORS), 2013

Pragmatics & Language Learning Volume 13 examines the organization of second language and multilingual speakers' talk and pragmatic knowledge across a range of naturalistic and experimental activities. Based on data collected among ESL and EFL learners from a variety of backgrounds, the contributions explore the nexus of pragmatic knowledge, interaction, and L2 learning outside and inside of educational settings.

292pp., ISBN 978-0-9835816-4-2 $30.

PRAGMATICS AND LANGUAGE LEARNING VOLUME 12
GABRIELE KASPER, HANH THI NGUYEN, DINA R. YOSHIMI, & JIM K. YOSHIOKA (EDITORS), 2010

This volume examines the organization of second language and multilingual speakers' talk and pragmatic knowledge across a range of naturalistic and experimental activities. Based on data collected on Danish, English, Hawai'i Creole, Indonesian, and Japanese as target languages, the contributions explore the nexus of pragmatic knowledge, interaction, and L2 learning outside and inside of educational settings.

364pp., ISBN 978-09800459-6-3 $30.

PRAGMATICS AND LANGUAGE LEARNING VOLUME 11
KATHLEEN BARDOVI-HARLIG, CÉSAR FÉLIX-BRASDEFER, & ALWIYA S. OMAR (EDITORS), 2006

This volume features cutting-edge theoretical and empirical research on pragmatics and language learning among a wide variety of learners in diverse learning contexts from a variety of language backgrounds and target languages (English, German, Japanese, Kiswahili, Persian, and Spanish). This collection of papers from researchers around the world includes critical appraisals on the role of formulas in interlanguage pragmatics, and speech-act research from a conversation analytic perspective. Empirical studies examine learner data using innovative methods of analysis and investigate issues in pragmatic development and the instruction of pragmatics.

430pp., ISBN 978-0-8248-3137-0 $30.

NFLRC Monographs
Richard Schmidt, series editor

Monographs of the National Foreign Language Resource Center present the findings of recent work in applied linguistics that is of relevance to language teaching and learning (with a focus on the less commonly taught languages of Asia and the Pacific) and are of particular interest to foreign language educators, applied linguists, and researchers. Prior to 2006, these monographs were published as "SLTCC Technical Reports."

NEW PERSPECTIVES ON JAPANESE LANGUAGE LEARNING, LINGUISTICS, AND CULTURE
KIMI KONDO-BROWN, YOSHIKO SAITO-ABBOTT, SHINGO SATSUTANI, MICHIO TSUTSUI, & ANN WEHMEYER (EDITORS), 2013

This volume is a collection of selected refereed papers presented at the Association of Teachers of Japanese Annual Spring Conference held at the University of Hawai'i at Mānoa in March of 2011. It not only covers several important topics on teaching and learning spoken and written Japanese and culture in and beyond classroom settings but also includes research investigating certain linguistics items from new perspectives.

208pp., ISBN 978–0–9835816–3–5 $25.

DEVELOPING, USING, AND ANALYZING RUBRICS IN LANGUAGE ASSESSMENT WITH CASE STUDIES IN ASIAN AND PACIFIC LANGUAGES
JAMES DEAN BROWN (EDITOR), 2012

Rubrics are essential tools for all language teachers in this age of communicative and task-based teaching and assessment—tools that allow us to efficiently communicate to our students what we are looking for in the productive language abilities of speaking and writing and then effectively assess those abilities when the time comes for grading students, giving them feedback, placing them into new courses, and so forth. This book provides a wide array of ideas, suggestions, and examples (mostly from Māori, Hawaiian, and Japanese language assessment projects) to help language educators effectively develop, use, revise, analyze, and report on rubric-based assessments.

212pp., ISBN 978–0–9835816–1–1 $25.

RESEARCH AMONG LEARNERS OF CHINESE AS A FOREIGN LANGUAGE
MICHAEL E. EVERSON & HELEN H. SHEN (EDITORS), 2010

Cutting-edge in its approach and international in its authorship, this fourth monograph in a series sponsored by the Chinese Language Teachers Association features eight research studies that explore a variety of themes, topics, and perspectives important to a variety of stakeholders in the Chinese language learning community. Employing a wide range of research methodologies, the volume provides data from actual Chinese language learners and will be of value to both theoreticians and practitioners alike. *[in English & Chinese]*

180pp., ISBN 978–0–9800459–4–9 $20.

MANCHU: A TEXTBOOK FOR READING DOCUMENTS (SECOND EDITION)
Gertraude Roth Li, 2010

This book offers students a tool to gain a basic grounding in the Manchu language. The reading selections provided in this volume represent various types of documents, ranging from examples of the very earliest Manchu writing (17th century) to samples of contemporary Sibe (Xibo), a language that may be considered a modern version of Manchu. Since Manchu courses are only rarely taught at universities anywhere, this second edition includes audio recordings to assist students with the pronunciation of the texts.

418pp., ISBN 978-0-9800459-5-6 $36.

TOWARD USEFUL PROGRAM EVALUATION IN COLLEGE FOREIGN LANGUAGE EDUCATION
John M. Norris, John McE. Davis, Castle Sinicrope, & Yukiko Watanabe (Editors), 2009

This volume reports on innovative, useful evaluation work conducted within U.S. college foreign language programs. An introductory chapter scopes out the territory, reporting key findings from research into the concerns, impetuses, and uses for evaluation that FL educators identify. Seven chapters then highlight examples of evaluations conducted in diverse language programs and institutional contexts. Each case is reported by program-internal educators, who walk readers through critical steps, from identifying evaluation uses, users, and questions, to designing methods, interpreting findings, and taking actions. A concluding chapter reflects on the emerging roles for FL program evaluation and articulates an agenda for integrating evaluation into language education practice.

240pp., ISBN 978-0-9800459-3-2 $30.

SECOND LANGUAGE TEACHING AND LEARNING IN THE NET GENERATION
Raquel Oxford & Jeffrey Oxford (Editors), 2009

Today's young people—the Net Generation—have grown up with technology all around them. However, teachers cannot assume that students' familiarity with technology in general transfers successfully to pedagogical settings. This volume examines various technologies and offers concrete advice on how each can be successfully implemented in the second language curriculum.

240pp., ISBN 978-0-9800459-2-5 $30.

CASE STUDIES IN FOREIGN LANGUAGE PLACEMENT: PRACTICES AND POSSIBILITIES
Thom Hudson & Martyn Clark (Editors), 2008

Although most language programs make placement decisions on the basis of placement tests, there is surprisingly little published about different contexts and systems of placement testing. The present volume contains case studies of placement programs in foreign language programs at the tertiary level across the United States. The different programs span the spectrum from large programs servicing hundreds of students annually to small language programs with very few students. The contributions to this volume address such issues as how the size of the program, presence or absence of heritage learners, and population changes affect language placement decisions.

201pp., ISBN 0-9800459-0-8 $20.

CHINESE AS A HERITAGE LANGUAGE: FOSTERING ROOTED WORLD CITIZENRY
Agnes Weiyun He & Yun Xiao (Editors), 2008

Thirty-two scholars examine the sociocultural, cognitive-linguistic, and educational-institutional trajectories along which Chinese as a Heritage Language may be acquired, maintained, and developed. They draw upon developmental psychology, functional linguistics, linguistic and cultural anthropology, discourse analysis, orthography analysis, reading research, second language acquisition, and bilingualism. This volume aims to lay a foundation for theories, models, and master scripts to be discussed, debated, and developed, and to stimulate research and enhance teaching both within and beyond Chinese language education.

280pp., ISBN 978–0–8248–3286–5 $20.

PERSPECTIVES ON TEACHING CONNECTED SPEECH TO SECOND LANGUAGE SPEAKERS
JAMES DEAN BROWN & KIMI KONDO-BROWN (EDITORS), 2006

This book is a collection of fourteen articles on connected speech of interest to teachers, researchers, and materials developers in both ESL/EFL (ten chapters focus on connected speech in English) and Japanese (four chapters focus on Japanese connected speech). The fourteen chapters are divided up into five sections:

- What do we know so far about teaching connected speech?
- Does connected speech instruction work?
- How should connected speech be taught in English?
- How should connected speech be taught in Japanese?
- How should connected speech be tested?

290pp., ISBN 978–0–8248–3136–3 $20.

CORPUS LINGUISTICS FOR KOREAN LANGUAGE LEARNING AND TEACHING
ROBERT BLEY-VROMAN & HYUNSOOK KO (EDITORS), 2006

Dramatic advances in personal-computer technology have given language teachers access to vast quantities of machine-readable text, which can be analyzed with a view toward improving the basis of language instruction. Corpus linguistics provides analytic techniques and practical tools for studying language in use. This volume provides both an introductory framework for the use of corpus linguistics for language teaching and examples of its application for Korean teaching and learning. The collected papers cover topics in Korean syntax, lexicon, and discourse, and second language acquisition research, always with a focus on application in the classroom. An overview of Korean corpus linguistics tools and available Korean corpora are also included.

265pp., ISBN 0–8248–3062–8 $25.

NEW TECHNOLOGIES AND LANGUAGE LEARNING: CASES IN THE LESS COMMONLY TAUGHT LANGUAGES
CAROL ANNE SPREEN (EDITOR), 2002

In recent years, the National Security Education Program (NSEP) has supported an increasing number of programs for teaching languages using different technological media. This compilation of case study initiatives funded through the NSEP Institutional Grants Program presents a range of technology-based options for language programming that will help universities make more informed decisions about teaching less commonly taught languages. The eight chapters describe how different types of technologies are used to support language programs (i.e., Web, ITV, and audio- or video-based materials), discuss identifiable trends in e-language learning, and explore how technology addresses issues of equity, diversity, and opportunity. This book offers many lessons learned and decisions made as technology changes and learning needs become more complex.

188pp., ISBN 0–8248–2634–5 $25.

AN INVESTIGATION OF SECOND LANGUAGE TASK-BASED PERFORMANCE ASSESSMENTS
James Dean Brown, Thom Hudson, John M. Norris, & William Bonk, 2002

This volume describes the creation of performance assessment instruments and their validation (based on work started in a previous monograph). It begins by explaining the test and rating scale development processes and the administration of the resulting three seven-task tests to 90 university-level EFL and ESL students. The results are examined in terms of (a) the effects of test revision; (b) comparisons among the task-dependent, task-independent, and self-rating scales; and (c) reliability and validity issues.

240pp., ISBN 0-8248-2633-7 $25.

MOTIVATION AND SECOND LANGUAGE ACQUISITION
Zoltán Dörnyei & Richard Schmidt (Editors), 2001

This volume—the second in this series concerned with motivation and foreign language learning—includes papers presented in a state of-the-art colloquium on L2 motivation at the American Association for Applied Linguistics (Vancouver, 2000) and a number of specially commissioned studies. The 20 chapters, written by some of the best known researchers in the field, cover a wide range of theoretical and research methodological issues, and also offer empirical results (both qualitative and quantitative) concerning the learning of many different languages (Arabic, Chinese, English, Filipino, French, German, Hindi, Italian, Japanese, Russian, and Spanish) in a broad range of learning contexts (Bahrain, Brazil, Canada, Egypt, Finland, Hungary, Ireland, Israel, Japan, Spain, and the U.S.).

520pp., ISBN 0-8248-2458-X $30.

A FOCUS ON LANGUAGE TEST DEVELOPMENT: EXPANDING THE LANGUAGE PROFICIENCY CONSTRUCT ACROSS A VARIETY OF TESTS
Thom Hudson & James Dean Brown (Editors), 2001

This volume presents eight research studies that introduce a variety of novel, nontraditional forms of second and foreign language assessment. To the extent possible, the studies also show the entire test development process, warts and all. These language testing projects not only demonstrate many of the types of problems that test developers run into in the real world but also afford the reader unique insights into the language test development process.

230pp., ISBN 0-8248-2351-6 $20.

STUDIES ON KOREAN IN COMMUNITY SCHOOLS
Dong-Jae Lee, Sookeun Cho, Miseon Lee, Minsun Song, & William O'Grady (Editors), 2000

The papers in this volume focus on language teaching and learning in Korean community schools. Drawing on innovative experimental work and research in linguistics, education, and psychology, the contributors address issues of importance to teachers, administrators, and parents. Topics covered include childhood bilingualism, Korean grammar, language acquisition, children's literature, and language teaching methodology. [in Korean]

256pp., ISBN 0-8248-2352-4 $20.

A COMMUNICATIVE FRAMEWORK FOR INTRODUCTORY JAPANESE LANGUAGE CURRICULA
Washington State Japanese Language Curriculum Guidelines Committee, 2000

In recent years, the number of schools offering Japanese nationwide has increased dramatically. Because of the tremendous popularity of the Japanese language and the shortage of teachers, quite a few untrained, nonnative and native teachers are in the classrooms and are expected to teach several levels of Japanese. These guidelines are intended to assist individual teachers and professional associations throughout the United States in designing Japanese language curricula. They are meant to serve as a framework from which language teaching can be expanded and are intended to allow teachers to enhance and strengthen the quality of Japanese language instruction.

168pp., ISBN 0–8248–2350–8 $20.

FOREIGN LANGUAGE TEACHING AND MINORITY LANGUAGE EDUCATION
KATHRYN A. DAVIS (EDITOR), 1999

This volume seeks to examine the potential for building relationships among foreign language, bilingual, and ESL programs towards fostering bilingualism. Part I of the volume examines the sociopolitical contexts for language partnerships, including:

- obstacles to developing bilingualism;
- implications of acculturation, identity, and language issues for linguistic minorities; and
- the potential for developing partnerships across primary, secondary, and tertiary institutions.

Part II of the volume provides research findings on the Foreign Language Partnership Project, designed to capitalize on the resources of immigrant students to enhance foreign language learning.

152pp., ISBN 0–8248–2067–3 $20.

DESIGNING SECOND LANGUAGE PERFORMANCE ASSESSMENTS
JOHN M. NORRIS, JAMES DEAN BROWN, THOM HUDSON, & JIM YOSHIOKA, 1998, 2000

This technical report focuses on the decision-making potential provided by second language performance assessments. The authors first situate performance assessment within a broader discussion of alternatives in language assessment and in educational assessment in general. They then discuss issues in performance assessment design, implementation, reliability, and validity. Finally, they present a prototype framework for second language performance assessment based on the integration of theoretical underpinnings and research findings from the task-based language teaching literature, the language testing literature, and the educational measurement literature. The authors outline test and item specifications, and they present numerous examples of prototypical language tasks. They also propose a research agenda focusing on the operationalization of second language performance assessments.

248pp., ISBN 0–8248–2109–2 $20.

SECOND LANGUAGE DEVELOPMENT IN WRITING: MEASURES OF FLUENCY, ACCURACY, AND COMPLEXITY
KATE WOLFE-QUINTERO, SHUNJI INAGAKI, & HAE-YOUNG KIM, 1998, 2002

In this book, the authors analyze and compare the ways that fluency, accuracy, grammatical complexity, and lexical complexity have been measured in studies of language development in second language writing. More than 100 developmental measures are examined, with detailed comparisons of the results across the studies that have used each measure. The authors discuss the theoretical foundations for each type of developmental measure, and they consider the relationship between developmental measures and various types of proficiency measures. They also examine criteria for determining which developmental measures are the most successful and suggest which measures are the most promising for continuing work on language development.

208pp., ISBN 0–8248–2069–X $20.

THE DEVELOPMENT OF A LEXICAL TONE PHONOLOGY IN AMERICAN ADULT LEARNERS OF STANDARD MANDARIN CHINESE
SYLVIA HENEL SUN, 1998

The study reported is based on an assessment of three decades of research on the SLA of Mandarin tone. It investigates whether differences in learners' tone perception and production are related to differences in the effects of certain linguistic, task, and learner factors. The learners of focus are American students of Mandarin in Beijing, China. Their performances on two perception and three production tasks are analyzed through a host of variables and methods of quantification.

328pp., ISBN 0–8248–2068–1 $20.

NEW TRENDS AND ISSUES IN TEACHING JAPANESE LANGUAGE AND CULTURE
HARUKO M. COOK, KYOKO HIJIRIDA, & MILDRED TAHARA (EDITORS), 1997

In recent years, Japanese has become the fourth most commonly taught foreign language at the college level in the United States. As the number of students who study Japanese has increased, the teaching of Japanese as a foreign language has been established as an important academic field of study. This technical report includes nine contributions to the advancement of this field, encompassing the following five important issues:

- Literature and literature teaching
- Technology in the language classroom
- Orthography
- Testing
- Grammatical versus pragmatic approaches to language teaching

164pp., ISBN 0–8248–2067–3 $20.

SIX MEASURES OF JSL PRAGMATICS
SAYOKO OKADA YAMASHITA, 1996

This book investigates differences among tests that can be used to measure the cross-cultural pragmatic ability of English-speaking learners of Japanese. Building on the work of Hudson, Detmer, and Brown (Technical Reports #2 and #7 in this series), the author modified six test types that she used to gather data from North American learners of Japanese. She found numerous problems with the multiple-choice discourse completion test but reported that the other five tests all proved highly reliable and reasonably valid. Practical issues involved in creating and using such language tests are discussed from a variety of perspectives.

213pp., ISBN 0–8248–1914–4 $15.

LANGUAGE LEARNING STRATEGIES AROUND THE WORLD: CROSS-CULTURAL PERSPECTIVES
REBECCA L. OXFORD (EDITOR), 1996, 1997, 2002

Language learning strategies are the specific steps students take to improve their progress in learning a second or foreign language. Optimizing learning strategies improves language performance. This groundbreaking book presents new information about cultural influences on the use of language learning strategies. It also shows innovative ways to assess students' strategy use and remarkable techniques for helping students improve their choice of strategies, with the goal of peak language learning.

166pp., ISBN 0–8248–1910–1 $20.

TELECOLLABORATION IN FOREIGN LANGUAGE LEARNING: PROCEEDINGS OF THE HAWAI'I SYMPOSIUM
Mark Warschauer (Editor), 1996

The Symposium on Local & Global Electronic Networking in Foreign Language Learning & Research, part of the National Foreign Language Resource Center's 1995 Summer Institute on Technology & the Human Factor in Foreign Language Education, included presentations of papers and hands-on workshops conducted by Symposium participants to facilitate the sharing of resources, ideas, and information about all aspects of electronic networking for foreign language teaching and research, including electronic discussion and conferencing, international cultural exchanges, real-time communication and simulations, research and resource retrieval via the Internet, and research using networks. This collection presents a sampling of those presentations.

252pp., ISBN 0–8248–1867–9 $20.

LANGUAGE LEARNING MOTIVATION: PATHWAYS TO THE NEW CENTURY
Rebecca L. Oxford (Editor), 1996

This volume chronicles a revolution in our thinking about what makes students want to learn languages and what causes them to persist in that difficult and rewarding adventure. Topics in this book include the internal structures of and external connections with foreign language motivation; exploring adult language learning motivation, self-efficacy, and anxiety; comparing the motivations and learning strategies of students of Japanese and Spanish; and enhancing the theory of language learning motivation from many psychological and social perspectives.

218pp., ISBN 0–8248–1849–0 $20.

LINGUISTICS & LANGUAGE TEACHING: PROCEEDINGS OF THE SIXTH JOINT LSH-HATESL CONFERENCE
Cynthia Reves, Caroline Steele, & Cathy S. P. Wong (Editors), 1996

Technical Report #10 contains 18 articles revolving around the following three topics:

- Linguistic issues—These six papers discuss various linguistic issues: ideophones, syllabic nasals, linguistic areas, computation, tonal melody classification, and wh-words.
- Sociolinguistics—Sociolinguistic phenomena in Swahili, signing, Hawaiian, and Japanese are discussed in four of the papers.
- Language teaching and learning—These eight papers cover prosodic modification, note taking, planning in oral production, oral testing, language policy, L2 essay organization, access to dative alternation rules, and child noun phrase structure development.

364pp., ISBN 0–8248–1851–2 $20.

ATTENTION & AWARENESS IN FOREIGN LANGUAGE LEARNING
Richard Schmidt (Editor), 1996

Issues related to the role of attention and awareness in learning lie at the heart of many theoretical and practical controversies in the foreign language field. This collection of papers presents research into the learning of Spanish, Japanese, Finnish, Hawaiian, and English as a second language (with additional comments and examples from French, German, and miniature artificial languages) that bear on these crucial questions for foreign language pedagogy.

394pp., ISBN 0–8248–1794–X $20.

VIRTUAL CONNECTIONS: ONLINE ACTIVITIES AND PROJECTS FOR NETWORKING LANGUAGE LEARNERS
Mark Warschauer (Editor), 1995, 1996

Computer networking has created dramatic new possibilities for connecting language learners in a single classroom or across the globe. This collection of activities and projects makes use of email, the internet, computer conferencing, and other forms of computer-mediated communication for the foreign and second language classroom at any level of instruction. Teachers from around the world submitted the activities compiled in this volume—activities that they have used successfully in their own classrooms.

417pp., ISBN 0–8248–1793–1 $30.

DEVELOPING PROTOTYPIC MEASURES OF CROSS-CULTURAL PRAGMATICS
Thom Hudson, Emily Detmer, & J. D. Brown, 1995

Although the study of cross-cultural pragmatics has gained importance in applied linguistics, there are no standard forms of assessment that might make research comparable across studies and languages. The present volume describes the process through which six forms of cross-cultural assessment were developed for second language learners of English. The models may be used for second language learners of other languages. The six forms of assessment involve two forms each of indirect discourse completion tests, oral language production, and self-assessment. The procedures involve the assessment of requests, apologies, and refusals.

198pp., ISBN 0–8248–1763–X $15.

THE ROLE OF PHONOLOGICAL CODING IN READING KANJI
Sachiko Matsunaga, 1995

In this technical report, the author reports the results of a study that she conducted on phonological coding in reading kanji using an eye-movement monitor, and draws some pedagogical implications. In addition, she reviews current literature on the different schools of thought regarding instruction in reading kanji and its role in the teaching of nonalphabetic written languages like Japanese.

64pp., ISBN 0–8248–1734–6 $10.

PRAGMATICS OF CHINESE AS NATIVE AND TARGET LANGUAGE
Gabriele Kasper (Editor), 1995

This technical report includes six contributions to the study of the pragmatics of Mandarin Chinese:

- A report of an interview study conducted with nonnative speakers of Chinese; and
- Five data-based studies on the performance of different speech acts by native speakers of Mandarin—requesting, refusing, complaining, giving bad news, disagreeing, and complimenting.

312pp., ISBN 0–8248–1733–8 $20.

A BIBLIOGRAPHY OF PEDAGOGY AND RESEARCH IN INTERPRETATION AND TRANSLATION
Etilvia Arjona, 1993

This technical report includes four types of bibliographic information on translation and interpretation studies:

- Research efforts across disciplinary boundaries—cognitive psychology, neurolinguistics, psycholinguistics, sociolinguistics, computational linguistics, measurement, aptitude testing, language policy, decision-making, theses, and dissertations;
- Training information covering program design, curriculum studies, instruction, and school administration;
- Instructional information detailing course syllabi, methodology, models, available textbooks; and
- Testing information about aptitude, selection, and diagnostic tests.

115pp., ISBN 0–8248–1572–6 $10.

PRAGMATICS OF JAPANESE AS NATIVE AND TARGET LANGUAGE
Gabriele Kasper (Editor), 1992, 1996

This technical report includes three contributions to the study of the pragmatics of Japanese:

- A bibliography on speech-act performance, discourse management, and other pragmatic and sociolinguistic features of Japanese;
- A study on introspective methods in examining Japanese learners' performance of refusals; and
- A longitudinal investigation of the acquisition of the particle *ne* by nonnative speakers of Japanese.

125pp., ISBN 0–8248–1462–2 $10.

A FRAMEWORK FOR TESTING CROSS-CULTURAL PRAGMATICS
Thom Hudson, Emily Detmer, & J. D. Brown, 1992

This technical report presents a framework for developing methods that assess cross-cultural pragmatic ability. Although the framework has been designed for Japanese and American cross-cultural contrasts, it can serve as a generic approach that can be applied to other language contrasts. The focus is on the variables of social distance, relative power, and the degree of imposition within the speech acts of requests, refusals, and apologies. Evaluation of performance is based on recognition of the speech act, amount of speech, forms or formulae used, directness, formality, and politeness.

51pp., ISBN 0–8248–1463 0 $10.

RESEARCH METHODS IN INTERLANGUAGE PRAGMATICS
Gabriele Kasper & Merete Dahl, 1991

This technical report reviews the methods of data collection employed in 39 studies of interlanguage pragmatics, defined narrowly as the investigation of nonnative speakers' comprehension and production of speech acts, and the acquisition of L2-related speech-act knowledge. Data collection instruments are distinguished according to the degree to which they constrain informants' responses, and whether they tap speech-act perception/comprehension or production. A main focus of discussion is the validity of different types of data, in particular their adequacy to approximate authentic performance of linguistic action.

51pp., ISBN 0–8248–1419–3 $10.

www.ingramcontent.com/pod-product-compliance
Lightning Source LLC
Chambersburg PA
CBHW081209170426
43198CB00018B/2899